Distancing Representations in Transgender Film

THE SUNY SERIES

HORIZONS OF CINEMA

MURRAY POMERANCE | EDITOR

RECENT TITLES

Tomoyuki Sasaki, *Cinema of Discontent*

Mary Ann McDonald Carolan, *Orienting Italy*

Matthew Rukgaber, *Nietzsche in Hollywood*

David Venditto, *Whiteness at the End of the World*

Fareed Ben-Youssef, *No Jurisdiction*

Tony Tracy, *White Cottage, White House*

Tom Conley, *Action, Action, Action*

Lindsay Coleman and Roberto Schaefer, editors, *The Cinematographer's Voice*

Nolwenn Mingant, *Hollywood Films in North Africa and the Middle East*

†Charles Warren, edited by William Rothman and Joshua Schulze, *Writ on Water*

Jason Sperb, *The Hard Sell of Paradise*

William Rothman, *The Holiday in His Eye*

Brendan Hennessey, *Luchino Visconti and the Alchemy of Adaptation*

Alexander Sergeant, *Encountering the Impossible*

Erica Stein, *Seeing Symphonically*

George Toles, *Curtains of Light*

Neil Badmington, *Perpetual Movement*

Merrill Schleier, editor, *Race and the Suburbs in American Film*

Matthew Leggatt, editor, *Was It Yesterday?*

Homer B. Pettey, editor, *Mind Reeling*

A complete listing of books in this series can be found online at www.sunypress.edu

Distancing Representations in Transgender Film

Identification, Affect, and the Audience

Lucy J. Miller

Published by State University of New York Press, Albany

For information, contact State University of New York Press, Albany, NY
www.sunypress.edu

Library of Congress Cataloging-in-Publication Data

Name: Miller, Lucy J., 1981– author.
Title: Distancing representations in transgender film : identification,
    affect, and the audience / Lucy J. Miller.
Description: Albany : State University of New York Press, [2023] | Series:
    SUNY series, horizons of cinema | Includes bibliographical references
    and index.
Identifiers: LCCN 2022024008 | ISBN 9781438491998 (hardcover : alk.
    paper) | ISBN 9781438492018 (ebook) | ISBN 9781438492001 (pbk. :
    alk. paper)
Subjects: LCSH: Transgender people in motion pictures. | Gender identity in
    motion pictures.
Classification: LCC PN1995.9.T684 M55 2023 | DDC
    791.43/653—dc23/eng/20220906
LC record available at https://lccn.loc.gov/2022024008

10 9 8 7 6 5 4 3 2 1

Contents

Acknowledgments

I want to thank some people who were instrumental in seeing me through the completion of this project. First and foremost is Sara Rowe, my best friend with whom I have shared all the joys of life and who has helped me survive all the trials and tribulations that life brings as well. I also want to thank Josh Heuman, Aisha Durham, Kristan Poirot, and Terence Hoagwood for guidance for completing my dissertation, which served as the genesis for this project. I want to thank Murray Pomerance, editor of the "Horizons of Cinema" series; James Peltz, associate director and editor in chief at SUNY Press; and the anonymous peer reviewers of the project for their help in bringing it to completion. I also want to thank all my friends for their support over the years, specifically Chris Silver, David Tarvin, Michael Rold, Andrea Calland, Joey and Corina Lopez, Anthony Ramirez, Jess Havens, and Anna Wolfe. Finally, I want to thank my family.

Along with thanking people for their support, I also want to acknowledge previous versions of material included in this book. An earlier version of the chapter "Ridicule in Transgender Comedies" was published in *Transgender Communication Studies: Histories, Trends, and Trajectories*, edited by Leland G. Spencer and Jamie C. Capuzza (2015, Lexington Books). An earlier version of the chapter "Fear in Transgender Horror Films" was published in *Spectator*, Special Issue on "Transgender Media," vol. 37, no. 2, 2017, pp. 40–47.

Introduction

I SINK INTO THE SEAT NEXT to my mom and sister at the strip-mall movie theater in Waco, Texas. I am twelve years old, and though movies are not an uncommon experience at this point in my life, the hour-long drive to Waco is just far enough that I relish any opportunity to see a movie. We are here this day in December 1993 to see the latest family comedy, *Mrs. Doubtfire* (1993) starring Robin Williams. The film tells the story of Daniel Hillard who, after he and his wife Miranda divorce, decides to disguise himself as the eponymous elderly British woman in order to be offered a job as a nanny that will allow him to spend more time with his children. I laughed along with the rest of the audience at the slapstick antics of star Robin Williams and enjoyed the film enough that it retained a warm place in my memories for years to come; the film was also significant to me personally because it was one of the first pieces of media I was aware of that portrayed a man dressing as a woman. I had been aware of my transgender identity since I was at least five years old, but I still struggled for many years to come out to my family and friends. The impact of seeing a character cross-dressing on screen was extremely important for me. While Daniel Hilliard would not have seen himself as transgender, seeing him cross-dress let me know, on some level, that I was not alone, that I was not the only person in the world who had the feelings I had and who understood themselves—even if I did not yet have the language to describe it—as transgender.

I continued to seek out representations of transgender people in film and other media. I was always very aware of new films that touched on transgender themes, such as *Ace Ventura: Pet Detective*

1

(1994), *To Wong Foo, Thanks for Everything, Julie Newmar* (1995), *Dr. Jekyll and Ms. Hyde* (1995), and *The Birdcage* (1996). I also enjoyed discovering older films that included transgender representations, such as *Some Like It Hot* (1959), *Psycho* (1960), and *Tootsie* (1982). To this day, I am still interested in consuming any media, no matter how bad, that includes some form of transgender representation, because I just have to see for myself how transgender people are being presented to the rest of the world.

Even though I have found enjoyment in transgender film and media representations over the years, I came to realize as I got older that most people in the audience were not processing films like *Mrs. Doubtfire* the same way that I was. All they saw was a silly man who barely looked like a woman finding himself in ridiculous situations because of his decision to wear a dress and makeup. Rather than a demonstration of the real possibility of existing as the gender that matches one's gender identity even when it was not the one given at birth, all that most moviegoers saw in *Mrs. Doubtfire* and similar films was a hilarious farce about something they would never experience for themselves. The very ridiculousness of its premise is the foundation of all its humor. I came to realize that while my experience with the film and others like it was a very important part of the development of my transgender identity, it was an oppositional reading of the film.[1] Marketed to a broad, primarily cisgender audience, the film's narrative and visuals were constructed to appeal to this audience, not to the small minority audience of transgender people desperately searching for any external acknowledgement of their identities. These films are not really about or for transgender people, even if transgender people's lives and experiences are an important part of the films. While the concept of representation generally refers to the inclusion of marginalized groups in media texts, more attention needs to be given to how representations are constructed to appeal to certain audiences who are generally not members of the same marginalized group. The purpose of *Distancing Representations in Transgender Film* is to show how the hopeful purpose of challenging binary understandings of gender seen in popular transgender film representations is not fulfilled in the texts themselves.[2] As a transgender woman myself, I want to see positive, realistic depictions of transgender lives in popular film and media, and identifying and acknowledging the shortcomings of existing tests is one important step toward attaining these positive representations.

I want to offer a note of explanation about the meaning of an important word in the title I've chosen. Distancing is the result of the centering of a dominant perspective on a marginalized group. The distancing I address in this book—that of transgender characters from the cisgender audience in transgender films—is accomplished through the use of specific narrative conventions and visual codes to deny an emotional investment or identification with the characters by audience members. The transgender characters are generally distanced from the audience by contrasting them with cisnormative standards of gender. The narrative conventions and visual codes of these films construct transgender identity in ways that prevent audience identification with the characters. The transgender identities of the characters are either discarded at the first available opportunity in order to better focus on the characters' cisgender identities, which are hidden until the last moments in order to create a shocking revelation, or shown to be the result of a tremendous amount of effort and suffering. Because of the prominence of the characters in most of the films analyzed here, audience members may be able to identify with them *despite* these issues, but how the characters are constructed does not *invite* this identification.

The transgender identities of the characters in transgender films are frequently delegitimized in contrast to their cisgender identities. The transgender characters are critiqued by cisnormativity for their poor performance of gender and their focus on outward appearance. The characters are also positioned as separate from cisnormative society, whether through the physical isolation of being forced to leave their homes and go to a new place, even somewhere as nice as a resort in Florida, or the interpersonal isolation of being rejected by others, through such acts as being bullied at summer camp. Finally, the transgender identities of the characters are presented as problems to be overcome rather than as legitimate identities; whether the characters actively claim a transgender identity or are positioned in that identity by external forces, their transgender identities are presented as the root cause of all the difficulties they must endure. All these issues represent an interest in highlighting clear distinctions between the transgender characters and cisnormative society. Making such clear distinctions supports the project of distancing the characters from the audience by arguing that the distinctions are impossible to overcome and that no true connection with the characters is possible.

An example from *Tootsie* illustrates this distancing effect. The main character Michael Dorsey's decision to adopt a transgender identity is based in his inability to find work as an actor, distancing him from the audience not only for his transgender identity but also for his lack of economic privilege. After adopting the transgender identity of Dorothy Michaels, Michael's transgender identity is made problematic through poor performance of gender, such as when he physically tosses a man out of a taxi after a long day of shopping as Dorothy, while his cisgender identity is privileged in his romantic pursuit of Julie. To pursue her successfully, Michael frequently discards his transgender identity even though Dorothy brings him more success and acclaim than he ever had before as an actor. Even with everything he learns through the experience, confessing to Julie that he was a better man as a woman with her than he ever was as a man, he discards his transgender identity for a final time in a dramatic reveal involving removing his wig on live television. By failing to treat Michael's transgender identity with the same respect given to his cisgender identity and having him frequently discard his transgender identity as an obstacle to a successful romance, the film does not allow the audience to make a connection with the character's transgender identity. The character's own privileging of his cisgender identity is reflected in the film's construction of Michael as a character. By working to keep Michael at a safe distance from his transgender identity, the film also works to keep the audience at a safe distance as well. Analyzing how transgender films are constructed to distance the transgender characters from the audience is the purpose of this book. To show how my argument differs, it is important to first look at the existing scholarship on transgender representation in film.

Overview of Transgender Representation in Film

Representation is constitutive of the events that surround us.[3] Representation does not create events; they do exist outside of their representation. But because events cannot signify on their own and must be *"made intelligible,"*[4] our understanding of events happens through the frame of representation. Events are framed in a particular way and given a particular meaning depending on how they are represented. For example, if a transgender person is attacked and beaten, the way the transgender person is represented in news media shapes how they are understood by members of society. Representation that focuses, for example, on the transgender person's presence in a gender-segregated space, such as a restroom or changing room, implies that the attack was justified because the transgender person deviated from cisnormative standards for gendered behavior. On the other hand, representation that focuses on the transgender person's attempt to eat dinner or purchase clothing in peace before suddenly being attacked implies that the person's freedom to express their gender without the threat of violence was violated. In both examples, the way the transgender person is represented impacts our understanding of the event. A single, hypothetical story may only reach a small audience, but the representation of transgender people found within can have a larger impact if it becomes the norm for how transgender people are represented in media. Representation is constitutive because it influences our understanding of events and people in significant ways.

The constitutive nature of representation shapes the way I approach filmic representations of transgender people in this book. Repeatedly representing transgender people as buffoons or liars impacts not only an audience's expectations of how transgender characters should act in film but also their expectations of the actions and motivations of transgender people in real life. This manner of representation leads to transgender people being seen as worthy of ridicule or mistrust.

Representations also provide scripts to guide our symbolic interactions. People who have little contact with transgender people often learn from film and other media texts how to treat and interact with transgender people. Furthermore, film and media texts provide scripts that transgender people also, consciously or not, adopt and adapt. Because films like *Mrs. Doubtfire* depicted transgender identity as the result of external motivations, I spent many years wishing and hoping for something external to happen to me, like winning a contest or finding a magic lamp, that would allow me to be the transgender woman that I knew I was, anything other than embracing my identity and coming out to my family. It was only through recognizing the impact of representations in such films on my own understanding of transgender identity that I was able to fully express my identity as a transgender woman.

Beyond constituting our understanding and impressions of events and people, representation is also constraining.[5] Representation orders events; it is impossible to perceive and understand everything, so representation provides the impression that all the random events in our lives are united by a coherent narrative.[6] No representation is ever completely accurate; something is always obscured to make the whole seem more intelligible. For example, a transgender woman choosing not to tell a potential romantic partner about her gender identity on a first date is often offered as evidence of the deceitfulness of transgender people. This representation ignores the possibility that the woman chose to wait before coming out to her date in order to protect herself; she may have feared the possibility of a verbal or physical attack, itself a constraining representation of her date.

As an example of the constraining nature of representation in film, Julia Serano and Kay Siebler argue that the representation of transgender people in film and other media is constrained by its focus on the desire of transgender women for greater femininity, such as Bree Osbourne's preference for wearing pink in *Transamerica* (2005).[7] Serano argues that, based on representations in the media, "most people believe that all trans women are on a quest to make ourselves as pretty, pink, and passive as possible."[8] Siebler adds that media represent transgender people as variously "unbalanced freaks" or people who surgically or hormonally modify their bodies to appear "'normal,' as happy, healthy and well-adjusted."[9] Siebler goes on to argue for moving beyond these two modes of representation to include more queer representations of people who are comfortable identifying outside of the cisnormative, binary gender system.[10] While I support the work of Serano and Siebler in critiquing the reinforcement of the binary sex/gender system through the representation of feminine transgender women, I hope through my own work to find a way of accomplishing this goal without alienating these women in the process.

Serano and Siebler's analyses serve as a good introduction to the scholarship on transgender representation in film and its connection to more general scholarly work on representation. Some scholars, like Serano and Siebler, focus on the constraining nature of trans-gender representations. Judith Butler argues that many transgender films deflect the homosexual possibilities in their narratives by "produc[ing] and contain[ing] the homosexual excess of any given drag performance."[11] What is constraining for Butler about the films she analyzes, primarily transgender comedies, is that they do not go far enough in embracing the queer potential of their narratives. Marjorie

Garber also finds transgender comedies constraining in their use of "progress narratives" in which individuals choose to cross-dress in order to avoid or escape economic or other external circumstances.[12] Instead of the characters' transgender identities developing internally, their transgender identities solely function as an "instrumental strategy" to address an external problem.[13] Instead of truly challenging dominant systems of gender and sexuality, the films revert back to the cis-heterosexual status quo and dispose of the characters' transgender identities when they are no longer needed.

John Phillips finds transgender films constraining in our understanding of transgender people's lived experiences through their reduction of transgender identity to a "necessary deception."[14] Whether it is cisgender characters who only take up transgender identities under extreme circumstances or characters who actively claim a transgender identity withholding that identity from others, the actions of the characters are presented as necessary to exist in a cisnormative society. Julia Serano argues that variations of this form of deception are at the root of her two main archetypes of transgender representation: the "pathetic transexual" and the "deceptive transsexual."[15] Pathetic transsexuals are unable to deceive others about their gender identity, even though they may want to, while deceptive transsexuals are not seen as successful in passing but rather as "'fake' women, and their 'secret' trans status is revealed in a dramatic moment of 'truth.'"[16] In this configuration, transgender characters are either mocked for failing to live up to cisnormative standards of appearance or punished for their success at meeting those standards. Transgender representations "go no further than to hint at a possibility that is ultimately closed off in the revelation of the body beneath the clothes."[17] Any opportunity the films may have at subverting cisnormative standards is undermined through reference to an essentialized gender identity.

Other scholars find more promise in transgender representations as a constitutive site for challenging dominant binary systems of gender. For Chris Straayer, transgender representation in film "offers spectators a momentary, vicarious trespassing of society's accepted boundaries of gender and sexual behavior" while remaining confident "in the orderly demarcations reconstituted by the films' endings."[18] In her foundational work *Hollywood Androgyny*, Rebecca Bell-Metereau supports Straayer's analysis by arguing that transgender films "allow us to enter into forbidden worlds of the imagination."[19] Bell-Metereau finds films like *Some Like It Hot* to be open to the new possibilities for gender that are presented in the texts.[20] Transgender films, from this perspective, are seen as open spaces in which the characters and the audience are free to experiment with new ways of being in terms of gender. Bell-Metereau reaffirms this perspective on transgender films in her recent work. While she does acknowledge that some films feature negative representations, she argues that the films ultimately "offer a sense of presence and inclusion over time" and also "offer inspiration, possible encouragement, and a sense of participation, visibility, and influence in the larger society."[21] Positive elements in transgender films, such as openness in terms of gender and the engagement of transgender people in the cultural conversation, help to create the positive future that LGBTQ+ people and their allies desire.

Sandra Meiri and Odeya Kohen-Raz locate this sense of openness in transgender films in Lacanian "feminine enjoyment," which "unlike desire, which can never be satisfied, and fantasy, which is doomed to remain in the imaginary, enjoyment . . . is a substance, not unlike Freud's notion of the libido, which achieves satisfaction in the body, functioning as a defense mechanism against desire."[22] Feminine enjoyment is found in transgender film through the characters "assuming responsibility" for their desire, either as a starting point for their journey or as a significant development on their journey.[23] As an example, Meiri and Kohen-Raz argue that Jerry in *Some Like It Hot* is able to find freedom in his transgender identity.[24] Like Bell-Metereau, they see the film, and other transgender films as well, as an open text that creates the possibility for freedom outside of the binary gender system once the characters are able to free themselves from their societally-imposed desires. The audience's continued viewership of transgender films also signals a tacit understanding of the freedom found within the texts.[25] Transgender films are awash in potentiality from this perspective.

While I sincerely hope that the positive potential found by these scholars in transgender films comes to fruition, I differ from them in the belief that this is all that is present within or can be read from transgender films. My concern is similar to that expressed by Joelle Ruby Ryan when she argues that, despite recent shifts in representation, "the *majority* of images of trans people repeatedly downplays the social, cultural and political implications of trans people's lives and focus instead on micro-level experiences and salacious personal details."[26] The images and narratives found in transgender films paint a more restrictive view of the lives of transgender people than what is found in positive and hopeful scholarship on transgender films. This restrictive view is often dismissive, hostile, and violent toward transgender people for failing to conform to the expectations of a cisnormative society. It is entirely possible to have multiple readings of the same film. It is entirely possible for you to read a film as opening up space for challenging gender norms while I see it as rejecting the possibility of acknowledging a transgender identity. It is entirely possible for you to read a film as presenting a queer character lashing out at the restrictive norms of society while I see it as perpetuating the framing of transgender people as violent and unstable. My argument in *Distancing Representations in Transgender Film* is that the trend up until this point in the texts of popular transgender films exhibits a more negative or restricted view of transgender people because the films are primarily created by cisgender authors for a cisgender audience. The readings of the films as offering positive potentials for challenging the binary system of gender are there, but as I show in my analysis, this is not the primary message being sent through the texts of the films. The potential is there for change in the future, but the trend so far has been supporting the cisnormative status quo.

My perspective on transgender representation in film is shaped by my experiences as a White, able-bodied, bisexual, transgender woman from a middle-class background. My understanding of gender and difference is shaped by the concept of positionality.[27] Positionality is an approach to identity that focuses on the connections between people created through gender, class, race, sexual orientation, and other identities and is similar to standpoint in its focus on connections between marginalized people in a society. Having been aware of my identity as a transgender person from a young age, I have never truly experienced the world in a cisgender way. As I struggled to understand who I was as a transgender person and even struggled to fully express my transgender identity, I often turned to popular film and media for support and escape. My identity as a transgender woman gives me unique insight into the topic of transgender representations in film, but it may also lead me to critique the characters or situations in the films in ways that differ from the analysis made by a cisgender scholar. Other aspects of my position may impact my awareness of race, class, and culture-based issues affecting the positions of the characters. As I try to use the insights available to me as a transgender woman, I also seek to be aware of the possible limitations this position introduces.

My analysis of transgender representations in film is grounded in my identity as a transgender woman. My focus on distance comes from my own feelings of distance from the characters. As transgender characters, I should feel a connection to them, but I often do not. My work on this book has helped me understand the ways the films are constructed to prevent that connection. Having experienced various forms of marginalization in my own life has also made me sensitive to the ways the characters are marginalized from others in the films. Cisnormativity, as with most dominant ideologies, works to build itself up by putting others down. Pushing for a place for transgender people in a cisnormative society is not necessarily the solution; finding ways to dismantle cisnormative privilege would be a solution that would benefit everyone, not just transgender people, but my experiences of marginalization have taught me that marginalization is more about the dominant group trying to stay in control than any actions on the part of the marginalized. Finally, my lived experience as a transgender woman makes me more critical of the ways transgender representations focus on transgender identity as nothing more than outward appearance and behavior. The experience of being transgender should be given the attention it deserves, rather than being glossed over in a quick cut between scenes, but there is more to being transgender than the amount of time it takes me to get dressed in the morning. My transgender identity influences all aspects of my analysis, but my analysis should not be dismissed because of my transgender identity. My experiences as a transgender woman give me unique insights into transgender representations, but these insights are grounded in the content of the films. My analysis is situated in a particular social and historical context that has shaped my position as a transgender woman.

Positionality is also important in examining characters in popular film because it enables a consideration of their gender identities as positions taken during the events portrayed in the films rather than presuming the presence of clues to their essential gender identities. Positionality moves beyond searching for a character's "true" or "real" identity and looks instead at the physical, social, and economic conditions that make up their position. A positional approach to gender accepts all the elements that make up a person's identity at face value without searching for an essential element that underlies and explains everything. Many of the characters under examination would not identify as transgender, but that does not mean being transgender does not make up part of their position at certain points in the narratives in which they are featured. I adopt the umbrella definition of *transgender* in this project, defined by Susan Stryker as "movement away from an initially assigned gender position,"[28] which includes everything from temporary cross-dressing to seeking permanent bodily change through hormone treatment and surgery. This umbrella definition is broad enough to encompass both self-identified transgender characters, such as Bree from *Transamerica* or Dil from *The Crying Game* (1992), to characters who are only engaging in transgender behavior to escape a temporary situation, such as Joe and Jerry from *Some Like it Hot* or Malcolm from *Big Momma's House* (2000). Rather than imposing a transgender identity on the characters, I make use of a broad definition of transgender identity to allow for the analysis of characters that communicate important ideas of what it means to be transgender to both cisgender and transgender audiences even in cases where the characters never personally identify as transgender.

My perspective on transgender representation in film is also shaped by my understanding of society as cisnormative. I define cisnormativity as "the systemic expectation that there are only two mutually exclusive genders and the gender of all members of a society will match the sex assigned to them at birth, with attendant benefits given to those who adhere and the labeling of those who do not, transgender and queer individuals, as deviant."[29] Cisnormativity is the current system through which gender is understood in American society. Clear expectations are created that people should adhere to a strict gender binary, and those who do not are often punished, both individually and systemically, for their failure to adhere to the standards. I use the term *cisnormative* in this book to refer to the system of expectations around gender and to certain patterns in the narrative and visual representation of transgender people in film and other media that follow this system. Cisgender people usually support these standards, whether consciously or unconsciously, but a person's identity or gender performance cannot fully embrace cisnormativity as a system, so I will not be referring to any people as cisnormative.

Cisnormativity as a concept is theoretically grounded in the concept of heteronormativity. *Heteronormativity* refers to the normalizing of heterosexuality as the assumed, "default" status of people.[30] While heteronormativity and cisnormativity as systems have negative effects for everyone because they limit how we perform, interact with, and express our identities, transgender activist Kate Bornstein argues that it is still transgender people who receive the fullest brunt of negative attention.[31] My position as a transgender woman living in a cisnormative society shapes my approach to transgender representation in film. From my position, I see transgender films less as hopeful spaces from which to challenge the binary system of gender and more as constraining texts that present transgender people as undermining cisnormativity. The constraining representations found in transgender film is the result of how the identification is created between the authors and the audience.

Identification, Affect, and the Audience

My approach to the audience in *Distancing Representations in Transgender Film* is at the intersections of the rhetorical concepts of identification and the first and second personae and the cultural studies approach of encoding/decoding. Filmic representations of transgender people are constructed with a primarily cisgender audience in mind. This is the main reason the cisgender identities of the characters are privileged throughout the films. Film, in general, seeks to reflect the interests and concerns of the audience, so if the audience is viewed as primarily cisgender, transgender representations are constructed to appeal to this dominant audience. Because those involved in the creation of popular films assume that a cisgender audience will find transgender characters to be shocking or disgusting, the narrative conventions and visual codes of the films are constructed in such a way that the transgender characters match these expectations. Trying to accurately represent the lived experiences of transgender people for a transgender audience is, at best, a secondary concern.

In the context of an ideology of cisnormativity, cisgender moviegoers are assumed to be unable to connect to or identify with transgender characters, thus leading to the distancing of the characters from the audience. The narrative and visual construction of film in general works to move the audience to connect with the characters on screen. The constant repetition of this feeling of identification is one reason millions of moviegoers continue to flock to theaters each week. Because the assumption is that members of a cisnormative society are incapable of identifying with transgender characters, the narrative conventions and visual codes in transgender films work to keep the characters at a distance from the audience. The audience watches the events in these films from a perspective far removed from the experiences of the characters on screen; they may laugh at the characters, scream in fear of them, pull away in disgust, or even feel sorry for them, but the message encoded into transgender films is that audience members can never see themselves as the characters.

The overarching assumption is that every member of the audience will react this way, viewing transgender characters as deviant and failing to identify with them. While this assumption may not be true (many audience members may identify with the transgender characters and may get angry about how these characters are represented), the basic assumption about how a cisgender audience perceives transgender characters shapes the entire narrative and visual structures of transgender films. A deeper understanding of the audience for transgender representations is important, but it is equally important to remember the ways each of our decodings are based on our own interpretations from identity positions that are embodied, specific, and historically situated. No matter the assumptions about who makes up an audience, each member brings their own experiences to their viewing of a film. Rather than making assumptions about the audience, we would do better to remember the variety of decodings that are possible. A rhetorical approach to identification helps us to understand how a text is constructed to appeal to an audience made up of certain identities.

Identification is important in analyzing film because it helps to explain the audience's experience of and connection to the film as a text. In contrast to approaches to identification based on the audience's subjective experience of viewing a film or on the characters,[32] I take a rhetorical approach to identification informed by the work of Kenneth Burke. For Burke, identification precedes persuasion and occurs across differences.[33] Two subjects, one of whom is attempting to persuade the other, search for real or perceived similarities through which to build persuasive arguments. In this process, which Burke labels *consubstantiation*, differences persist while similarities are enhanced.[34] Consubstantiation can be read through the text in terms of the first and second personae. According to Edwin Black, the first persona is the implied author, and the second persona is the implied auditor or audience.[35] The first and second personae do not encompass everything about the author or the audience but instead reflect the image of themselves the author wants to present and the ideal audience they envision for the text. The images of the author and audience found in the text are intended to increase connection and the likelihood of persuasion.

In a rhetorical approach, identification is not found with the characters or the camera but in the relationship between the implied author and audience. Here *author* refers to all those who have a hand in the creation of a film (the director, cinematographer, editor, screenwriter, actors, etc.), and *audience* refers to those members (not as individual people but as a group) of the undifferentiated mass audience to whom the author is trying to appeal.[36] The appeal is made across certain similarities between the author and the audience that serves as the point of identification. A film is then constructed narratively and visually in line with the identification between author and audience, within certain constraints like genre.

For dominant identities like being cisgender, the identification that exists between the author and the audience is often not explicitly stated. Most mainstream Hollywood films are produced to appeal to as broad a group as possible. The ideal audience would be White, male, straight, cisgender, middle to upper class, and so on. The widest group of people can find some category with which they identify in this ideal audience, so declaring mainstream films to be for this audience would be redundant. The audience for a film is usually only explicitly stated for films aimed at a minority or marginalized group, such as films labeled Black films, women's films, gay films, and so on. Dominant group members can, therefore, assume that all movies are meant for them unless a marginalized audience is identified. Even if a film centers on a member of a marginalized group, it is still generally constructed to appeal to the largest audience possible since the point of identification for mainstream films is that dominant ideal audience. As a result of trying to appeal to a broad audience, messages about the marginalized group that are consistent with maintaining the dominant hierarchies and power structures in society are built into the film through its narrative and visual construction. In terms of gender identity and expression, the point of identification for transgender films is a cisgender, not transgender, identity. Dominant cultural ideas about transgender people are still mistaken or purposefully negative, and transgender films reflect this dominant perspective back to audience members, who are most likely of the dominant group themselves.

The point of identification between the cisgender authors and audience often leads cisgender audience members to be distanced from the transgender characters. While a space for difference may exist in the contemporary media environment, audience members may still find representations of difference bothersome, particularly those of marginalized groups with whom the audience members have little or no direct personal contact. Transgender representations produce distancing effects between the transgender characters and the audience because of this lack of ability to identify with the characters. Identification becomes tenuous when the representation is so far removed from its referent, as literary theorist Edward Said argues in his landmark analysis of Western perceptions of the Orient. "The value, efficacy, strength, apparent veracity of a written statement about the Orient therefore relies very little, and cannot instrumentally depend, on the Orient as such. On the contrary, the written statement is a presence to the reader by virtue of its having excluded, displaced, made super-erogatory any such *real thing* as 'the Orient.' "[37] Since representations themselves have no necessary connection to their subject, it is not surprising that audience members may not feel a connection with the representations. Transgender films support the distancing of the characters from the audience, and this distancing effect is rooted in a lack of legitimacy ascribed to the transgender identities of the characters. The narrative conventions and visual codes of the films do not help audience members look past the perceived differences between themselves and the transgender characters, and the distance that results from the cisgender audience's identification with the films' authors risks leading to a lack of engagement or interest with the film. Emotion provides a means of addressing this lack of engagement.

According to Aristotle, emotions shape how the audience responds to persuasion.[38] Affect theory provides a useful means of understanding how emotions and feelings shape the audience's responses to a film. Affect is the primary motivator of human beings, shaping even our processing of basic drives like hunger and sexual desire.[39] Affect consists of unconscious, physical reactions to stimuli, such as jumping at a loud noise or gagging when smelling milk that has gone bad. The affect system provides a great degree of freedom in shaping our identities since a wide variety of stimuli can produce different affects that persist for varying amounts of time for different people.[40] Films are constructed to evoke a specific affective response, and the experience of watching a film, from the construction of the theater itself to the passive engagement encouraged by the film, enhances the feelings experienced by audience members.[41] Individual audience members, though, may respond differently to the narrative and visuals found in a film that were intended to prompt a specific affective response. I am interested in this book in analyzing how transgender films are narratively and visually constructed to prompt affective and emotional responses that support a cisnormative ideology, not in determining if every audience member responded to the films in the ways intended by the author.

Affect shapes the audience's initial response to what is seen on screen. When audience members jump in fright after a monster pops out from behind a door to menace a stranded sorority girl or when they laugh at a nerdy hero's bumbling pratfalls as he tries to match his debonair rival in wooing the attractive woman who moved in next door, affect is at work, but there is more to affect than just the basic reactions to such events. Affect also shapes how people see themselves and are seen by others through their affective responses, thus shaping who we are and how we understand our identities by anticipating and expecting certain responses to specific events in particular contexts. We understand ourselves better through seeing what makes us laugh, cry, and scream, and others come to understand us more deeply based on our reactions to different stimuli. How we are prompted to feel about those we see on screen also helps the audience to move beyond representation's call to see and recognize others toward a deeper knowing of their lived experience.[42] How affect shapes the self is not unique to us as people but reflects existing cultural ideologies.

According to feminist scholar Sara Ahmed, emotions function as a "form of cultural politics or world making."[43] Through contact with others, the "surfaces and boundaries" of our bodies take shape.[44] We come to understand who we are and who others are through the impressions left behind through our contact with them, so the emotions we experience and expect are shaped by dominant ideologies that regulate this contact. Even in projects intended to try to understand the experiences of LGBTQ+ people from a variety of cultural contexts, for example, the feelings of White people are privileged over the experiences of people of color as reflective of the systemic Whiteness of the culture in the United States.[45] If affect is a person's immediate, bodily response to stimuli that is interpreted through cultural ideologies, our affective responses are transformed into emotion through rhetoric. As with our affective responses, our emotions are best understood in relation to others. Our affective responses form the foundation and are only understood as emotions when we communicate to and with others about our responses to different stimuli.[46] Rhetoric provides a means for analyzing these roles as reflective of both cultural ideologies and relationships among people and groups. I differentiate in this book between affective responses (the physical, immediate responses an audience member has to a stimulus seen in the film) and emotional responses (the cultural meaning applied to those physical responses once they are consciously processed) in order to reflect these differences.

A useful method of analyzing the ideological dimension of affect and emotion can be found in Brigitte Bargetz's concept of a "political grammar of feelings" in which she distinguishes between "*feeling politics*" and "a politics *of* feelings."[47] By feeling politics, Bargetz is interested in the historical, hierarchical power relations that are reflected in our affective responses.[48] The panic a young woman feels when a man, whether her father, a romantic partner, or a stranger, raises his voice in anger and a Black man's anger as a result of constant surveillance by others while in public can be understood as feeling politics, since both reflect long histories and cultural hierarchies that shape what feelings they are supposed to express and what feelings they should expect from others. Both people must contend with the weight of the expected feelings as they move through their everyday lives. A politics of feelings, on the other hand, emphasizes "that power and politics work through feelings" by focusing on how feelings "are produced within specific normative frames."[49] When taking a politics of feelings approach to the previous examples, the young woman's panic arises because society has given more attention to teaching young women how to protect themselves from acts of aggression and violence instead of teaching young men to not be violent, and the Black man's anger is the result of centuries of systemic racism that treats Black lives as less valuable and more suspicious than White lives. In terms of an analysis of affect and emotion in film, feeling politics enables, for example, an analysis of how transgender people can feel angry or depressed at constantly being presented in film and other media as people to be laughed at or scared of while a politics of feelings enables an analysis of how transgender people are constructed as objects of ridicule, fear, disgust, and sympathy in the film texts in line with the dominant views of a cisnormative society.

In *Distancing Representations in Transgender Film*, I use a politics of feelings to analyze how an ideology of cisnormativity shapes the narrative and visual constructions of transgender films and the affective and emotional responses by the audience to transgender films. Transgender films are made by a cisgender author for a cisgender audience.[50] Being transgender is not the point of identification in these films; being cisgender is the point of identification. Even though transgender characters feature prominently in these films, they are not who the audience identifies with. Instead, identification for the audience lies with a cisnormative understanding of gender identity shared with the implied cisgender author. The affective and emotional responses by the audience to transgender films is then shaped by the decisions made by the cisgender author in constructing the narrative conventions and visual codes of the films, further reinforcing a cisnormative ideology.

Gender studies scholar Elspeth Probyn, in her study of shame, reminds scholars that "different affects make us feel, write, think, and act in different ways."[51] It is not enough to refer to "general Affect"[52]; instead, scholars must be specific about the effects specific affects and emotions have on people. In this book, I aim to take Probyn's admonishment seriously by analyzing how different affective and emotional responses are generated by different narrative and visual constructions and how these different affects and emotions reflect differing components of cisnormativity. The specific affects and emotions I analyze in transgender films are ridicule, fear, disgust, and sympathy. Rather than analyzing a specific text to represent each affect and emotion, I instead analyze narrative conventions and visual codes across a variety of texts.

My argument is that because popular transgender films are made for a cisgender audience by cisgender authors, the films support a cisnormative ideology that views transgender and gender nonconforming people as existing outside the norms of a binary gender system. Being cisgender serves as the point of identification between the audience and authors, so the transgender characters are distanced from the audience because they do not fit within this point of identification. The specific affective and emotional responses of ridicule, fear, disgust, and sympathy are prompted by the narratives and visuals in the films as a means of keeping the audience engaged even though they do not identify with the transgender characters. These affective and emotional responses are also in line with a cisnormative ideology as they encourage negative feelings toward the transgender characters specifically and transgender people in general.

Narrative Conventions and Visual Codes

To analyze the narrative conventions and visual codes of the films under study, I use an approach to textual analysis guided by the work of Alan McKee. McKee's poststructuralist approach to textual analysis "seeks to understand the ways in which these forms of representation take place, the assumptions behind them and the kinds of sense-making about the world that they reveal."[53] Unlike the form of textual analysis found often in rhetoric and film scholarship, I analyze groups of texts in this book as guided by what literary historian Franco Moretti calls "distant reading," which he argues constitutes *"a specific form of knowledge:* fewer elements, hence a sharper sense of their overall interconnection."[54] While I do not engage in the analysis of hundreds, if not thousands, of texts as Moretti does, I agree with his argument that taking a wider view of a group of texts can reveal information about them that is not available through the detailed analysis of individual works. The detailed reading of individual texts is still a highly valuable form of analysis, but it is not the goal of the current project.

In *Distancing Representations in Transgender Film*, I analyze narrative conventions and visual codes as constructed meanings that an audience decodes from a film text. Meaning can be understood from a cultural studies perspective as encoded into a text to be decoded by audience members. Stuart Hall defines encoding as "selecting the codes which assign meaning to events" while decoding assigns meaning to the message that may or may not agree with the intended meaning that was encoded into the message.[55] Meaning in film can also be understood as the *"construction* of meaning out of textual cues."[56] For Hall, meaning is created by audience members from the information available in the film text but may differ greatly from the meaning encoded into the text by the director or performers. The meaning decoded by the audience from the information available to them is not inferior to the "preferred reading" encoded into a text.[57] My approach in this book seeks to recognize strong textual cues in a film that lead the audience toward a particular reading while still acknowledging that it is the audience's prerogative to decode meaning from the text either in line with this reading or in opposition to it. This approach allows for the focus of analysis to be on the meanings found within the text while still being aware that individual audience members have the freedom to read the text as they choose. Narrative conventions and visual codes are the strong textual cues that I analyze in this book.

Narrative conventions consist of the unfolding of story elements relative to similar film texts, including everything from significant plot events to the dialogue and interactions between characters. Examples of narrative conventions in transgender films include a character deciding to cross-dress in order to win a school contest, a character bloodily getting revenge on her earlier attackers, or a character taking a classmate's place in a school play in order to kiss the boy she likes. Visual codes are divided among three different gazes (discussed in more detail below) and consist primarily of mise-en-scène. I am concerned with what the audience sees on screen, how the characters are presented including costuming, facial expressions, and body movements. References to camera movements (such as a slow tilt up a character's body from feet to head), transitions (such as cuts between scenes), and camera positioning (such as an overhead shot of a couple in bed together) are used when necessary to understand how the characters are visually presented to the audience, but the focus of my analysis of visual codes is on the information presented on screen rather than on the ways the camera was manipulated to capture that information. Narrative is discussed when necessary to place the visual information in context. Recognizing the way narrative conventions and visual codes work together furthers our understanding of how media texts construct representations of marginalized groups. When conducting a textual analysis, the texts should always be considered within the social and cultural context in which they are produced and consumed.

The broad range of research about minority stereotypes, which includes transgender representations, provides a means of understanding the narrative construction of marginalized groups. Communication scholars John Downing and Charles Husband argue that the term representation is "mostly used either to signal presence or absence of people of color from media, or constructive vs unconstructive portrayal."[58] The use of stereotypes, the belief that members of a group all exhibit certain positive or negative traits, is one of these unconstructive portrayals. Film historian Donald Bogle argues that the stereotypes of African Americans in film are meant "to entertain by stressing Negro inferiority."[59] Sociologist Herman Gray identifies three discursive practices that structure contemporary media representations of African Americans: "assimilationist (invisibility), pluralist (separate but equal), and multiculturalist (diversity)."[60] These three practices demonstrate the varying ways marginalized groups are represented in relation to the dominant group in a society. Discussions about racial representations in film and television are important because they make clear that gender identity is just one of the many ways that people can be represented; *Distancing Representations in Transgender Film* draws on this larger body of research on representations of marginalized groups.

Extending earlier discussions about minoritized representations, communication scholar Larry Gross argues that LGBTQ+ people remain particularly vulnerable to stereotyping because as "self-identified" minorities, LGBTQ+ people may lack adequate information about their identities in their immediate social environment and are forced to rely more on mass media for information.[61] The constraining nature of stereotypes limits the information available to people as they come to understand their identity. Gross, Gray, and Bogle point to the productive aspects of representation as well as the constraints by examining the ways stereotypes can limit how people see members of certain groups and affect how members of those groups see themselves.

Scholars exploring minority representations argue for images and stories that are as complex as our everyday lives. Damaging stereotypes present a homogeneous view of a marginalized group. Black lesbian feminist scholar and activist Audre Lorde argues that we have all been programmed to respond to difference either by ignoring, copying, or destroying it.[62] American society's failings to properly relate to difference lead Lorde to conclude that "our future survival is predicated upon our ability to relate within equality."[63] Stuart Hall distinguishes between difference that "makes a radical and unbridgeable separation" and difference which "is positional, conditional and conjectural."[64] Similar to Hall and Lorde, communication scholars

Victoria DeFrancisco and Catherine Palczewski argue, in their study of gender and communication, that it is important to be aware of the differences in people's gender identities while also identifying similarities in the binary categories of man and woman.[65] Dismantling these binary oppositions is, according to feminist literary scholar Sneja Gunew, "facilitated by the proliferation of differences."[66] An analysis of transgender representations is helped by an awareness of the different experiences and circumstances of the characters in the films under study by making it clear that difference can be just as important and informative as similarity. Since this project focuses on the legitimacy of transgender identities, difference is addressed through the various experiences of being transgender for the characters in these films rather than arguing for different conceptions of what it means to be transgender. A character in a transgender comedy whose adoption of a transgender identity is prompted by external circumstances and a character in a transgender drama who makes an active claim to a transgender identity are analyzed in this book as different experiences of being transgender rather than separated according to illegitimate and legitimate conceptions of transgender identity.

In contemporary media, "the primary emphasis" is on "the management of difference through incorporation or even its regulation through recognition."[67] Transgender representations fit within the management of difference; transgender characters are not incorporated into cisnormative systems of representation, but these representations do present a variety of experiences of being transgender. A space has been opened up in contemporary media, including film, for explorations of difference, and this project takes up difference by viewing transgender identity as a heterogeneous rather than homogeneous category. Transgender identity is accepted as legitimate in this project, but no one way of being transgender is necessarily privileged over any other, with criticism of the transgender characters focusing on their positions within cisnormative society rather than on their transgender identities. The selected films depict transgender people across race, class, sexual orientation, and gender identity and expression. Drawing from communication, queer, and cultural studies scholars, *Distancing Representations in Transgender Film* identifies ruptures across and within social categories, such as gender. These ruptures provide a fuller picture of how transgender people are represented in film.

Stereotypes and difference have shaped my understanding of how marginalized groups are narratively constructed in film and other media. My understanding of visual construction has been primarily influenced by the work of feminist film theorist Laura Mulvey on the gaze. Many film theorists discuss the constructed nature of film reality and viewing.[68] Film theorist Todd McGowan locates work on the gaze in "the work of French theorists such as Christian Metz, Jean-Louis Baudry, and Jean-Louis Comolli, as well as British theorists associated with the journal *Screen* such as Laura Mulvey, Peter Wollen, Colin MacCabe, and Stephen Heath."[69] Mulvey's conceptualization of the male gaze addresses how film guides the audience to look at characters in particular ways.[70] Mulvey argues that there are two ways of looking at women in film: voyeurism and fetishism. The male character controls the gaze and gains pleasure either from the act of looking or from the object being looked at. Film viewing in itself is often equated with voyeurism; fetishistic looking often involves the reduction of female characters to individual body parts.[71] Mulvey is not making an absolute claim for how audiences view films, but her arguments about the ways films are constructed to privilege certain viewing positions is useful to our understanding of the constructed nature of representation.

Criticisms of Mulvey's work have been made for decades. Substantive critiques were made from the perspectives of Lacanian psychoanalysis and feminist and queer film theory. According to McGowan, early Lacanian film theory focuses on desire as an expression of power.[72] Instead of being an expression of power, desire in Lacanian terms comes from the lack that is the product of the subject never being able to obtain the object so desired.[73] From this perspective on desire, the gaze "is not the vehicle through which the subject masters the object but a point in the Other that resists the mastery of vision. It is a blank spot in the subject's look, a blank spot that threatens the subject's sense of mastery in looking because the subject cannot see it directly or successfully integrate it into the rest of its visual field."[74] Film, functioning like a dream, allows the audience to surrender control of what happens on the screen while still embracing the world created there, but by doing so, the audience also cannot "turn away from the traumatic encounter" revealed by the gaze.[75] This traumatic encounter is with the Lacanian real, which is "the point at which signification breaks down, a gap in the social structure."[76] The potential of film is in this encounter with the real, but most popular film fails to achieve this by instead offering a "fantasmatic support for the ideology of capitalist society."[77]

My approach to visual construction in film is in line with this perspective on the gaze. I locate the gaze in the text of the film and not in the audience. "Understood in Lacan's own terms, the gaze is not the spectator's external view of the filmic image, but the mode in which the spectator is accounted for within the film itself."[78] The audience encounters the gaze through the film but does not possess it themselves. While film can facilitate an encounter with the Lacanian real, in most popular, commercial films, the "spectator's lack of conscious control renders the spectator extremely vulnerable to ideological manipulation while at the cinema."[79] The gaze has the potential to challenge ideology, but as found in popular films, it reinforces the status quo. The status quo in terms of gender is cisnormativity, so popular transgender films reproduce this ideology in their texts. The different gazes employed in transgender films visually construct film worlds that reproduce different aspects of cisnormativity. The visual construction of the films around these gazes communicates specific, cisnormative messages to the audience about the transgender characters.

Another critique of Mulvey's approach to the gaze from the perspective of feminist and queer theory is that the male gaze is limiting to our understanding of male audience members. For example, men's identities are also linked to how women see them.[80] According to Mulvey, the pleasure gained from the gaze by the male subject places the gaze within the realm of desire; it is the desire for the woman that gives men control over the gaze.[81] Kaja Silverman argues instead that the look is within desire while the gaze exists outside of desire.[82] The separation of the gaze from the male subject has important implications for feminist film theory, particularly that the problem is not the desire men direct toward women "but that male desire is so consistently and systematically imbricated with projection and control."[83] Instead of reducing the gaze to the possession of one group, we should instead be trying to understand how all kinds of people are constructed within the gaze.

While research on different gazes is useful to increasing our understanding of how the gaze functions in film to construct different groups of people in different ways, it should not be the end of research on the gaze. "By elaborating ways of seeing other than the male gaze, gaze theorists miss the most interesting point for thinking about how the body is produced in visual power relations. In gaze theory spinoffs, sight is held constant while gender, race, and sexuality become the variables."[84] What matters in Mulvey's work is her identification of the "structures of seeing" that privilege male perspectives in film.[85] The male gaze is one particular structure of seeing that constructs women in film according to "an aesthetic canon of female corporeity" that is "middle class, white and young, with fine facial features and unwrinkled skin, fit and well toned and especially slim."[86] If the gaze exists within the text of the film, what matters is how different groups are constructed within that text according to dominant ideologies, not the identities of the audience members.

J. Jack Halberstam adds to this line of analysis with his concept of the "transgender gaze."[87] Halberstam argues that the transgender gaze works either by forcing the audience to "rewind" the narrative of the film to make sense of the newly revealed transgender identity of a character, by allowing the audience to "look *with* the transgender character," or by constructing a gaze that does not directly reference either the male or female gazes.[88] Halberstam further develops Mulvey's concept of the gaze by taking a more developed account of those characters and audience members who do not fit easily into the categories of male and female.

I seek to identify another structure of seeing in *Distancing Representations in Transgender Film* that has been constructed in support of a cisnormative ideology. This structure of seeing takes the form of three gazes found in popular transgender films: trans-misogynistic, transphobic, and trans-pathetic. Trans-misogyny is "when a trans person is ridiculed or dismissed not merely for failing to live up to gender norms, but for their expressions of femaleness or femininity."[89] An example of the trans-misogynistic gaze is the shot in *Some Like It Hot* focusing on Joe and Jerry's legs as they walk along the train platform dressed as women for the first time. The trans-misogyny in the shot comes from using cisgender men to replicate how cisgender women are often presented visually in film; Joe and Jerry are critiqued in the shot for attempting to appear feminine even though they can never be as attractive as cisgender women. Transphobia is "an irrational fear of, aversion to, or discrimination against people whose gendered identities, appearances, or behaviors deviate from societal norms."[90] Transgender activist and legal scholar Dean Spade argues that transphobia functions through three forms of power: situating the person within a perpetrator/victim relationship, disciplining the person according to societal norms of behavior, and exclusion or inclusion from broad population management programs designed to benefit society.[91] It is primarily perpetrator/victim and disciplinary power at work in the transphobic gaze; an example of the transphobic gaze would be the image, toward the end of *Psycho*, of Norman Bates dressed as Mother with his knife raised high above his head in the fruit cellar of their house. The fear the audience feels from the shot attaches to Norman as he stands in the doorway with Mother's housedress over his clothes and her wig hastily placed on top of his head. A trans-pathetic gaze is one that directs the audience to feel sympathy for the transgender characters for all the effort they put into deviating from cisnormative standards; an example of the trans-pathetic gaze is the headless image of Bree as she gets dressed at the beginning of *Transamerica*. While the amount of effort Bree puts into getting ready in the morning is not that different from other women, the amount of attention given to it through the medium shots and close-ups gives each action additional weight that makes it seem excessive. Bree is given sympathy as a result of the extraordinary amount of work she goes through to present herself as a woman.

In what follows, the transgender gaze serves as a structuring element for the visual codes because it is important to understand how transgender characters are being looked at and how they are looking at others. I do not intend for the audience's affective and emotional responses and the three transgender gazes to appear to be a one-to-one match, with the trans-misogynistic gaze conveniently appearing in transgender comedies and so on. In order to accomplish the larger goal of this book in examining the ways transgender characters are distanced in filmic representations, I necessarily focus on the primary gaze in each category, but this does not mean that there is only one gaze present in the films. For example, *Mrs. Doubtfire* and *Big Momma's House* both feature scenes in which the disguises of the transgender characters are revealed when their latex masks begin peeling off of their faces. These scenes might rightfully be considered examples of the transphobic gaze, with Daniel's daughter Natalie in *Mrs. Doubtfire* bursting into tears at the sight of her father's face peering out from beneath the face of her nanny, but that does not change the fact that the primary gaze in these films and other transgender comedies is trans-misogynistic. In order to maintain the clarity of my argument, I avoid lengthy discussions of these deviations.

In order to help the reader better understand my position as a transgender woman as it relates to my analysis of transgender representations, I begin with a reflection of my own personal experiences with film and other media and how these experiences have shaped and been shaped by my transgender identity. I then analyze how the narrative conventions and visual codes are used in transgender comedies to prompt ridicule in the audience, how fear is prompted in transgender horror film, disgust in transgender thrillers, and sympathy in transgender dramas. I end with some brief suggestions of how to improve transgender representation in film and offer some suggestions for how the approach I use in this book can be applied to other films.

Many of the films analyzed in this book, such as *Some Like It Hot, Psycho, Sleepaway Camp* (1983), *The Crying Game, Mrs. Doubtfire,* and *Boys Don't Cry* (1999), are now two or more (in some cases, *several* more) decades old. I believe it is important to focus my analysis on these texts rather than more contemporary ones because they serve as the foundation for the patterns in transgender representations that I identify. These are the texts that are familiar to most people and are the ones most frequently referenced when discussing transgender representations in film. In order to clearly establish the patterns of identification with the audience and affective and emotional responses found within the film texts, it is important to begin with the foundational texts analyzed in this book. This is not to say that contemporary films should not be analyzed; films like *Tangerine* (2015), *A Fantastic Woman* (2017), and *Bit* (2019) are definitely deserving of analysis. I plan to continue my research on transgender representations in film by looking at these and future texts, and I hope other scholars join me as well. These more contemporary texts are not the focus of this book, and I hope it is clear through my analysis why it is important to focus on the foundational texts.

Transgender representations in film have an impact on the lives of transgender people because of the distance they create between a cisgender audience, whose only experience with transgender people is often through such media as film and because the affective and emotional responses prompted in the audience lead to negative associations with transgender identity. Films teach audiences to laugh at, be afraid of, be disgusted by, and have a distanced sympathy for transgender people. I am not claiming here a strong sense of the effect of film in that these films create these feelings within the audience. Instead, what I am arguing is that the affective and emotional responses are prompted by the narrative and visual constructions of the film and are located within the transgender identities of the characters by cisgender audience members. The distancing of the cisgender audience in terms of identification supports the location of the affective and emotional responses within the transgender identities of the characters because the cisgender audience is not encouraged to find a sense of commonality with the transgender characters. The films prompt responses of ridicule, fear, disgust, and sympathy in the audience and then attach those feelings to the transgender identities of the characters. The narrative and visual constructions of transgender films must change if the distance between the audience and the transgender characters is going to be reduced and if the affective and emotional responses in these films are going to be located in the situations instead of the characters.

1

My Transgender Experience
with Film and Other Media

I OPENED THIS BOOK WITH A brief anecdote about the role that *Mrs. Doubtfire* played in my earliest understandings of the public perception of transgender people, but this was far from the only time my transgender identity intersected with film and other media. I have been aware of my transgender identity since I was around five years old, at least as much as I could be aware without the language necessary to describe my experiences, which I would not acquire until I was a high school student just starting to poke around on the internet on the Macintosh Performa with the dial-up modem in my family's den. Media has been with me throughout my journey to understand and express my transgender identity.

One of my earliest memories of being aware of my nascent transgender identity came while watching an episode of the TV cartoon *Teenage Mutant Ninja Turtles* (1987–1996) when I was five. I remember thinking as I watched the episode that I would be more like the character of Irma, the nerdy secretary at a New York news station, rather than April O'Neil, the attractive reporter at the same station who befriends the Ninja Turtles. It was my realization that I was thinking about the woman I would one day be, rather than considering such a future an impossibility, that brought the first glimmers of my awareness of my transgender identity. In order to help readers better understand my perspective on transgender representation in film, I want to share more of my experiences with film and other media that have played a role in shaping my transgender identity.

Searching for Transgender Representation

One thing I remember as I reflect on my childhood experiences is my desire to see as many examples, good or bad, of transgender representation as I could. This was not always easy to do as a kid growing up in a small town in central Texas in the 1980s and 1990s. At first, awareness was my primary barrier; it is hard to search for something that you do not even know exists. After seeing *Mrs. Doubtfire* and realizing that films like it even existed, I used any means available to find more. I remember furtive searches in encyclopedias and library card catalogs, quick glances in bookstore fashion/beauty sections, and hastily deleted internet search histories. One valuable tool was a *People* magazine CD-ROM that was included with my family's Performa home computer. The disk functioned as a pop-culture encyclopedia, and its search function led me to other films that included elements of cross-dressing. I read with great interest about films like *Some Like It Hot, La Cage aux Folles* (1978), and *Psycho*, always ready to click over to material on a more mundane subject if my parents came into the room. The *People* disk opened my eyes to the existence of transgender representation in film, and I was always on the lookout, whenever I was watching a cable movie channel or perusing the offerings at a video rental store, for titles I had seen mentioned in its database.

One particularly fruitful outlet in my search for transgender representation was late-night TV. In those days, films about or featuring transgender people were often shown late at night on cable channels like HBO and Cinemax. This made clear to me, on some level, that transgender identity was taboo, a topic to be explored only in darkness and privacy. But I was so desperate for any examples of transgender people that I was grateful for any chance to see them on screen. One film I watched multiple times on HBO was Lee Grant's 1985 documentary, *What Sex Am I?* The film told the stories of several transgender women and men, and I was particularly drawn to a young transgender woman who underwent gender confirmation surgery during the film. I remember thinking how pretty she was and hoping I could be like her in the future. I was still too young to understand the film's presentation of the struggles of the transgender people it featured, which was the primary theme of the film, but I was still drawn to it whenever I was able to catch it.

At this time, my mom subscribed to a monthly broadcast guide for all of the cable channels, so I didn't have to rely on simply stumbling across transgender films by accident. It was while perusing this guide one month that I found that *The Christine Jorgenson Story* (1970), the true story of an American World War II veteran who was one of the first people to publicly transition and undergo medical treatment and surgery, would be airing on Turner Classic Movies one night at around two a.m. My plan was to use my VCR to record the film and watch it later, but I was so excited to see it that I woke up in the middle of the night to watch it when it aired. My desire to see any transgender representation I could was so strong that being exhausted at school the next day seemed like a worthwhile sacrifice to make. The film dramatizes Jorgenson's life and her fame after returning from her surgery in Denmark in the 1950s, but it stumbles a bit by identifying sexual frustration as Jorgenson's primary motivation for pursuing transition and surgery. I also remember being disappointed with how much time the film spends on Jorgenson's pre-transition life.

Recalling these late-night TV viewing experiences reminds me now of how clandestine and furtive my attempts to find examples of transgender representation were at this time. I was never able to openly express my interest in transgender representation because my family has never been supportive of my transgender identity. I tried to come out to my family as a kid, somewhat clumsily since, as a kid in early 1990s central Texas, I did not have the language to communicate what coming out even meant. To this day, it is difficult even to think of that effort as an attempt to come out, since I was so unable to understand, much less articulate, the feelings I was trying to express. One day when I was eleven, I enthusiastically told my dad that I wanted to show him what I wanted to be when I grew up. As he waited, annoyed because he wanted to finish mowing the yard, I went to the bathroom and emerged several minutes later wearing one of my mom's dresses that I had hidden there and happily exclaimed, "I want to be a girl!"

My dad reacted with a look of shock on his face and told me angrily, "Take that off immediately!" Then he tried to explain to me that my behavior was a phase that showed I was starting to be interested in girls. I was sad and confused at the time, because while I had known for a long time that I wanted to be a girl, I had always thought of it as a wish that could only be granted magically, supernaturally. Seeing films like *Mrs. Doubtfire* and transgender representation in other media made me realize that being a woman was something I could achieve in my real life, and I did not expect my family to not be supportive. My feelings did not go away, of course, but my ability to express my identity and to see other people like me in film and other media became more repressed as I grew up. My understanding of my identity and my interest in transgender representation did not go away, but they became hidden interests that I could not openly express.

Since my interest in transgender representation had to stay covert, I often thrilled when hints of transgender people appeared in unexpected places. One of those places was popular music. The 1987 Aerosmith song "Dude (Looks Like a Lady)" has a crass, transphobic message about its narrator being shocked at finding out that the person he is attracted to is a transgender woman, but when you are as starved for any transgender representation at all, as I was as a kid, you can find some small degree of pleasure even in a song like this. One particular context where it was often thrilling to hear the song was as part of the Rock 'n' Roller Coaster Starring Aerosmith ride experience at Walt Disney World's Hollywood Studios. The ride takes guests on a wild ride through the streets of Los Angeles to get to a sold-out rock show as Aerosmith music plays through speakers in each guest's headrest. During my visits to Walt Disney World in the early 2000s, I always enjoyed the "Dude (Looks Like a Lady)" part of the ride, knowing that all the other guests were also listening to a song about a transgender woman, even if the overall message of the song was negative. I think when I first heard the song, I tried to reinterpret it in a positive way, with Tyler's repeated exclamation intended to express admiration at the beauty of the transgender woman. But I soon accepted that there was no realistic understanding of the lyrics that made it positive. Despite this, I still took pleasure in hearing it, because its transgender theme was open and clear rather than coded and hidden.

Other songs allowed for even more covert enjoyment. One that was a particular stretch was No Doubt's "Sunday Morning" (1995). In the song, lead singer Gwen Stefani sings about a partner, "I'd never thought you could be that way / But you looked like me on Sunday." The song is actually about a woman who really liked someone and wanted to be like them, but they never gave her the time of day; now that she's moved on, they want her, so their roles have reversed. However, as a teenager starved for any hint of transgender representation, it was easy to reinterpret it to be about a woman discovering that her partner is transgender, that her partner literally looked like her. It was definitely a stretch, but my desire to express my true gender identity pushed me to find validation anywhere I could.

The Beatles have been one of my favorite bands since high school, so I delighted to find hints of transgender identity in a couple of their popular songs. In the final verse of the 1968 song "Ob-La-Di, Ob-La-Da," the main characters of Molly and Desmond switch places, and Molly now runs the stall in the marketplace, while Desmond "stays at home and does his pretty face / And in the evening she's a singer with the band." Meanwhile, the second verse of "Get Back" (1969) is about Sweet Loretta Martin who "thought she was a woman / But she was another man." The Beatles are an exceedingly mainstream band, so finding these little hints of transgender identity provided a secret pleasure for me.

A more contemporary example is the Killers' 2004 song "Somebody Told Me." In the chorus, lead singer Brandon Flowers sings about a potential partner whose boyfriend "looked like a girlfriend / That I had in February of last year." As with the Beatles, transgender identity is only hinted at in what was a popular song when it was released. These hints of transgender identity were especially important to me when I had to be more covert about my interest in transgender representation and when I was still in the closet about my own transgender identity.

I also enjoyed discovering songs that addressed a transgender identity in a more direct way. One example is Garbage's "Cherry Lips" (2001). Lead singer Shirley Manson sings of the title character (who is based on the fictional transgender character Cherry Vanilla in the 2000 JT LeRoy novel, *Sarah*), "You could make grown men gasp." The reason she is able to do this is "Because you looked just like a girl." It was easy for me to listen to the song and dream of being sexy and desirable.

Another I remember discovering was Green Day's song "King for a Day," from their 1997 album, *Nimrod*. I'd had the album for a few years before listening to the song, as I tended to just listen to a few of the popular songs at the beginning of the album before skipping to "Good Riddance (Time of Your Life)" toward the end. Imagine my surprise—as a college student in the early 2000s, listening to the album all the way through on the long drive from central Texas to Fayetteville, Arkansas—to discover the lines in the chorus, "King for a day, princess by dawn / Just wait 'til all the guys get a load of me."

While I had been surviving for years finding hints of a transgender identity in popular music, a song that made clear reference to cross-dressing had been hiding under my nose the whole time! The lines in the bridge of the song about femininity not being exclusive to women also served as a balm during my time in the closet as a means of declaring my femininity without having to completely come out yet. I even used lines from the song as the heading of a now long-abandoned LiveJournal blog that I maintained as another semipublic attempt to express my continually developing identity. Revisiting that blog recently in preparation for writing this book was an interesting look into a time capsule, as it is mostly me writing about what is going on in my life and what anime I am watching. The identity-related posts are private, so they are not visible if you find the blog online, but they were definitely an important means of expression for me at that time. It was through that blog that I officially came out to my group of friends at the time. I came out initially as a cross-dresser, because I still was not fully ready to come out as a transgender woman, but this was still a big first step. I almost had a panic attack, though, when I checked the post later and found dozens of comments. It was only visible to my friends, so I immediately worried that someone was very upset and unsupportive of my identity. My panic quickly turned to annoyance, though, when I found that a few of my friends had chosen to use that post's comment box, of all posts, to debate some random topic. Beyond the use of the lyrics for "King for a Day" in my blog, songs that made more direct references to transgender identity felt like progress from trying to find vague references and hints in a song's lyrics. Those were still few and far between and still were not openly supporting transgender people, but they served as at least some actual representation in media.

Many other forms of media were part of my search for any transgender representation I could find. One example that I remember well is the role-playing video game *Final Fantasy VII* (1997). In an early part of the game, the player character Cloud Strife sees a fellow party member named Tifa Lockhart being escorted into the mansion of the mafia boss Don Corneo. With help from another party member named Aerith Gainsborough, the player undertakes a quest to find the clothing needed to disguise Cloud as a woman and infiltrate the mansion. If the player finds clothing of high enough quality, they are able to play through the scenario as a cross-dressed Cloud, with the scene stopping right before Cloud is forced to kiss Corneo. I was extremely excited to find an extended cross-dressing segment in a video game and even created a separate save file right before the segment began so that I could replay it whenever I wanted. My experience with transgender representation was still limited to brief moments like this one in much larger texts, but each one I encountered, especially when it was unexpected, as in this case, sent a shiver of joy down my spine.

Another medium that has been important to my experience with transgender representation has been anime. Transgender representation in anime is generally limited to cross-dressing, and the shows exhibit some of the same issues that I will be discussing in my analysis of transgender representation in film. But I still got a thrill from discovering transgender representation of any kind in a medium I have enjoyed since I was in high school. It is, of course, annoying that many transgender characters in anime seem to be annoyed to be cross-dressing or only do so because of external reasons. For example, the main characters of *Princess Princess* (2006) are made to dress up as girls to break up the monotony of their all-male high school, and the main character in *Otoboku* (2006) cross-dresses as a condition of receiving his inheritance in his grandfather's will. As with other forms of transgender representation in media, these external reasons often make the characters more reluctant to cross-dress, which can be especially tough to accept for an in-the-closet transgender person like me who would have loved to have been in their positions. Reluctance can also be seen in anime in characters whose gender expression is more masculine or feminine than would be expected but who have clearly cisgender identities. One example is the character of Megumu in *If Her Flag Breaks* (2014); he is very feminine and often dresses as a girl (which he claims is the result of teasing by his older sisters) while also asserting his male identity and aspirations to manliness. Another is the character of Yukimura in *Haganai* (2011), who initially identifies as a boy and dresses as a maid as a way of proving his true manliness, but then, when it is discovered in the second season, *Haganai Next* (2013), that Yukimura is actually a girl, she is disappointed that she can no longer be a man and begins to dress as a butler to continue her quest for manliness. My point here is not to question the avowed identities of the characters themselves but to point out that the creators of these series generally use external reasons or a reluctance to identify as transgender as a means of providing the audience with the thrill of finding out that the characters are cross-dressing without risking alienating audience members by asking them to identify with a truly transgender character. Anime fans also have not always been great in their response to characters like these, frequently using the term *trap* to refer to any cross-dressed characters, with the clear implication that the fan was caught unawares by the character's gender identity and could therefore easily deny the authenticity of any attraction they may have felt to them. The two aspects of the characters, cross-dressing for external reasons and hiding that they are cross-dressing until they are discovered, work together to create the pleasure for many audience members.

Despite these issues with transgender representation in anime, I have still found pleasure myself in the abundance of the medium's cross-dressed and transgender characters. Seeing cute cross-dressers in anime gave me hope that I could be similarly cute as a transgender woman once I was able to come out. Anime also served as one of my first outlets for expressing my transgender identity as I began cosplaying (dressing up as some of my favorite anime characters) at anime conventions starting in 2005. I cosplayed exclusively as female characters, which was a surprise to many who knew me before I came out, and these opportunities to dress up in the safe space of an anime convention were fundamental to my understanding and embrace of my transgender identity.

I must also note that anime does include texts with characters who openly identify as transgender. *Genshiken: Second Season* (2013) includes a trans character named Hato who starts the series cross-dressing for external reasons but then grows to accept her transgender identity more by the end, while *Wandering Son* (2011) tells the story of a young transgender boy and transgender girl who struggle to understand their gender identities. An interesting recent example can be found in the character of Lily Hoshikawa from *Zombie Land*

Saga (2018). Lily is part of a group of young women resurrected as zombies to perform in an idol group. While she was assigned male at birth, Lily found success as a child actress because of her cuteness and energetic, feminine personality. Her death ties into her transgender identity, because she dies of shock upon discovering her first facial hair as her body begins going through puberty. She had stated previously that she never wanted to go through puberty and become an adult, because the changes it would bring would not match her gender identity. Lily's death touches on the trauma of puberty that many transgender people experience, a rare thing for any media text to address, and the show continues to support Lily's identity by having the other characters accept her for who she is and never question her gender identity. While these shows may be the exception in terms of transgender representation in anime, they show that the medium still has the potential for growth and will not always stay trapped in limiting forms of representation. Anime has been an important part of my life and my understanding of my transgender identity, and I hope to see even more positive examples like Lily in the future.

As should be clear by now, I seek out transgender representation wherever I can find it, and I generally want to see it for myself, even if it is not positive. One of the few consistent places to see transgender people in media when I was a teenager in the mid-1990s were trashy syndicated talk shows like *Jerry Springer* (1991–2018) and *The Maury Povich Show* (1991–2022). These shows presented transgender people as oddities for the audience to gawk at. One recurring feature of *Jerry Springer* was transgender people coming out to their romantic partners in front of the studio audience, often with violent results as their partners physically assaulted them and had to be physically restrained by the show's security. *Maury Povich* often featured transgender people encouraged to dress "one last time" as the gender assigned to them at birth for the benefit of their family members and friends, who could not accept their transgender identities. The episodes ended with the reveal of the transgender people appearing in clothes that matched their gender assigned at birth and the inevitable tears of joy of their family and friends getting to see them dressed again in a manner that matched how their family and friends wanted to remember them. These shows were cruel toward and exploitative of the transgender people who agreed to appear on them, as they were to most of the marginalized people who made up the majority of their guests. Despite the fact that I easily recognized this cruelty, I still watched the shows religiously in high school, in the hopes of catching any glimpse of an actual transgender person. The cruelty eventually outweighed my desire to see a transgender person on screen, and I stopped watching the shows. But my willingness to watch them for so long, no matter how negative, says a lot about how desperate I was for *any* representation.

Even as I have continued to seek out transgender representation in film and media, I have not ignored the fact that it is often negative toward transgender people. When the film *The Danish Girl* was released in 2015, I chose to go see it in the theater even though I agreed with the general sentiment that it would be bad. I exited the theater having confirmed that negative sentiment to be true, and I remember being most upset about Lili Elbe being presented as only discovering her identity as a woman after her wife gets her to wear a dress for a painting and, more importantly, that the film's vagueness about Lili's surgeries made it seem like all gender confirmation surgery is inherently deadly. This film also raises another issue that often contributes to negative representation of transgender people: the casting of cisgender actors as transgender characters—in this case, Eddie Redmayne as Lili. There has been a long history of cisgender actors playing transgender characters in film, with Matt Bomer in *Anything* (2017) and Michelle Rodriguez in *The Assignment* (2016) as two particularly troubling recent examples, and the continued casting of cisgender actors in these roles contributes to the negative representation of transgender people as the actors often help to perpetuate stereotypes about transgender people in their performances.

Even when a representation is good overall, there can still be issues. The film *A Fantastic Woman* is a very positive representation featuring a transgender actress, Daniela Vega, in the lead role, but I did not enjoy the scene in which Marina disguises herself as a man in order to enter a men's locker room of a sauna to try to find out what her partner Orlando left her when he died. Marina starts out in the women's locker room, but she then pulls her towel down around her waist, exposing her bare chest, and slicks back her hair to sneak into the men's locker room. She is ultimately disappointed as she finds Orlando's locker empty. While other members of the audience may have found the scene thrilling as they worried about whether Marina would be caught, I found it uncomfortable, as transgender women already have to work hard to be seen as women, so a scene in an otherwise positive film that implicitly reinforces the perception of transgender women as men was disappointing.

My desire to see any transgender representation I could has often meant enduring a lot of negative representation or searching for any hints of a transgender identity where I could find them. The lack of high-profile positive representations in media and of role models and acceptance in my own life contributed to this need to see any form of transgender representation available, no matter how bad. If there had been a handful of high-profile positive representations available at the time or if I had been accepted for who I am by my friends and family, I might not have needed to see transgender representations in media as badly as I did. My familiarity with transgender representation may not have been as well developed as it is now if I had experienced greater acceptance in my own life, but the lack of those positive experiences fueled my interest in the subject of transgender representation that led directly to this book.

Interest in Transformation

My identity as a transgender woman not only influenced my interest in transgender representations in film and other media but also shaped my enjoyment of other texts in significant ways. Another way my engagement with film and media texts was influenced by my transgender identity was in my interest in seeing narratives that involved transformation. After my clumsy, naïve attempt to come out to my dad as a kid, I turned more and more inward as I tried to process the experience and understand my transgender identity. I framed coming out to my dad around what I wanted to be when I grew up because wanting to be a girl seemed like, at the time, just as valid a goal for the future as anything else. I had expected my desire to be validated and for plans to be put in place to help me more freely express my identity, so when that did not happen, I was completely caught off guard. A lack of support from my family made becoming the woman I knew myself to be seem like less and less of a possibility, and as I withdrew into myself, I began to dream of other forces intervening in my life to help me become a woman. I was raised as an Evangelical Christian, so this meant a lot of praying for God to make me a girl, for me to just wake up one morning and be a girl. Alongside praying to be a girl was a lot of wishing and daydreaming about often fantastical events occurring that would allow me to be the person I was inside. This wishing persisted well into my mid-twenties as I struggled to find a way out of the closet, and I cannot say that such wishes are entirely gone even as I have been out publicly as a transgender woman for over a decade now. Wishing to be a girl was such a formative experience for me as a transgender person that I still find myself idly daydreaming about similar fantastical events—such as being transported to a fantasy world and transformed into a magical girl to save the kingdom or receiving a rich heiress's offer to cover all of my transition-related medical needs and then pay me a large salary to work as her personal maid—even to this day. These experiences manifested in my engagement with film and other media through an interest in texts involving transformation.

One film that resonated strongly with me in this way was Disney's *Aladdin* (1992). I loved the film as a kid, and I watched my family's VHS copy whenever I was home sick from school. The film itself was enjoyable on its own, but what sparked my imagination were the magic lamp and the theme of being a diamond in the rough. I fantasized about finding my own magic lamp that would grant my wish to be a girl, but I also connected with the film's theme of people being overlooked and not having their worth recognized by others. I was already beginning to feel that not being able to express my transgender identity meant that an important, creative, expressive part of myself was being bottled up and that it might take a magic lamp to release it. To this day, I still do not think that I am always able to express myself as fully as I want to because of years of trying to keep my feminine side under control lest someone find out the truth about me and hate me for it. Those daydreams I still have often revolve around being able to fully embrace the feminine person that I am without the limitations that came from having to live as someone that I am not. My dream may no longer be to find a magic lamp, but it is still similar to the dreams I had after watching *Aladdin* as a kid.

I was so desperate for a way to be myself that it did not even take a text as developed as a feature-length film to capture my interest. Sometimes, it could be the smallest snippet of a text in an advertisement. I read a lot of video game magazines as a kid, and I remember seeing an ad for a game based on the manga and anime series *Ranma ½* (1989–1992) in one of the magazines. The ad featured a few panels from the manga that summarized the story of Ranma Saotome and his father Genma doing martial arts training in China when Ranma falls into a cursed spring and turns into a girl when cold water is poured on him. I had not heard of the series and did not even know what anime was at the time, though I would soon be a huge fan, but it only took a handful of panels in a video game ad for my imagination to start running wild. I immediately began to dream about having a similar experience and happily staying a girl as compared to Ranma's constant complaining about his situation. A candidate for such a place could even be found in our backyard, where an old storm shelter had been filled in with dirt, creating a small hill. I began to imagine that it was not a storm shelter that had been filled in but a spring that had been covered up after a girl drowned in it. My dream was that I would be playing on the hill when the ground beneath me would suddenly give way, and I would fall into the water of the spring and take on the form of the girl who had drowned. The dream was short-lived, but this small snippet in an ad was all it took to spark the fantasy. I did eventually get to see the *Ranma ½* anime when it was released on DVD nearly a decade later, and I was even able to play the game that had been the subject of the magazine advertisement all those years before, though it could never live up to the vivid fantasies I had built up in my head about it. Even if the text itself did not live up to expectations, as with the *Ranma ½* video game, it could still serve as fodder for my imagination.

Another small text that sparked my imagination regarding transformation was a 1992 Nike ad campaign featuring Bugs Bunny and Michael Jordan that preceded the film *Space Jam* (1996). In the ad, Bugs is asleep when he is awoken by the racket of a basketball game being played above his home. When he confronts the players, Bugs is comically abused by them, so he seeks his revenge by slipping on a pair of the new Air Jordan sneakers and teaming up with Michael Jordan. In the midst of their antics, including replacing the ball with a cartoon anvil and pies in the face, Bugs quickly cross-dresses in a blonde wig, frilly purple top, and blue skirt with a slit up the right leg and poses flirtatiously in order to distract the other team—a reference to Bugs's frequent cross-dressing in the old Looney Tunes cartoons. I remember drawing a cross-dressed Bugs in my school notebooks over and over again, along with other Looney Tunes characters in the same style. I eventually began to imagine myself in the sexy pin-up style Bugs adopts in the ad and dreamed of being able to transform as easily as him into an attractive woman. Even though Bugs was cross-dressing, the *ease* with which he transformed is what drew my attention. My experience had not been so easy, so the wishes inspired by the ad seemed just as fantastical as a magic lamp.

The fantastical daydreams of my middle-school years eventually led to an interest in films more explicitly about transformation. *My Fair Lady* (1964) was my first Audrey Hepburn film and remains my favorite film to this day. The amazing music, gorgeous costumes, and stellar cast are all wonderful, but what excited me most about the film was the story of an average person who is able to transform into a beautiful, sophisticated woman. I hoped for a long time to find my own Henry Higgins, someone whose coaching would help me fully be the woman I wanted to be. In reality, I have had to figure things out as a transgender woman mostly on my own, and I do not know if I have fully reached the level that I dreamed of when I was younger (it definitely would help to already be as beautiful as Audrey Hepburn), but I was eventually able to overcome the mental barriers that prevented me from coming out, one of which was the idea that I should not try unless I could be beautiful. This feeling was reinforced when I was sent to a Christian psychologist by my parents after trying to come out as a freshman in college. The psychologist told me there was no point in transitioning because I would always be physically seen as a man; he told me he also gave similar advice to a young transgender man that his feminine features would always prevent him from being seen as a man. Having yet another authority figure try to quash my transgender identity was upsetting to say the least, and this, combined with my wishes for a transformation, probably prolonged the time until I came out publicly. As I reflect on these experiences, I feel that my true desire at the time was for someone to support me and accept me for who I am, demonstrating that support by helping me transform into a beautiful woman. For that reason, the films felt hopeful for me instead of limiting my ability to come out through wishful fantasies.

As I became a bigger fan of Audrey Hepburn, I was surprised to discover other films starring her that focus on transformation. *Sabrina* (1954) tells the story of the daughter of a rich family's chauffeur who, after a suicide attempt, leaves for Paris and returns as an attractive, sophisticated young woman. *Funny Face* (1957) features Hepburn as a clerk at a bookstore who ends up becoming a model in a fashion magazine. Even *Roman Holiday* (1953) tells the story of a princess who disguises herself in order to explore Rome on her own. I soon discovered other films with a makeover theme, with Cher's makeover of Tai in *Clueless* (1995) and Laney's transformation from nerd to prom queen in *She's All That* (1999) as standouts. Makeover and transformation films like these remain enjoyable to me because it took a lot to overcome the messages that I have received for most of my life telling me that I should not bother coming out because I will never be seen as a woman. These films gave me a little bit of hope that those messages were not true.

Along with enjoying makeover and transformation stories in film and other media, songs in films about transformation and the desire for change resonated strongly with me. *The Little Mermaid* (1989) and *Beauty and the Beast* (1991) feature songs about this kind of longing. In the former, in the song "Part of Your World," Ariel sings, "When's it my turn? / Wouldn't I love, love to explore that shore up above?" In the latter film, in the song "Belle (Reprise)," Belle sings, "I want adventure in the great wide somewhere / I want it more than I can tell." Films like *The Hunchback of Notre Dame* (1996) and *Pocahontas* (1995) had similar messages, with Quasimodo, dreaming of getting to leave the cathedral, singing, "Just one day and then / I swear I'll be content." Meanwhile Pocahontas wonders, "Why do all my dreams extend / Just around the riverbend?" Kids growing up in the 1990s got a lot of messages from popular film and media that you should be yourself and not give in to the constraints of those around you. A more recent song that features a similar sentiment is "Let It Go" from *Frozen* (2013). I remember sitting in the theater with my mom and my three-year-old nephew completely stunned as Elsa, one of the princess protagonists of the film, sang, "Can't hold it back anymore" and "I don't care what they're going to say." The defiance in her song as she declared that she was going to be herself in spite of what anyone else thought stood out to me and made the song feel like it could be a queer/transgender anthem. I spent years as a kid and into my twenties dreaming of being able to finally be myself, so songs like these will always resonate with me.

A song that touches on the difficulties of transformation is "Reflection" from *Mulan* (1998). The song takes place right after

Mulan has ruined the meeting with a matchmaker that her family set up for her to find her a husband, and she is still wearing the makeup and outfit chosen for her in order to impress the matchmaker. As she walks home, Mulan reflects on her unsuitability for the role she is expected to play. As she sits in front of the graves of her ancestors and wipes off her makeup, she ends the song wondering if she will ever truly be able to be herself. The message in this song is similar to the one found in other Disney films about the desire for change and transformation, and I have often felt a similar sense of disappointment at the image I see in a mirror not matching how I see myself inside.

This element alone, giving voice to the desire for change being not just about the yearning for something new but also a need to be true to yourself, would be enough to make the song resonate with me. But its additional theme of the fear that underlies that desire takes the song to another level. As Mulan leaves the matchmaker's house, she sings about not being able to be the perfect daughter that her family wants, and she looks over to see her parents consoling each other over how she ruined their plans for her future. She then sings, "Now I see, that if I were truly to be myself / I would break my family's heart." These lines always get me choked up because my family is still important to me, even if they do not accept me for who I am. This is a fear that has shaped a lot of my decisions throughout my life. The desire to be bold and decisive, to stand up for myself and for who I am, and to not let anyone prevent me from being myself is counterbalanced by a feeling of not wanting to hurt people I care about. It would be nice if we were in a place as a society where being transgender was not seen as something hurtful, but we are still not there for the most part. My family most definitely is not there yet, and I do not know if they will ever get there. I obviously have not completely repressed my identity and stayed in the closet to appease my family, but I still see how I limit myself out of concern for hurting them. The fear is still there, and that is why this song still gets to me whenever I hear it.

Transformation stories have long been an important part of my engagement with film and other media. Especially when I could not express my transgender identity freely, these stories offered a feeling of hope and possibility for the future. These hopes and dreams, however fantastical they may have been, were an important part of helping me get through some of the hardest times of being in the closet. When I did not have anyone to really turn to or offer support, I could at least imagine a future where I could be myself. This interaction between media and my dreams for the future also happened in more tangible ways.

When I was in junior high school, I wrote and sent a letter to Walt Disney World in which I said how much I loved the character of Alice from *Alice in Wonderland* (1951) and requested the company's help to get hormone treatment and gender confirmation surgery so I could play her at its theme parks. Around the same time, I also sent a letter to Saban Entertainment, the creator of the kids' martial arts action show *Mighty Morphin Power Rangers* (1993–1996), in which I offered my ideas for a similar show and my request for gender confirmation support so I could play one of the female characters. I do not remember whether I ever heard back from Saban, but I did receive a reply from Walt Disney World, politely turning me down and thanking me for my love of Alice, along with a photo of her and the other *Alice in Wonderland* characters. It did not seem ludicrous to me at the time to reach out to media companies in this way, because it was through media that I found any hope for change at all. I was obviously very naïve, but at the time, being able to be myself seemed like an equally impossible achievement. I found solace in these stories of transformation, so I still think of them fondly rather than worrying about being somehow misguided. Along with hope through stories of transformation, film and other media also offered role models and opportunities to express my femininity.

Looking for Role Models and Expressions of Femininity

I obviously did not have any transgender role models to look up to growing up, either in real life or in media, so I had to look for other role models for how to be a woman in film and other media. Like many other nerdy kids in the 1990s, I was immediately drawn to Belle from *Beauty and the Beast* for her love of books and because she becomes a princess. Another character I wanted to be like was Rory from the comedy-drama series *Gilmore Girls* (2000–2007) both for the fact that she embraced her intelligence and that she had a close relationship with her mother, Lorelai. (I have always had a close relationship with my mom, but her feelings about my transgender identity has always created a bit of a barrier to my fully opening up with her.) A few other characters I remember wanting to be like growing up include Nona from the comedy series *The Adventures of Pete and Pete* (1992–1996), Patty Mayonnaise from the animated series *Doug* (1991–1994), Cher from the movie *Clueless*, and Willow and Tara from the series *Buffy the Vampire Slayer* (1997–2003). A more recent character I have wanted to be like is Jessica Day from comedy series *New Girl* (2011–2018). I always admired Jess because she was able to stay true to her feminine identity while still showing strength and the ability to stand up for herself. In a season one episode, Jess asks Julia, a lawyer who is dating her roommate Nick, for help getting out of a ticket. When Jess messes up their plan by pleading guilty, Julia mocks her for her feminine style and cutesy attitude. I was proud in that moment that Jess stood up for herself by not denying her femininity and insisting that being feminine does not mean that she also cannot be strong. I have always seen myself as a feminine person and have had to overcome a lot of barriers, both internal and external, to be able to fully embrace my femininity. Even after coming out, I still felt pressure to downplay my femininity in order to be more professional and create a proper persona for the classroom and other professional settings. I have been making more of an effort in the last few months to reject the idea that my kind of femininity means I am not suitably professional or should not be taken seriously. I have reached a point where I just do not care anymore what people think as trying to fit in did not really work for me either. If I am not going to be accepted either way, I should at least be happy being myself instead of worrying about others. I have characters like Jess to thank for helping me understand that about myself.

Film and other media also provided a space for me to express my femininity while I was in the closet without raising many real questions about it. Enjoying Audrey Hepburn and Disney princess films was mainstream enough that no one really questioned it. Two forms of media that particularly created space for me to express my femininity were video games and anime. I have played video games since I was a kid, and I got my first video game console, a Nintendo Entertainment System, for my seventh birthday. Video games were heavily marketed in the 1980s and 1990s as a pastime for boys, which actually provided cover for the feminine space I was able to create for myself within the medium. The first form this feminine space took for me was in simple character choice. When playing *Super Mario Bros. 2* (1988), for example, I would always pick the player character of Princess Peach, and I continue to prefer playing as female characters when given the choice. A specific memory I have related to character choice is racing my cousin to choose Julie over Zeke when playing *Zombies Ate My Neighbors* (1993) together. I am not sure why my cousin, who was a boy, was so determined at the time to play as Julie, but I know that I always enjoyed it because I was able to imagine myself as a girl for as long as we were able to stay alive in the game. There were not a lot of games at the time that gave you the option to play as a female character, so I was always excited to find a game that did. *Threads of Fate* (1999) let you play as the magic-wielding princess Mint along with the sullen, sword-wielding Rue. A genre that provided a surprisingly high number of opportunities to play as female characters were fighting games. Most fighting game series would start off with only one female character, but that was still more than most other game series included. I remember wanting to get a Super Nintendo and *Street Fight II* (1992) after seeing the inserts about the game in *GamePro* magazine and wanting to play as Chun-Li. *Rival Schools: United by Fate* (1997) included a high number of female characters in its roster and also allowed players to add a seemingly endless number of random clone characters. I even remember getting frustrated at times when I was not as good as I wanted to be with a particular female character. *Garou: Mark of the Wolves* (1999) featured two female characters in its roster of fighters: Hotaru Futaba and Bonne Jenet. Hotaru is a cute, spritely young woman searching for her brother while Bonne is a sexy pirate in high heels and a dress with a slit up her left leg. I wanted to play as Hotaru because she fit my style better, but I found that I played better as Bonne. Even when multiple female characters are available in a game, I still have to make decisions about who I want to play by weighing aesthetic preferences against gameplay effectiveness.

Another way that video games created a space for me to express my femininity was when more games included character creation options. These games allowed you to design a character that fit your preferences, so my ability to express myself increased even more. After a period of waning interest in video games, I got back into gaming with the release of the Nintendo Switch in 2017. One game I spent hundreds of hours with that first year was *Splatoon 2* (2017). The game has you competing against other teams to paint as much of the terrain as you can using a creative set of weapons, and I had a lot of fun making my Inkling (the squid-kid avatars in the game) as feminine as I could within the game's sporty-punk aesthetic. I also enjoyed that the game allowed for effective participation in multiplayer matches without the need for voice chat. Voice chat is often a touchy subject for transgender people, as it can often lead to harassment and abuse when others learn about your transgender identity. I had generally avoided multiplayer games because of not wanting to use voice chat, so I was pleasantly surprised when *Splatoon 2* allowed me to play without needing it. *Animal Crossing: New Horizons* (2020) provided a wider range of style options to customize your characters than those found in *Splatoon 2*, and I have enjoyed dressing my avatar up in sailor dresses, maid outfits, and giant hair bows. The number of games that allow for feminine character customization is high enough now that I find myself getting frustrated when a game limits your options. When the popular battle royale game *Fortnite* (2017) came to Switch in 2018, I tried the game out, but one reason I lost interest in it pretty quickly is that when playing as a default character, players do not have any options to customize the character or even make choices about their basic appearance or gender. I remember getting a female character the first time I played and being frustrated when I came back to the game to find her replaced with a male character. Character customization has allowed me to express my femininity even more fully in games, so I find myself frustrated whenever those options are limited.

A game that I was surprised by my reaction to was *Pokémon: Sword* (2019). I played *Pokémon* on the Nintendo Game Boy when the game debuted in 1998, but I had not really kept up with the series until playing the remake of the original game, *Pokémon: Let's Go, Eevee!* (2018). The remake did allow you to choose a female avatar, unlike the original version, but the customization options were fairly limited. When I started playing *Pokémon: Sword*, I was able to choose a female character, as this had become a staple of the series in the twenty years since I had really played one of the games, but an avatar's appearance initially was mostly restricted to the default version of the character. The character was cute enough and I enjoyed playing the game, but I did not feel a strong connection to the character at first. I was surprised, then, when I got out of the starting town and was able to customize my character for the first time. I honestly got choked up upon seeing my character after making the customization changes because she looked like how I had always imagined I would have looked as a kid. As I set off to catch as many Pokémon as I could and become a champion, I also found myself wistfully imagining the adventures I could have had if I had been able to be this version of myself.

Video games have provided meaningful opportunities to express my femininity. The interactive nature of games helps me to see myself as the character on screen and gives the opportunity to express my femininity with even greater impact. Video games are still mostly marketed to and revolve around boys and men, but I will always appreciate the feminine spaces I have been able to create for myself within games.

Anime is another medium that has offered me a number of opportunities to express my femininity. Like video games, anime has not been understood well by those around me, so my enjoyment of anime as a whole was seen as weird, regardless of how feminine it was as a product. The first anime series I ever saw that I recognized as anime was *Sailor Moon* (1992–1997), when it first appeared on Cartoon Network's Toonami block of programming in 1998. I had seen other anime series before *Sailor Moon*, but I did not know they were anime at the time. When I saw *Sailor Moon*, though, I was floored, and my love of anime has continued to this day. What stood out to me about the show was not only its magical action featuring teenage girls (something hardly seen at the time in American media) but also the aesthetics and themes of femininity that it offered. The characters start off wearing outfits based on Japanese sailor-style school uniforms to fight monsters, and their outfits get even more feminine, with added ribbons, bows, and weapons based on makeup, as the series goes on and the characters get stronger. The power of friendship is a major theme of the series, with the characters repeatedly sacrificing themselves for each other, and even though Usagi, the main character, starts off the series as a lazy crybaby, her friends stick with her and support her as she grows to be a competent leader. The fact that the show did not shy away from femininity in its designs and in the characters left a major impression on me about how femininity could be used effectively in telling a story. While I would go on to watch a lot of anime series that are more traditionally masculine, such as *Dragon*

Ball Z (1989–1996), *Bleach* (2004–2012), and *Demon Slayer: Kimetsu no Yaiba* (2019), *Sailor Moon* will always hold a special place in my heart and has led me to other great anime series centered around feminine characters, including *Cardcaptor Sakura* (1998–2000), *Revolutionary Girl Utena* (1997), and *Paradise Kiss* (2005), just to name a few.

What always excited me about how femininity is presented in anime is the predominant focus on being cute as compared to the focus in American media on being cool. There is a lot of influence in aesthetic and character design from Japanese street fashions like Gothic/Sweet Lolita and maid culture, so the designs mostly focus on ribbons, bows, sparkles, puffy skirts, and Mary Jane-style shoes. These design elements fit my personal style better and have probably influenced it a lot as well, so I find myself attracted more to the style of femininity found in anime. The desire to be cute is often a character trait for female characters who are tall and perceived as cool. Sakaki from *Azumanga Daioh* (2002) and Erza from *Fairy Tail* (2009–2019) are both characters who have to hide their interest in cute things because of the way others idolize them for being cool. This desire to be cute is also a major part of the plot of *Sword Art Online Alternative: Gun Gale Online* (2018). The main character, Karen Kohiruimaki, is a tall woman who is self-conscious about her height and ends up playing the online VR game Gun Gale Online because it is the only one that allows her to have an avatar that is cute and little. This desire to be cute even when you physically do not fit the expectations of who can be cute is definitely something I can relate to. Karen's interest in being cute and little is even turned on its head when she meets a group of short high school girls who play together in the game as tall, masculine women. The series does a good job of reminding viewers that your own personal desires may not be shared by others but that does not make either any less valid. This interest in all things cute was even tested while I was still in the closet in college. I went to my local Best Buy to browse the anime section one day and decided to buy a new series called *Super Gals!* (2001–2002) after enjoying a trailer I had seen for it earlier. The first disc for the series came in a collector's box that was meant to hold the rest of the series, and when I picked up the box, I found it was pink and covered with flowers and other girly artwork. Since I was still in the closet, I thought to myself for a moment about what others would think of me if I bought it and even wished that the designers had chosen a more subdued design, but I quickly shook those thoughts off and told myself that if I really was the woman I knew myself to be, I should not be embarrassed to buy something so feminine. With that thought in mind, I marched straight to the cashier to buy the series without a second thought.

Anime and video games created useful spaces for me to express my femininity at times when I could not express it openly in my own life. Film and other media also provided me with useful role models as I tried to understand what kind of woman I wanted to be. Even as I have been able to express my gender identity more openly for the last few years, the media I have listed here and many others continue to serve a useful purpose in my journey to better understanding myself.

I hope these recollections of how my transgender identity has shaped my experiences with film and other media provide a better understanding of who I am and the context of my work that follows. I also want to acknowledge that my experiences with media are not universal. Other transgender people may have had a wide range of transgender role models available to them that I was unaware of. Other transgender people may have also had different reactions to some of the texts I have mentioned in this chapter; the same texts that felt freeing to me as a space to express my femininity may have felt suffocating to someone else as a reinforcing of binary gender expectations. My purpose here is not to provide an all-encompassing look at how transgender people have understood film and other media but to provide an honest assessment of my own experiences with media and the role they have played in shaping my understanding of my transgender identity. I have tried to provide a snapshot here of the author that I am, for good and bad, before moving into my analysis of transgender representations in film.

I want to end with a recent experience that gives me some hope for my own future as a transgender woman. I was at home visiting my family, and my mom and I were talking when she excitedly told me about a show I needed to watch. We had talked about the 2021 sitcom *Call Me Kat* starring Mayim Bialik and some of the strange decisions the creators made in the first episode. The show was based on a British sitcom called *Miranda* (2009–2015), and my mom had just finished watching it on Hulu and said that it explained some of the decisions made in *Call Me Kat*. We started watching the first episode, and many of the jokes of the show centered on how much taller the main character, Miranda, is compared to other women. At one point in the episode, Miranda gets a date with a guy she is interested in, and her friend tells her she needs to get a new outfit for her date. Miranda is reluctant to go shopping because the stores usually do not have anything nice in her size, so she is excited to find out about a store that carries larger sizes. Cut to Miranda arriving at the store as someone who is very obviously a man leaves in a sequin-covered gown. I guess my expression was one of dismay, because my mom looked over at me at that point and actually said, "I'm sorry." It was just a small gesture, but it actually made me feel a little hopeful, because it is still rare for my mom or my family as a whole to acknowledge anything about transgender issues or to even notice when a negative portrayal makes me feel uncomfortable. I am not expecting any major shift in behavior or acceptance from my family anytime soon, but it was nice to feel a little hopeful.

Ridicule in Transgender Comedies

OMEDY IS THE MOST common genre of representation of transgender people in film.[1] Films like *Some Like It Hot, Tootsie,* and
Victor/Victoria (1982) have become both financial and critical
successes. *Some Like It Hot* grossed $25 million (earning the highest
weekly box office grosses for five weeks of 1959) and received six Oscar
nominations, winning one; *Tootsie* grossed $117 million (becoming the
second-highest grossing movie of 1982), received ten Oscar nominations, and won one; and *Victor/Victoria* grossed $28 million, received
seven Oscar nominations, and won one. Even a critically panned film
like *Big Momma's House* (2000) grossed $117 million and spawned two
sequels. Hollywood rakes in money as audiences laugh at images of
a man in a dress or a woman wearing a tuxedo.

While these films have been successful, the success of each has
relied on the distancing of the transgender characters, making them
objects of ridicule. John Phillips argues that cross-dressing in film
reflects the needs of comedy and society to have a subject to ridicule.[2]
He dismisses any transgressive readings of these films, *Some Like It Hot*
in particular, because the effect of comedy is to not take the actions
of the characters seriously.[3] By not taking the characters seriously,
any threat present in their transgender identities is controlled. This
control is exerted not only through the ridiculing of the characters'
transgender identities but also through the privileging of their cisgender

identities. The films construct the cisgender identities of the characters to appeal to the mostly cisgender audience while still allowing them to laugh at the transgender identities of the same characters.

According to Sara Ahmed, affective responses reflect a sense of "stickiness" based on how they connect us to others.[4] Laughter and happiness produce stickiness by connecting us to the people and objects we are closest to.[5] In the distancing representations found in transgender comedies, the audience is not encouraged to identify with the transgender identities of the characters, so the films provide a source of identification within their texts that is consistent with the cisnormative identification that exists with the implied author. The distinct cisgender identities of the characters serve as this additional point of identification and shape the narrative conventions and visual codes used to prompt the emotional response of ridicule from the audience.

Humor has the clear rhetorical function of telling the audience how it should respond to the characters; in the case of transgender characters, the lack of seriousness attributed to their actions, making them the objects of the humor rather than active participants in the humor, creates a separation from the audience. Ridicule, laughing at the characters, implies a negative relationship between the audience and the characters that runs counter to the closeness that is expected from laughter. John Meyer expands on our understanding of humor's rhetorical function by identifying four potential effects of humor based on the relationship between the laughing subject and the object of that laughter: identification, clarification, enforcement, and differentiation.[6] Humor works through the audience recognizing similarities with the characters, encountering new situations through the characters' experiences, disciplining the characters for violating society's norms, or ridiculing the characters for diverging from the dominant society. Whether humor comes from similarity or difference, it is ultimately used to reinforce conformity to social norms.[7] The humor in transgender comedies is usually the result of the enforcement and differentiation effects; audience members laugh because they are happy to see a character facing difficulty while cross-dressed or because the experiences of the characters while cross-dressed are so distant from audience members' own lives that mocking the characters is acceptable. Because the point of identification for these films is being cisgender, the transgender identities of the characters can only be viewed as different and in need of disciplining to conform to social norms. Humor based in difference is often used to assuage audience fears; what is feared "must be made fun of to exorcise the fear" with laughter providing a way of "asserting power over terrible threats."[8] Victoria Flanagan argues that, ultimately, "male cross-dressing films replicate the general cultural construction of male cross-dressing as an amusing joke."[9]

Prompting Ridicule through Narrative Conventions

The narratives of transgender comedies may seem to be aiming only for laughs, but through the use of specific conventions, messages are sent to the audience that clearly privilege the cisgender identities of the characters over their transgender identities. At various moments throughout the films, the cisgender identities of the characters are given greater weight and importance than their temporarily adopted transgender identities. These moments range from the characters leaving their normal lives in face of a crisis by adopting transgender identities to regularly discarding those identities in order to pursue heterosexual romances. At the end of these narratives, the characters are portrayed as having learned important lessons and grown as people through their experiences, but their transgender identities are cast aside as inconsequential, just part of their personal growth.

The separation that is created narratively between the cisgender and transgender identities of the characters leads to their transgender identities being the objects of ridicule, thus supporting the distancing of the transgender characters from the audience. Most of the comedy in the films is either performed by the characters in their transgender identities, such as stumbling down the street while trying to walk in high heels, or directed at their transgender identities, such as making fun of how they look as their transgender alter egos. Jerry gleefully frolicking as one of the girls at the beach in *Some Like It Hot* is a good example of the former, while a good example of the latter is the reply of the cameraman in *Tootsie* when asked how far back he can pull the camera to make Michael Dorsey look good for his screen test: "How do you feel about Cleveland?" By doing this, the emotional response of ridicule remains focused on the transgender identities of the characters. Judith Butler argues that transgender comedies "are functional in providing a ritualistic release for a heterosexual economy that must constantly police its own boundaries against the invasion of queerness."[10] Audience members must continue to differentiate themselves in order to maintain clear cisgender identities, and they accomplish this through laughter. Transgender comedies assist in the work of maintaining a cisgender identity by providing clear examples of people who privilege their own cisgender identities over any alternatives. By laughing at the transgender identities of the characters while seeing how the characters work to maintain their cisgender identities, the audience is encouraged to maintain a cisgender point of identification with the films with no danger of shifting the point of identification to being transgender. The narrative conventions first communicate this separation between the characters' cisgender and transgender identities through a crisis that requires cross-dressing.

Crisis Requiring Cross-Dressing

External crises requiring cross-dressing, such as Joe and Jerry needing to go on the run from gangsters in *Some Like It Hot* or Daniel's wife asking for a divorce in *Mrs. Doubtfire*, allow the characters to adopt transgender identities for specific purposes while keeping these identities separate from their cisgender identities. Such crises allow the audience to maintain identification with the characters in terms of their cisgender identities while viewing their transgender identities as temporary. The characters in transgender comedies never choose to cross-dress unless prompted by an external crisis. Marjorie Garber argues that transgender comedies function as a "phenomenon of rationalization" to explain away transgender identity and deny it as a legitimate experience.[11] The key element in the films is that the characters "are said to embrace transvestism unwillingly," as an "instrumental strategy."[12] Chris Straayer argues that "the necessity for disguise is the genre's most fundamental narrative element."[13] The crisis that leads a character to cross-dress is never an internal identity crisis but is always external, including everything from a desperate search for employment to trying to find an unknown one-night stand. Each character in the films under analysis must face their own unique crisis. These characters would not choose to cross-dress on their own, and they protest mightily when questioned about it, a feature that distinguishes them from characters in other transgender films (such as horror, thriller, or drama). The protests by the characters in transgender comedies work to reinforce the existing gender binary through the assertion that the characters have one "natural" gender.[14] A man returning to living as a man at the end of a film after spending time dressing as a woman is usually presented as a return to the character's true gender. The narrative crisis that is constructed to require cross-dressing further reinforces the gender binary by providing an external explanation for the adoption of a transgender identity.

The external explanations for the crises faced by the characters in transgender comedies are structured around economic privilege: those with low economic privilege are desperate enough to cross-dress while those with high levels of economic privilege have the freedom to cross-dress. The economic privilege of the characters is rooted in their cisgender identities and attendant heteronormativity. Part and parcel with heteronormativity's privileging of heterosexual romance and the nuclear family is the conception of the family as middle class, with the steady job and suburban home that accompanies traditional family values. The assumption being made by these films in constructing their narratives is that the majority of the audience is middle class and has neither experienced the economic desperation that might lead to cross-dressing as a remedy nor the extravagant wealth and leisure that might lead to cross-dressing as a solution to simple problems. The narratives are constructed to allow the audience to laugh at the characters' actions and decisions while never feeling that their own values are threatened since their experiences, particularly economically, are so different from those of the characters on screen.

Joe and Jerry in *Some Like It Hot* choose to cross-dress when faced with unemployment. Unemployment, another form of marginalization, creates a liminal space that allows for the subversion of gender norms. Liminality is a space and time that is "betwixt and between,"[15] meant in these films to mitigate any possible harm to cisnormativity. By removing the characters from their everyday lives, transgender comedies privilege cisnormativity by presenting transgender identity as temporary and existing outside of the norm. The employment status of many characters at the start of transgender comedies is tenuous at best. Joe and Jerry are performing in a speakeasy that is raided by the police. While they manage to escape the raid, demonstrating their ingenuity when faced with danger, they do not get paid for the speakeasy gig and are desperate to obtain other work. Michael is seen in *Tootsie* auditioning for a number of jobs and doing anything he can to make ends meet, from waiting tables to teaching acting. He tells his students, "There's no excuse for not working." Adopting a transgender identity in these films is presented as a last recourse for the economically desperate. Because the characters adopt their transgender identities in moments of desperation, they can discard those identities in favor of their cisgender identities when their situations improve. The lack of doubt the characters have that their situations will improve is further evidence of their cisnormative privilege.

For Joe and Jerry, the marginality offered by unemployment frees them up to adopt a transgender identity. They are on the way to a new gig when they witness the St. Valentine's Day Massacre. Now faced with death, Joe decides that he and Jerry should take jobs playing sax and bass, respectively, in a girls band that he had been opposed to earlier. Getting out of Chicago and staying alive trumps Joe's aversion to dressing as a woman, which Rebecca Bell-Metereau deems "cross-dressing as a necessary survival mechanism."[16]

Cross-dressing by those with low economic privilege is presented as a final act of desperation in order to improve their situations. For those characters with higher economic privilege, cross-dressing is presented as an almost fantastical solution to mundane problems. Wealth and steady jobs give these characters the freedom to explore nontraditional solutions to the crises they face. Terri in *Just One of the Guys* (1985) comes from a wealthy family. Her family's wealth is evidenced by the enormous size of the house she lives in and the fact that her parents go away for a two-week vacation, leaving her and her brother home alone and giving Terri the freedom to cross-dress. When she fails to win a journalism competition at her high school, she questions why her article was not selected, and her journalism teacher says that while it was well written, it was not outstanding. Infuriated, Terri asks, "Why? Because a pretty girl can't possibly have a brain?" She later complains to her brother Buddy about not being taken seriously because she's cute: "Sometimes I just wish I were a guy." When Terri tells Buddy that she has decided to attend another school in town disguised as a boy, Buddy says, "Makes perfect sense. You got a problem, you get in drag." Buddy's sarcastic comment reveals the ludicrousness of Terri's plan; she feels so entitled to the newspaper internship that she goes to the extreme measure of cross-dressing to ensure that it is hers.

Through the crisis requiring cross-dressing, the characters are presented as firmly cisgender people, often through their resistance to cross-dressing, who decide to cross-dress only when faced with external forces beyond their control. The characters are then differentiated from the audience through their economic status, either higher or lower, freeing the audience up to laugh at them without calling their own positions in society into question. The audience is also prompted to ridicule the characters by laughing at the consequences of their decisions to solve their problems by adopting identities outside of the gender binary norm. The crisis is important narratively for creating a space in which ridicule becomes possible. Without the crisis, it would be impossible for the characters to adopt transgender identities that can be ridiculed while also maintaining their cisgender identities. While characters who identify as transgender may differ from the audience, thus making ridicule possible, they would differ from the audience too much and would take their identities seriously in ways that the characters in transgender comedies do not. These differences would combine to make the ridicule by the audience seem to be mean-spirited and coming from a place of superiority. The crisis creates a safe space in which a cisgender audience can freely ridicule the transgender identity of a character while not feeling guilty since the character is actually cisgender like them. The crisis forcing a cisgender character to adopt a transgender identity allows for guilt-free ridicule. That ridicule is mostly directed narratively at the struggles the characters have in performing their transgender identities.

Challenges to and Reassertion of Cisnormativity

The cisgender identities of the characters are challenged by the need to master behaviors consistent with another gender, so the films find ways for the characters to reassert their cisgender identities, frequently through failure to convincingly master their newly adopted identities. Such failure to master their transgender identities, rather than being a comment on restrictive gender roles or the struggles newly-out transgender and gender-nonconforming people face in a binary society, privileges the cisgender identities of the characters and prompts the affective response of laughter. The distance created in transgender comedies between the transgender characters and the audience is a product of the humor encoded into the transgender identities of the characters. This distance creates problems of identification for audience members in these films because the transgender characters are also the protagonists. The transgender positions of the characters challenge the system of cisnormativity, but the characters find other ways of reasserting their own cisnormativity. Feeling distanced from a character's transgender alter ego, the audience is encouraged to support the cisgender identity of a character. Watching *Tootsie*, the audience may laugh at Michael dressed as Dorothy while also rooting for him to end up with Julie, an actress he falls in love with, in his cisgender identity. The challenges to cisnormativity are overcome through the privileging of the cisgender identities of the characters.

One way the films privilege the cisnormative identities of the characters is by demonstrating the difficulty the male characters have mastering feminine attire, particularly footwear. *Tootsie*'s Michael stumbles as he walks down the street for his audition as Dorothy, and in *Some Like It Hot*, Jerry stumbles as he and Joe walk along the train platform to join the girls band. In *Mrs. Doubtfire*, Daniel complains bitterly upon returning home after his interview to be his children's nanny: "If I find the misogynistic bastard who invented heels, I'll kill him." Jerry, too, raises questions about how easily women walk in heels: "How do they walk in these things, huh? How do they keep their balance?" Joe responds, "Must be the way the weight is distributed." Jerry ultimately comes to an essentialist conclusion about the difference between men and women after watching Sugar sashay down the platform: "I tell you it's a whole different sex!" Poor performance makes clear the disinterest these characters have in successfully adopting identities as women, even though the risks of being found out are often great. The audience's laughter is encouraged by making it clear that the characters do not take their transgender identities seriously. The characters also engage in actions in public that would be perceived as unfeminine. Michael, for example, pulls his panties out of his crotch while walking down the street as Dorothy and adjusts his stockings in public. The lack of concern for public perception further reinforces the lack of seriousness with which the characters take their transgender identities. The audience feels free to laugh when Daniel, while walking down the street as Mrs. Doubtfire, breaks character and yells at a mugger in his masculine voice in order to stop the man from stealing his purse. Poor performance also positions the transgender identities of the characters as artificial since they do not have equal difficulty in their performances of masculinity. The cisgender identities of the characters are protected as the audience is invited to laugh at the ridiculous antics of the characters' transgender alter egos.

Poor performance of masculinity by Terri in *Just One of the Guys* is also constructed through her inability to contain her cisgender identity, demonstrated in her case not through the bodily actions of characters like Joe and Jerry but through her knowledge of subjects unknown to and unappreciated by cisgender men. Terri nearly gives herself away through her knowledge of feminine fashion. While playing the role of the supportive friend, she goads her friend Rick, whom she has a crush on, to tell her who he likes, and he points out a girl in a red sweater. Terri notices her "cute shoes," which leaves Rick baffled. Her knowledge of fashion also almost gives her away on her second day of class when she offers advice to another girl about using an eraser to replace a lost back to an earring. The girl looks at her funny until she explains that she has sisters. Greg, the girl's boyfriend, is upset that she was talking to another boy, but she defends the conversation as innocent. "He knew how to fix my earring," she says, to which Greg responds, "That's cause he's a little tulip." It is interesting to note that one of the few attacks on a cisnormative form of knowledge, a woman knowing how to fix a piece of jewelry, comes as a result of Terri's poor performance of masculinity. While the characters' cisgender identities in general may be privileged, the films also demonstrate a privileging of masculine interests and behaviors over their feminine counterparts.

Though they may not recognize the ways their cisgender identities are being challenged, the poor gender performances of the characters demonstrate their lack of interest in fully adopting their transgender identities. Adam in *Sorority Boys* (2002) is one of the few characters to openly discuss the danger to cisnormativity posed by the amount of time he, Dave, and Doofer are spending as women. As the three give each other makeup tips and outfit suggestions, Adam brings a sudden halt to the conversation. "Do you know what this could do to us? We're not supposed to know about makeup or periods or self-esteem issues. We're not supposed to see behind the curtain." Learning too much about what it means to be a woman or actually enjoying it is seen by Adam as a clear threat to their masculinity and the cisnormative status quo.

A second way transgender comedies privilege the cisnormative identities of the characters is the quickness with which they discard their transgender disguises. Michael is able to find a safe space to discard his identity as Dorothy at home, often having conversations with his friend Jeff in his male voice while getting ready as Dorothy. Allowing the characters to spend extended periods of time not in their transgender disguises helps the audience identify with their cisgender identities rather than their transgender identities.

Joe's ditching of his transgender alter ego in *Some Like It Hot* is one of the better-known examples. Even though he faces a big threat (death) should his identity be discovered, the allure of Sugar Kane is too much for him, and he quickly adopts a second disguise as impotent millionaire Junior in order to seduce her. Like the other characters in transgender comedies, Joe frequently switches back and forth between his disguises and nearly gets caught. As he rushes to his rendezvous with Sugar on Osgood's yacht, Joe nearly forgets to take off the earrings he was wearing while performing in the girls band, snatching them off his ears at the last second. This constant switching between identities not only creates the potential for comic mishap but also makes clear the main heteronormative element in these films: heterosexual romance.

Having shown the characters to be uncommitted to their transgender identities through poor gender performances and the frequent discarding of those identities, the narratives reinforce cisnormativity and attendant heteronormativity one final way through the heterosexual romances featured in the films. Though the characters may adopt their transgender identities to escape a crisis, what they usually get out of the experience is a romantic relationship. The clearly heterosexual romances the characters are engaged in are intended to assuage any fears the audience might have about the characters because of their adoption of transgender identities. Audience members are not distanced further from the characters through same-sex romances on top of cross-dressing.

Many of the characters make use of their transgender alter egos to help in their romantic conquests. Terri takes the opportunity to check out her friend Rick as he gets out of the shower after P.E. class; he passes muster better than the bully Greg. Michael even tries to make use of the intimate knowledge about Julie's preferences in men he gained through his friendship with her as Dorothy to hit on her at a party, which earns him a drink tossed in his face.

The use of their transgender identities to further their heterosexual romances can occasionally backfire, so the characters must make appeals to heteronormativity to tamp down any confusion the objects of their affection might have in their own sexual orientations. Michael complicates his potential relationship with Julie by kissing her as Dorothy. Julie freaks out, assuming that Dorothy is a lesbian because she perceives her to be a woman, and backs away from Michael as he tries to explain that her attraction to Dorothy is "a good impulse" because it is ultimately heterosexual. The audience can laugh at the mishap Dorothy finds herself in because they agree with Michael that Julie's attraction ultimately conforms to societal norms. The privileging of the characters' cisgender identities is intended to rectify any possible confusion that may result from the attraction the characters feel for each other; as ultimately heterosexual, the relationships are approved of by the films while any lingering same-sex attractions are discarded along with the characters' transgender identities.

In *Some Like It Hot*, a relationship that Jerry experiences provides the clearest alternative to heteronormativity, but his cisgender identity is privileged as he tries to ignore the implications of his attraction. While Joe tries to seduce Sugar, Jerry becomes "one of the girls," hosting a party in his sleeping compartment on the train and joining the girls for a swim in the ocean. After arriving at the Florida resort where the band will be playing, Jerry as Daphne acquires an ardent admirer in the form of eccentric millionaire Osgood. Joe returns one morning after spending the night with Sugar to find Jerry on his bed still dressed as Daphne, shaking maracas and humming a tango tune. Jerry is on cloud nine because Osgood has proposed, but Joe is quick to bring him back to Earth by reminding him that two men cannot get married. Jerry's own motives then come into question. He talks about marrying Osgood for his money and then getting a quick annulment, but his initial happiness, concern for Osgood's feelings when he has to break the relationship off, and anger at Joe for giving his engagement bracelet to Sugar show that Jerry's feelings for Osgood are not quite so opportunistic. Osgood's reply to Jerry's revelation that they cannot marry because he is a man—"Nobody's perfect"—also hints that, to some, a fluid gender identity may not dissuade them from romance.

Since Jerry's relationship with Osgood is discarded at the end of the film along with his wig, the audience is prompted to laugh at the chaos the relationship creates. The laughter prompted in the audience by transgender comedies is intended to ridicule the transgender identities of the characters. While the characters may still identify as cisgender and the narrative works to privilege that identity, the audience is laughing at a transgender woman struggling as she walks in heels for the first time or a transgender man trying to sort out the misunderstandings caused by his attraction to his friend who is a cisgender man. The lack of seriousness with which the characters may take their gender expressions in their transgender identities may give the audience license to ridicule those identities, but this does not change the object of their ridicule. The audience is being encouraged to laugh at transgender characters as they try to express their gender identities. The inclusion of heterosexual romances supports the privileging of the characters' cisgender identities at the expense of their transgender identities. Any mishaps that occur in the progress of the characters' romances can be blamed on their transgender identities, allowing the audience to laugh at the events transpiring on screen while not questioning cisnormativity. The use of heterosexual romance as a means of reinforcing the privileging of the characters' cisgender identities is supported by their encounters with cisnormative rivals.

Cisnormative Rivals

The cisnormative rivals faced by each of the characters may seem redundant when compared with the privileging of the characters' cisgender identities, but these rivals are generally positioned in opposition to the characters' transgender identities as a way of further privileging their cisgender identities. The rivals are positioned as the villains of the films, usually either initiating or intensifying the crises that led to the characters cross-dressing in the first place. Lieberfeld and Sanders call these characters "norm enforcers" to the gender transgressions of the other characters.[17] Their role is to enforce the standards of cisnormativity, but since the cisgender identities of the characters have been positioned as sites of identification for the audience, the rivals must play the role of the villain by harassing the transgender characters for daring to violate the standards of cisnormativity. These rivals and other norm enforcers perform an important role in privileging the cisgender identities of the characters by providing a clear distinction from the cisgender gender performances the audience should support and those they should not.

Violence is the method of choice for most rivals. Spats and the other gangsters in *Some Like it Hot* represent an over-the-top masculinity hidden behind a façade of gentility. They drink milk in a speakeasy to avoid getting arrested by the police while also having a man shot for spilling a drink on their shoes. The gangsters' violence serves to make any flaws in Joe and Jerry's masculinity, such as their open leering at women, seem less consequential.

Joe functions as another norm enforcer in *Some Like It Hot*, though he is not directly a rival to either of the transgender characters. Joe's quick discarding of his disguise as Josephine to pursue Sugar as the millionaire Junior establishes Joe's greater commitment to his cisgender identity than that of Jerry, who quickly becomes "one of the girls." After Joe creates the identity of Junior to hit on Sugar, Jerry brings Sugar back to their hotel room, hoping to catch Joe still in his Junior disguise. Joe quickly hides himself in a bubble bath in full clothes with only his face showing. After Sugar leaves, Joe emerges from the bath dripping wet and, using his taller stature, physically intimidates Jerry by grabbing him by the neck and lifting him off the ground for threatening to tell Sugar the truth. Joe clearly establishes himself as the dominant man between the two and positions his masculine pursuit of a woman as superior to Jerry's concern for her feelings. As the only transgender character to take on the role of norm enforcer, Joe's violence is expected to be excused by the audience as a defense of his cisgender identity, which would be in jeopardy if Jerry told Sugar the truth. Since some audience members may be turned off by an act of physical intimidation eerily similar to the kind practiced by Spats and the other gangsters, Joe quickly abandons the role of norm enforcer and focuses instead on asserting his cisgender identity by seducing Sugar rather than intimidating Jerry.

It is telling that Joe is in his cisgender identity in the scene while Jerry is still in his transgender disguise as Daphne. The laughter that is prompted in the audience is the result of Jerry having to beg for Joe's forgiveness that is in line with his gender performance as a woman. The hints of domestic violence are tempered by the fact that both of the characters still identify as cisgender men; society is more tolerant of violence between men than between men and women, so the appearance of the latter is implied while the fact that it is the former makes it more acceptable. Transgender comedies allow the audience to indulge in humor they would (hopefully) not find funny if both characters were not cisgender men. The laughter is still at Jerry's expense, though, since he is inhabiting his transgender identity, placing the blame as much on that identity as Jerry's scheming.

Greg in *Just One of the Guys* is another violent rival, but violence is not the only behavior available to rivals. Other rivals try to present themselves as the paragons of cisnormativity, but since the audience most likely supports the main characters, the rivals' actions come across as arrogant and pompous instead. Kevin, Terri's wealthy college boyfriend, places his masculine sexual desires ahead of any of Terri's concerns. His lack of concern for her feelings crystallizes after she stands him up on a date. Though she spent hours getting made up in a tight, white dress for their date, she has to quickly change back into her transgender alter ego when Sandy, a girl who has a crush on her, comes over to her house. After getting rid of Sandy, Kevin arrives to find Terri in sweats. He makes his disappointment in her abundantly clear, saying "You know, a long time ago, I knew this girl named Terri, she wore dresses and makeup. She was hot. Then one day, she disappeared. You know where she went?" Kevin's purpose may be to chide Terri for failing to live up to cisnormative standards, but he comes across as a jerk to audience members who have seen everything she has done to try to live up to his expectations. By privileging his own cisgender identity, Kevin fails to recognize that Terri is doing everything she can to keep her cisgender identity dominant. Kevin's inability to understand Terri leads her to choose Rick over him at the end of the film.

Debra, the most attractive girl in school and the object of Rick's affection, is another rival who makes appeals based on gender performance. Terri is occasionally jealous of her for getting to wear cute clothes and shoes and attracting the attention of Rick while Terri must continue to perform her role of Rick's supportive male friend. Debra reminds the audience that by adopting a transgender position, another, more obviously cisgender person can swoop in and steal the person you are attracted to from under your nose.

Ultimately, rivals are exaggerations meant to make the cisgender identities of the transgender characters seem natural by comparison. The exaggerated performance of the rivals is intended to make the cisgender identities of the characters appear to be the most reasonable gender performances in the films. The rivals function as counterbalances to the transgender identities of the characters, but through their attacks on the characters, they increase the support for the characters from audience members who see their attacks as unwarranted. The rivals may appear to be redundant at first glance, since the films already privilege cisgender identities, but they play an important role in privileging the cisgender identities of the characters by providing an exaggerated contrast. Though the characters have discarded their transgender identities numerous times throughout the films, even risking attack by their cisnormative rivals, they reach a point where they must leave the liminal space of transgender identity and return with lessons learned about being a better member of cisnormative society.

Lessons Learned

At the end of each film, the characters have made positive changes in their lives. Many have entered relationships with the people they love. Almost all have learned something about the struggles of the opposite sex. While self-improvement is all well and good, the lessons are applied to the characters' cisgender identities while their transgender identities are discarded for good. Few attempts are made to incorporate their transgender identities as they return to their cisnormative lives.

The endings of the films are marked by returns. The characters clearly leave the liminal space of transgender identity and return to the cisgender lives they left behind, such as Joe and Jerry riding across the waves in Osgood's boat with the Florida resort clearly in the background. The settings of many transgender comedies support viewing the cross-dressing of the characters as a liminal escape from reality, whether it be sunny Florida, a sorority house, or any other number of unusual locations that take the characters outside of their everyday existence. Cross-dressing in film is read by audiences as socially acceptable "so long as it occupies a liminal space and a temporary time period."[18] Joe must remind Jerry in *Some Like It Hot* that, despite his dreams of wealth and security, he cannot marry Osgood because they are both men. Jerry is trying to extend his cross-dressing beyond the limited space and time that the audience finds acceptable, so Joe must bring him back down to Earth.

Within this liminal space and time, moments of rupture exist that reveal that society is not as homogeneous as it seems. A temporary dream world is created for the characters in which these ruptures take place, but it is ultimately erased by the film.[19] One instance of this dream world is the previously mentioned example of Jerry wanting to marry Osgood, and another is Sugar's enjoyment of her lesbian kiss with Joe disguised as Josephine;[20] both are also clear examples of Chris Straayer's bisexual relationships that force the audience to wrestle with ideas of gender fluidity.[21] While *Some Like It Hot* goes to great pains to elide moments like these and other films seek to minimize the impact of similar moments in their narratives, the constraining forces of cisnormativity cannot completely eliminate the potentially subversive readings made available through these moments. While in these dream worlds of luxury and frivolity, the characters are free to experiment with new identities. All dreams must come to an end, though, and cisnormativity must be restored. The wigs and makeup are removed, and the cross-dressed character returns to their cisgender identity. The endings of the films function as closure for the transgender identities of the characters. The happy endings are meant only for the cisgender identities of the characters, so their transgender identities must be left behind.

Rebecca Bell-Metereau finds more promise than I do in the dream world created by *Some Like It Hot* through the openness created by the film's ending.[22] As Joe, Sugar, and Jerry escape the mobsters at the Florida resort with Osgood in his boat, Joe and Sugar kiss in the back of the boat while Osgood make plans for his marriage to Jerry as Daphne. Jerry protests every plan he makes in an effort to let Osgood down easy, but when Osgood is undeterred, Jerry plainly states that he cannot marry Osgood because he is a man. Osgood responds with the classic line that ends the film, "Nobody's perfect!" Bell-Metereau describes this scene as "one of liberation from a variety of restrictions,"[23] and she argues that the ending constitutes "the beginning of a trend toward more open sexuality in movie cross-dressing."[24] Sandra Meiri and Odeya Kohen-Raz argue that the ending represents the beginning of Jerry's "journey of self-creation."[25] Having experienced the freedom possible through feminine enjoyment during his time spent as Daphne, Jerry is now able to seek fulfillment on his own terms, outside of the constraints of society.[26] It is here that my analysis of the film and transgender comedies as a whole differs from those of Bell-Metereau and Meiri and Kohen-Raz. While the promise of a more open sexuality is a positive outcome of the film's ending, the promised openness is not extended to the transgender identities of the characters. Jerry is able to experience what it means to be loved as a woman while spending time with Osgood as Daphne, and Osgood's matter-of-fact acceptance of Jerry's identity as a man does exhibit more interest in the object of his affection than in the labels expected in a heteronormative society. But Jerry is not able to make the decision for himself to come out as a transgender woman and marry Osgood as Daphne because the narrative of the film would not let him. The narrative of transgender comedies is built around the inherent superiority of the cisgender identities of the characters over their transgender identities. Having Jerry find joy and pleasure as a transgender woman would complicate that message, so Jerry must adamantly reject his transgender identity as Daphne. Daphne's story ends with Jerry's declaration to Osgood that he is a man, so the narrative for the transgender identity of the character is no longer open. My analysis does not deny the progressiveness of Osgood's final line or the openness in terms of sexuality that it represents, but it is important to distinguish between openness in terms of sexuality and openness in terms of gender identity. The narrative conventions of transgender comedies require that the cisgender identities of the characters be constructed as superior to their transgender identities. The endings of the films are meant to provide closure for the transgender identities of the characters. Closure does not mean the characters have not learned anything from their experiences; Joe in *Some Like It Hot* and Bob in *All-American Co-Ed* (1941), for example, are both much less misogynistic as a result of their experiences temporarily adopting transgender identities, and their more progressive attitudes in terms of gender help improve their chances romantically. What closure means in transgender comedies is that the happy endings of the films focus entirely on how the characters' lives have improved in terms of their cisgender identities. Their transgender identities may have enabled the happy endings of the films, but these identities are generally not included in those happy endings.

Love is the most common happy ending in transgender comedies, but these new relationships are not without complications. Rick in *Just One of the Guys* clearly delineates cisnormative roles before entering a relationship with Terri. When she tries to make plans for their date, he says, "I'm the guy here. Let me just try this." She then offers him a ride in her car, and he responds, "As long as I get to drive." The message seems to be that if there is a true connection, all is forgiven, even if one partner spent time cross-dressing. The transgender identities of the characters remain in the liminal space and do not come back to haunt the characters in their cisgender lives.

Personal achievement also comes from time spent in a transgender alter ego. Terri's journalism teacher apologizes for misjudging her when she turns in her article, "I Was a Teenage Boy." As one of the few characters to try to incorporate his transgender identity into his cisnormative life, Daniel becomes the host of a successful kids TV show as Mrs. Doubtfire. He makes it clear, though, that this is just a performance; after taping an episode, he walks off set, still dressed as Mrs. Doubtfire, high-fives a crew member, and is enthusiastically patted on the back by the station owner for the success of the show.

Most transgender comedies show the improvement in the lives of the characters without direct reference to their transgender identities. *Tootsie* and *Mrs. Doubtfire* are the only films to feature explicit statements about how living as a woman made the male characters better. Michael tells Julie, "I was a better man with you as a woman than I ever was with a woman as a man. . . . I just gotta learn to do it without the dress." Miranda tells Daniel that Mrs. Doubtfire "brought out the best in you." Even though the adoption of transgender identities has clearly helped the characters improve their lives in ways that include positive new relationships and positive new jobs, the positive influences are generally swept under the rug along with these discarded identities. Having constructed the narratives to privilege the cisgender identities of the characters, suddenly acknowledging the positive benefits of their transgender identities would call the other events of the films into question. The positive effects of their transgender identities must be diminished or else risk calling their cisgender identities into question.

Having laughed at the antics of the characters in their transgender identities, from stumbling in their high heels to having to escape the violence of cisnormative rivals, the conclusion of the narrative is constructed to maintain cisgender identity as the audience's point of identification. The characters return to their previous lives, which are much improved from their experiences, and often also fall in love. Cisnormativity is preserved as the transgender identities of the characters have been thoroughly ridiculed while their cisgender lives are even better than they were at the beginning of the films. By primarily focusing the audience's laughter at the transgender identities of the characters, any gender transgression that is implied by the characters having amazing adventures while in their transgender identities is contained. The transgender identities of the characters can only exist in the liminal space of the film's events and are mostly abandoned at the end. Adopting a transgender identity in transgender comedies is a temporary existence that is mostly the object of ridicule, reinforcing cisnormativity by making transgender identity the focus of the audience's laughter. Along with the narrative conventions, the visual codes of transgender comedies construct the transgender identities of the characters as objects of the audience's ridicule.

Visual Codes: The Trans-Misogynistic Gaze

The visual codes of transgender comedies distance the transgender characters from the audience through the use of the trans-misogynistic gaze. Trans-misogyny involves a transgender person being objectified not only for their appearance but also for failing to perform femininity or masculinity according to cisnormative standards. Much of the visual humor in these films comes from framing shots and scenes as if the male gaze is in operation as it objectifies a woman then once it has been made clear that the object of the gaze is transgender, mocking the character for failing to live up to cisnormative standards of beauty. The trans-misogynistic gaze distances the transgender characters from the audience through this combination of objectification and ridicule. As with the narrative conventions, the visual codes privilege the cisgender identities of the characters through the lack of attention to their transformations, the situating of the characters as objects and possessors of the gaze, and the final big reveal of the characters' transgender identities.

Successful Transformation

The successful transformation of the characters into their transgender alter egos is key to the narratives of the films. If the other characters do not believe the transformations, then the characters' plans will be all for naught. The successful transformation generally works only within the diegesis of the films; the audience is given too much information, whether it is hearing the characters devise their plans or seeing them don their disguises, to believe that a character has transformed into a man or woman. The transformations in these films work to distance the audience from the characters by reminding them that what they are seeing on screen are disguises rather than allowing them to identify with the characters as the men or women they appear to be as the other characters in the films are able to do. The transformations, therefore, are constructed in such a way to only be successful within the diegesis of the films and not for the audience. The cisgender identities of the characters are preserved through the clear disconnect with their transgender identities. Particular visual techniques are used to ensure that the transgender identities of the characters are not presented to the audience without clearly establishing the primacy of their cisgender identities.

The successful transformations of the characters into their transgender identities usually happens off-screen and is communicated through a cut or other scene transition, which maintains identification with the cisgender identities of the characters by not allowing the audience to see the struggle that went on during their transformations. These transitions use the technique of montage to help the audience make the connection between the man or woman they were watching in the previous scene and the woman or man who appears on the screen now. The cisgender identities of the characters are presented first before their transgender alter egos are ever seen. After Joe, in *Some Like It Hot*, accepts the job in the girls band by talking in a high-pitched voice over the phone, there is a fade-out from the scene and a fade-in to the next one of Joe and Jerry walking down a train platform dressed as women. Montage is clearly used in the scene transition as the audience is able to connect Joe and Jerry to the two women seen from behind before they even see their faces. No attempt is made to explain how Joe and Jerry acquired their disguises, but it is not necessary, as the connection between the characters and their transgender alter egos is made visually. Likewise, in probably the best-known example of this technique, after Michael in *Tootsie* has been told that no one will hire him by his agent, there is a quick cut to Michael dressed as a woman in the center of the frame walking down a crowded New York street. While a sequence in which Michael applies his makeup to become Dorothy occurs later in the film, the initial transformation remains in the realm of fantasy. The use of the quick cut represents a general lack of interest in the process of transgender transformation and a desire to surprise the audience into laughter upon seeing either the man they just saw on screen now wearing a dress and heels or the woman they just saw now with slicked-back hair and wearing a suit.

Just One of the Guys features two such cuts. After Terri complains to her brother Buddy about how difficult it is to be taken seriously as a girl, there is a cut to Buddy answering the front door to find Terri standing there with a baseball cap on her head, wearing a white T-shirt and jeans. She asks for herself, and Buddy does not initially recognize her. He soon mocks the ridiculousness of her disguise when he asks, "Who do you think you are, Tootsie? . . . Yentl?" The second cut happens after Buddy gives Terri lessons on how to act like a guy, followed by a dapperly dressed Terri arriving at her new school. Her transformation is more drastic this time—including a haircut and new clothes that are obviously not Buddy's—and continues the trend of a lack of attention to the actual transformation. Through the use of these cuts, the film is able to privilege Terri's cisgender identity since the audience knows that it is Terri disguised as a boy on screen and not Terri after coming out as a transgender man. The scene transitions often combine with the narrative convention of the characters struggling with their transgender identities, such as Joe and Jerry stumbling in their heels on the train platform after the fade-in, to prompt the affective response of laughter in the audience. Focusing so quickly narratively on the characters' struggles prevents the audience from responding to the characters' transformations with anything but laughter.

The audience's response to the characters' transformations is also modeled on screen in many transgender comedies through the use of reaction shots. The reaction shot consists of the characters on screen reacting to a transformation before the audience has seen it for themselves. In *Sorority Boys*, to confirm their innocence after being kicked out of their fraternity for embezzling money, Adam, Dave, and Doofer decide to sneak into a frat party dressed as women. After they decide on this plan, there is a cut to a frat guy opening the door with a smile on his face then giving them a disgusted look and saying "Geez, ass!" Only after this comment does the audience see the guys' transformations for themselves. The reaction shot is intended to model the appropriate reaction for the audience. The surprised and disgusted reactions in this example sends the message to the audience that they should find the transgender alter egos of the characters ridiculous, whether audience members actually feel that way or not, and laugh accordingly.

Mrs. Doubtfire is one film that does show an extended initial transformation scene while continuing the trend of privileging the cisgender identities of the characters. In the film, there is a cut from Daniel showing up at his brother's house asking to be made a woman to a series of outrageous parodies of femininity. Daniel treats the transformation process as a standup comedy routine and creates entire personalities and backstories for these women, based on Barbara Streisand and a stereotypical Jewish mother, mainly for the entertainment of his brother and the audience since none of these women match the alter ego he created during his phone interview with his ex-wife Miranda. There is a final cut and Mrs. Doubtfire is seen for the first time. The transformation process for Daniel is meant to serve his own amusement rather than accomplishing his goal of reuniting with his children.

The lack of attention given to the process of transformation for the characters helps to preserve the privilege given to their cisgender identities. Since the transformations happen during a transition between scenes, they can be treated as almost magical, the result of some external power, rather than seeing the characters struggle to pull a pair of pantyhose up their legs, close the clasps of a bra, or experiment with the correct way to apply lipstick, all of which might undermine their cisgender identities. The characters may have to don transgender disguises, but the films are not concerned with the details of completing their transformations. When the process is seen, it is treated as a joke or as close to torture. Even then, the final transformations are saved for a big reveal. Daniel may joke around with his brother, but the sequence still avoids the full details of his transformation into Mrs. Doubtfire.

Even when adopting transgender identities, the cisgender identities of the characters must be privileged, which is accomplished visually through a lack of attention to the process of transformation. This lack of attention sends the message that the characters' transgender identities should be treated with a similar lack of attention; the cisgender identities of the characters are what matters while their transgender identities are more insubstantial. Their transgender identities appear as if by magic and disappear just as quickly. Once they have donned their transgender disguises, the characters now become objects and possessors of the gaze.

Objects and Possessors of the Gaze

Cross-dressed characters in transgender comedies problematize the standard workings of the male gaze. While they maintain their cisgender identities, their transgender identities make it difficult for audience members to fully adopt their point of view. This dual identity allows these characters to be both objects and possessors of the gaze. For the characters in transgender comedies, their "positions as subjects or objects of the gaze constructs their gender."[27]

The trans-misogynistic gaze is most evident in the scenes where the characters are the object of the gaze as their transformations are revealed. As is often the case with women in film, the characters are revealed via a tilt or camera movement that begins at the characters' feet and moves slowly up their bodies before reaching their faces, positioning them as objects to be looked at. As Joe and Jerry walk along the train platform dressed as women for the first time in *Some Like It Hot*, the audience is invited to stare at their legs in the same way that Joe leered at the legs of the dancing girls at the speakeasy earlier in the film. This use of the gaze privileges the cisgender identities of the characters by subjecting them to a fetishistic gaze that encodes humor into their transgender identities through a substituting of the expected objects of the male gaze, attractive women, with transgender women. This use of a fetishistic gaze further reinforces the distance that exists between the audience and the characters' transgender identities when the same camera movement is used as Sugar Kane sashays down the platform and walks by Joe and Jerry as they stare at her butt. Having been prompted to laugh at Joe and Jerry's masculine faces at the top of bodies coded visually as feminine, the audience is now rewarded with the expected combination in the form of Sugar's overly feminine body and face. Joe and Jerry seem even more ridiculous to the audience in comparison to Sugar.

Other characters are also subject to this fetishistic gaze as their bodies are reduced to their individual parts. Along with Joe and Jerry's aforementioned legs, the extended makeover scenes in *Tootsie* and *Mrs. Doubtfire* feature extreme close-ups of Michael's and Daniel's bodies, particularly their lips, eyes, and legs, as they apply makeup and get dressed. This focus on individual body parts rather than the characters as a whole communicates the message that the characters' transgender identities are nothing more than the sum of their parts. The cisgender identities of the characters, on the other hand, are generally presented as complete people rather than as disembodied body parts; in the scene that opens *Tootsie*, for example, Michael is seen applying stage makeup to make himself look like an older man.[28]

The positioning of the characters as objects of the fetishistic gaze is part of these films' larger construction of the gaze as a common characteristic of men's behavior vis-à-vis women. As Joe and Jerry play at the speakeasy, Joe openly leers at the dancing girls, forgetting even to play his sax. Stu, the rich alpha male to Daniel's sloppy loser in *Mrs. Doubtfire*, openly stares at Miranda while she tries to explain her decorating ideas for his newly purchased mansion. As a cisnormative rival, Stu's employment of the gaze is intended to make Daniel look better by comparison for caring more about his children than ogling women.

Adam is repeatedly subjected to a trans-misogynistic gaze as he walks to campus in *Sorority Boys*. A guy honks his car horn at Adam while his friend yells "Fat ass, DOG girl!" and throws a drink at him. Adam gets angry and, upon his return to the sorority house, scolds the other members of the sorority, "Why do you let them treat you like this? You can't be a bunch of pussies your whole lives!" While Adam places the blame for street harassment on women for their acceptance of it, the other sorority members write off his anger to hormones: "Whoa, PMS!" The guy in the car returns later, yelling "Fat City! Clear the way for Buttzilla!" This comment gets to Adam; back in his room, he examines his buttocks in a mirror and then uses a Thighmaster to exercise. Adam's concern about his appearance is a product of his inability to be perceived with the cisnormative privilege to which he is accustomed. He is not used to people laughing at him or harassing him because of his appearance; in fact, he is used to being the one who harasses others.

Adam is often treated as the least attractive member of the group, often because he is the one who tries the hardest to live up to traditional standards of beauty. Adam is the one who spends the most time getting ready each day, but he is also usually the target of the trans-misogynistic gaze. Doofer seems to be given a pass for not even trying, though he is upset after being ignored by the staff at a department store makeup counter while trying to pick out the right makeup for a fraternity event, while Dave is presented as the most conventionally attractive. A moment of Dave and Adam exiting a building is illustrative of the different treatment they receive. A random man holds the door open for Dave but lets it slam in Adam's face, even though Adam is seen running toward the door asking the man to hold it open. Dave does not face the same negative consequences of the gaze as Adam because of his more conventional attractiveness and because he is more likely to discard his transgender identity when in public.

By presenting the transgender identities of the characters as failing to meet the standards of conventional attractiveness, their cisgender identities are privileged by not being disparaged in the same way. The audience is prompted to laugh at the characters' transgender identities for these failures. The critique of the characters' appearances is rooted in the films' inversion of the male gaze that frames the characters in the same objectifying manner that attractive women are usually subject to in order to highlight their failures to live up to cisnormative standards. The visual code of replicating the male gaze is so frequently used not only because it provides a cheap laugh but also because of the clear privileging of the cisgender identities of the characters.

The cisgender identities of the characters are also privileged through the manner in which they possess the gaze. As cisgender people, they are uncomfortable with and unaccustomed to being the object of the gaze, but this does not prevent them from possessing the gaze and objectifying other women. In *Some Like It Hot*, Joe and Jerry both stare at Sugar Kane's butt as she sashays past them on the way to the train and at her legs when they catch her sneaking booze in the women's restroom; Jerry also openly ogles the girls in the band as they undress on their first night on the train to Florida. During his audition for a soap opera in *Tootsie*, Michael as Dorothy lowers his glasses to stare at the butt of fellow actress Julie as she walks away after helping him pick up some papers he dropped. The lowering of the glasses makes it clear that he is staring at her; Michael has no trouble seeing through the glasses so the action is meant to highlight the direction of his gaze. These moments are funny because the characters carry out these actions while they are disguised as their transgender alter egos; they would be unusual actions for the heterosexual women they are positioned as. Yet again, a visual code is used to privilege the characters' cisgender identities as impossible to contain in the presence of an attractive woman. This objectification of women might be seen as justification for the treatment of the characters discussed previously (the transgender characters in these films do not have a right to complain about being objectified since they have objectified women themselves) except for the fact that cis-normativity approves of their behavior. The characters' objectifying gazes help support the very standards of beauty they are criticized for failing to live up to.

Even a costume can reveal how attractive women are objectified in transgender comedies. The final musical number in *The All-American Co-Ed* is about farm girls who are lonely when the farmers go off to war. The farm girls are dressed in short skirts while the farmers are wearing satin overalls, but to ensure that the girls playing the farmers are still seen as attractive, one pants leg is long while the other is short in order not to completely hide their sexy legs. In this scene, Bob, a fraternity brother disguised as a student at a women's college, is originally supposed to perform as one of the farm girls as his alter ego Bobbie. But once his identity is revealed to Virginia, the woman he has fallen for, he switches costumes with another girl in order to dress in a more masculine fashion, or at least as masculine as one can be in satin overalls. Bob's new costume, though, is the only farmer costume with two full pants legs, since seeing Bob's legs holds no interest for the audience. While the women in the film are objectified by the gaze, Bob's cisgender identity is privileged down to the costume he wears. Through the visual codes in transgender comedies, the trans-misogynistic gaze is defined as the objectification of attractive women and the criticism of less attractive women for failing to conform to the same standards of beauty. The sharp divide between attractiveness and unattractiveness structures the entire approach in these films to who should be looked at and how they should be looked at.[29]

Finally, Terri's experiences as an object of the gaze in *Just One of the Guys* provides further support of its construction in these films as cisnormative. She is able to escape the gaze as her transgender alter ego, but since her cisgender identity is as a woman, she becomes the object of it again when reasserting that identity. The opening scene of the film is a camera movement up Terri's sleeping body, wearing nothing but her bra and panties, and a lot of attention is given to her appearance when she is getting dressed in a tight, white dress for her date with Kevin. Every opportunity is taken to objectify Terri in the few moments she is not seen in her transgender alter ego in the film. Given her objectification by the gaze, it comes as no surprise that Terri spends the most time as her transgender alter ego and is least likely to discard this identity in public. Her objectification in these fleeting moments when she is not seen as her transgender alter ego is a stark reminder that cisnormative privilege does not mean the same thing for women as it does for men.

In order to privilege the cisgender identities of the characters, their transgender identities are belittled and mocked as objects of the gaze while their cisgender identities are positioned as sites of power and control as possessors of the gaze. The intended joke is the apparent ridiculousness of a male-bodied person being the object of the gaze. The power located in the cisgender identities of the characters transcends the limits of those identities, allowing them to objectify others as their transgender alter egos. This visual code calls into question any lessons the characters may have learned narratively, with the characters being able to masquerade as transgender people while still enjoying the benefits of cisgender privilege.[30] Being unaccustomed to the objectifying gaze, the characters are, not surprisingly, quick to discard their transgender identities. The final discarding of these identities is accomplished visually through a big reveal.

The Big Reveal

The trans-misogynistic gaze makes the transgender characters in transgender comedies uncomfortable by positioning them as the objects of heterosexual male desire and by judging them for failing to live up to cisnormative standards of femininity. This positioning is only temporary since their transgender identities can be discarded as a means of exiting the liminal space created by their identities. The final abandoning of these identities is not done in private but in a big public reveal meant to confirm the cisgender identities of the characters for any who might have questioned them. Marjorie Garber links the big reveal to the narrative convention of the characters seeking heterosexual love, even at the risk of revealing their identities. During the time spent cross-dressing, the character's heterosexual desires remain unfulfilled "so that it becomes necessary for him or her to unmask" by discarding their transgender identity in favor of a cisgender identity.[31] The motivations for these reveals may be self-serving or somewhat altruistic, but the ultimate goal is to forcefully reassert the cisgender identities of the characters. While images of the characters in the process of transformation are generally avoided in these films, images of the characters in a transitional identity that blurs their transgender and cisgender identities during the big reveal are intended to privilege their cisgender identities by framing the scenes as an inability to contain their cisgender identities within their transgender identities any longer. By removing their wigs, the characters definitively assert their cisnormativity.

The removal of a wig or mask is the most common form of big reveal for male-to-female cross-dressers in transgender comedies, making the argument that the hair and face are stronger signifiers of femininity than other aspects of a transgender woman's body. In *Some Like It Hot*, Joe takes his wig off after Sugar follows him to Osgood's boat while he is being chased by gangsters. Upon confirming his cisgender identity, Sugar instantly falls in love with Joe, needing no further information than this visual proof. Jerry removes his wig on Osgood's boat as a last desperate attempt to convince Osgood, who has fallen madly in love with him, that they cannot get married. The image of Jerry with his short hair and masculine features in a dress is not enough to dissuade Osgood, opening up the potential for a non-heteronormative relationship, but Jerry's big reveal sends the message that he is no longer interested in pursuing any kind of relationship with Osgood. The ambiguous ending of the film has left many critics to ponder the possibilities for Jerry and Osgood after the screen fades to black, but the definitive manner in which Jerry removes his wig and asserts his cisgender identity makes it clear that any potential future together will not be with Jerry as a transgender woman.

A dramatic wig removal is not an option for Terri in *Just One of the Guys*, since—like Victoria in *Victor/Victoria*—she has adopted the greatest visual sign of her commitment to her transgender identity through cutting her hair. Regardless of her inability to accomplish her big reveal through wig removal, she still needs to reassert her cisgender identity. Terri accomplishes this goal by exposing her breasts. After Kevin has outed her to Rick and the rest of her classmates at prom, Terri is desperate to find a way to convince Rick that she is a woman and that she loves him, so she rips open her tuxedo shirt and exposes her bare breasts. This visual presentation of a female secondary sex trait convinces Rick of her cisgender identity better than her words ever could.

Dave's big reveal in *Sorority Boys* is in service to the woman he has fallen in love with. During a fraternity party on a boat, a group of alumni, led by Dave's father, decide Leah, the woman Dave has fallen for, should be removed from the party using the fraternity's dog-catcher routine of tossing a net over her to identify her as unwanted. Since the party takes place on a boat, this means throwing Leah overboard, but Dave, dressed in a lavender party dress, steps forward to stop them. The other men ignore him until he uses his masculine voice and dramatically removes his wig. His father is suddenly able to recognize Dave, as if his transgender alter ego were some kind of superhero disguise, and the other alumni cease attempting to throw Leah overboard. Having been ignored as his transgender alter ego, Dave now reasserts his cisnormativity. Even wearing a dress is not enough to undermine the privilege associated with his cisgender identity. Though his actions may be for Leah's benefit, they are also a clear assertion of his cisnormativity; unaccustomed to being ignored when making demands, Dave discovers that what is hindering him are the trappings of his transgender disguise. Removing his wig restores the cisnormative privilege he feels entitled to.

Michael's big reveal in *Tootsie* is more self-serving. Looking for a way out of the one-year contract he has been offered as Dorothy, he decides to reveal his identity during a live broadcast of the soap opera Dorothy has become the star of. After delivering a dramatic monologue involving long lost twins and other typical soap opera fare while dressed in a long lavender dress and holding a bouquet of flowers, Michael removes his wig and reveals his identity to the live television audience. His ulterior motive, convincing Julie that her attraction to him is okay, initially backfires as she angrily knees him in the crotch, but she changes her mind by the end of the film. Michael experiences the greatest success of his acting career as Dorothy, but he chooses to give that up by revealing his cisgender identity. The cisgender identities of the characters must be privileged over their transgender identities no matter what financial or emotional costs may result from that decision.

The big reveal is the final visual confirmation of the cisgender identities of the characters. The fact that these reveals often involve very dramatic actions, such as wig removals or exposing breasts, sends the message that the cisgender identities of the characters were very much as risk of being subsumed by their transgender identities. Bold and decisive action is needed to make their cisgender identities crystal clear to any who might have doubts.

Laughter is prompted in the audience as the characters are pushed to the limits of their transgender identities. Jerry is desperate for Osgood to no longer be in love with him, Dave and Terri want to support and reveal themselves to the ones they love, Daniel can no longer keep up the charade of living two lives, and Michael wants to find a way out of his unexpected acting success. Finding no way out, the characters abandon their transgender identities and reveal their cisgender identities, often accompanied by physical humor like Julie's knee to Michael's groin. The fact that the big reveal happens visually on-screen, rather than as information delivered in the narrative, allows the audience one last opportunity to ridicule the characters for adopting their transgender identities. The narrative ending of the film is a celebration of the characters in their cisgender identities, so in order to reinforce the privileging of those identities, the visual climax of the films focuses on ridiculing their transgender identities. The laughter serves as closure for the audience since this is generally the last time the characters' transgender identities are seen on screen. This ridiculing of the characters' transgender identities also reflects the cisnormativity that underlies the narrative and visual construction of transgender comedies.

Possible Effects of Transgender Comedies

The distance produced by transgender comedies has potential negative impacts on the lives of transgender people. As a transgender woman, I have experienced my fair share of ridicule. One time as I entered the local mall to do some shopping, a man who was heading toward the exit saw me, covered his mouth with his right hand while pointing at me with his left, and repeatedly said "What the fuck!" Another time when I was shopping at Target, a group of teenage girls followed me all over the store trying to get a photo of me with their smartphones. They finally achieved their goal when I stopped to pay at the self-checkout, and they hurried away giggling with their prize. I have been ridiculed multiple times at restaurants, from the McDonald's employee who broke down laughing when I pulled up to the drive-thru window to the Chipotle employee who had a huge grin on her face when I stepped up to pay for my meal and she asked if I had lost a bet, assuming that my feminine attire was some kind of college prank. These are just a few examples of my experiences with ridicule, and the effect they have for me is generally to make me more self-conscious of my appearance, as if I would not have been the target of ridicule were I to conform more closely to cisnormative standards of beauty. I was once told this directly early in my transition. While on a road trip to a friend's wedding, I stopped to eat lunch at a Wendy's, and as I ordered my food, the cashier, over the chuckles of her coworkers, told me I would look much better if I grew my hair longer. Ridicule can make transgender people feel unwelcome in public space, so the fact that the humor in transgender comedies is directed at the transgender characters leads to the films reinforcing cisnormativity and not challenging the existing system or revealing new possibilities in terms of gender identity and expression. The narrative conventions and visual codes used in the films also create specific potential effects.

The crisis requiring cross-dressing gives the impression that transgender identity is the product of external factors, such as child-hood trauma or perverse desires, rather than as a legitimate gender identity. This is problematic for transgender people because the search for an external reason is often extended to their own gender identities. A young transgender woman may search desperately for an external cause to explain her initially confusing feelings or a transgender man may be asked what caused him to become transgender after coming out to family or friends. The distancing of transgender characters in transgender comedies is supported by the external nature of the crisis that leads to cross-dressing; audience members can reassure themselves that they would respond differently when faced with similar situations. Instead of helping audience members understand the characters by attributing the actions of the characters to the desperateness of their situations, the external nature of the crisis can be decoded by audience members as justification for the ridiculous choices the characters make in response to their situations.

The crisis also positions the adoption of a transgender identity as a viable option only for those at the polar ends of economic privilege. Only the economically desperate or the economically privileged would consider cross-dressing as an appropriate solution to their problems; middle class people, in contrast, are too busy working and raising their families to ever consider cross-dressing. This message is particularly dangerous for economically disadvantaged transgender people whose plight can be ignored because of the connections to their transgender identities; either their economic disadvantage is a product of their transgender identities or their transgender identities are viewed as an attempt to improve their situations. Situating cross-dressing within the economic privilege of the characters also distances them from the audience through a lack of shared experiences; the audience is assumed not to share a connection with the characters either in gender identity or economic terms and so would not be expected to connect with them. The only connection the audience is expected to find with the characters is their striving to reclaim or retain the privileges of cisnormativity.

With such a focus in these films on privileging cisgender identity through cisnormative or heteronormative actions, a transgender person may be constantly reminded of any previous actions or activities that could be perceived as cisnormative or heteronormative, such as being in a heterosexual relationship or playing football. Such cisnormative or heteronormative behavior is used as evidence of a true cisgender identity. By presenting transgender identity as an easily discarded disguise that exists only within a liminal space, the films may also lead those close to a transgender person to wait anxiously for them to remove their disguise.

Transgender people are also positioned in these films through the use of the visual codes of the trans-misogynistic gaze as people to be looked *at*, encouraging even total strangers to openly stare at any transgender people they encounter. This looking at is frequently tied to and produces laughter in the audience from the failures of the characters to reach certain levels of cisnormative attractiveness in their transgender identities. The message is that if transgender women are unable to achieve a certain level of cisnormative attractiveness then they should not be seen in public.

The visual code of the characters possessing the male gaze while in their transgender identities, in particular, problematizes the identities of transgender people in the real world when they enter gender-segregated spaces. By raising the specter of the objectifying gaze, this visual code raises the possibility that a transgender woman is in a changing room to harass or assault other women rather than to try on clothing or that a transgender man is in a men's restroom to look at other men's penises. The visual privileging of the characters' cisgender identities comes at the cost of real harm to transgender people.

Finally, the endings of these films, in which the characters abandon their transgender alter egos, give the impression that transgender identity is temporary and will eventually end, often leading family and friends to hold out hope that the transgender people in their lives will abandon their transgender identities as well. Given the popularity of transgender comedies, transgender people have a lot of work to do to overcome the distance created for the important people in their lives.

3

Fear in Transgender Horror Films

A N IMAGE OF TRANSGENDER people that is well known to film
audiences is that of a transgender woman with knife raised
high, ready to plunge it into the unsuspecting body of a
victim. Most memorable from the shower scene in *Psycho* (1960),
similar images can be found in such films as *Dressed to Kill* (1980)
and *Sleepaway Camp* (1983).[1] The fear felt by the audience comes not
only from the shock of an unexpected event occurring but also from
an unexpected encounter with the Other. Fear is the result of the
Other coming too close and the accompanying turning away in order
to protect oneself from harm.[2] The fear felt by audience members
upon seeing the shadowy figure of Norman Bates as Mother throw
open the shower curtain to stab an unsuspecting Marion Crane to
death also forces a reconsideration of the events that preceded the
shower scene that the audience must engage in to make sense of what
they have just seen, which must be done later when it is revealed that
Norman is Mother. This rethinking of a film after the revelation of
a transgender character's identity shapes how the audience views the
transgender characters in these films.[3] The fear the audience experiences
in transgender horror films reflects the cisgender lens through which
the films are constructed and viewed, an approach that reinforces an
ideology of cisnormativity.

The reconsideration is necessary because unlike in transgender comedies, the audience for transgender horror films generally does not know about the transgender identities of the characters until the moment of revelation. While transgender comedies are constructed to privilege the cisgender identities of the characters over their transgender identities, the transgender identities of the characters in transgender horror films are withheld in order to construct the transgender characters as objects of fear. The audience fears the killer in these films as they would in any horror film, so when the transgender identities of the killers are revealed, that fear is then transferred to their transgender identities. The audience is distanced from the transgender characters in these films out of fear of the harm that might befall them if such characters get too close.

The affective response of fear involves a turning away in anticipation of injury from an encounter with an unfamiliar Other.[4] The affective response to the threat of danger persists even if the threat proves not to be true, since the feelings are still real,[5] so in response to the potential threat of injury, the mobility of some bodies must be restricted.[6] Transgender horror films construct the transgender characters as a threat, thus prompting fear in the audience that persists even after the specific threat is contained. Audience members have been able to feel "sympathy and sometimes covert admiration" for the transgender characters in transgender horror films,[7] but as I show in this chapter, the primary construction of the transgender characters in these films is intended to prompt a feeling of fear in the audience. I am not saying that positive feelings for the characters are not supported by the texts or that an audience member could not find pleasure in seeing a marginalized group member striking back at their oppressors, but I am saying that these are not the primary purposes for which the texts were constructed.

Transgender identity is presented in transgender horror films as the root cause of the audience's fear, rather than the inflexibility of cisnormativity, marking it in these films as "a site of cultural anxiety so profound that it manifests itself in psychosis."[8] Locating fear in perceived psychosis did not begin with films like *Psycho*,[9] and such films drew on larger anxieties during the Cold War era.[10] The anxieties in transgender horror films centered in transgender identity can apparently only be assuaged by locating it in psychosis.[11] Transgender comedies present a narrative in which the characters travel through the liminal space of transgender identity to be reincorporated into cisnormative society. Transgender horror films, on the other hand, present the possibility of unassimilable transgender characters who cannot be fully incorporated into cisnormative society and may not even desire to be part of it. Scholars locate this tension between the transgender characters and cisnormative society in the difficulty members of the audience have in identifying with the characters. The characters' psychoses and their gender transgressions are identified in the films as reasons why the characters should be distanced from the audience as objects of fear.

The fear of transgender characters is built up in these films through the genre tropes of the horror film, which "presupposes a *threat*, building tension with its promise that something hideous will occur, and there is no escape."[12] While for some scholars horror films ultimately confirm audience suspicions,[13] Altan Loker argues that the fear in these films is the result of the audience's guilt felt as the result of "conflicting wishes related to a story event that has morally acceptable and unacceptable components that are inseparable from each other."[14] In the case of transgender horror films, the audience may have wished for the characters to face danger and death, and by aligning their emotional reaction with the films' cisnormative ideology, which tells them that the transgender character is the one they should fear, any guilt about such wishing is tempered. The transgender character must then be contained in order to assuage the audience's fear. The transgender characters, as the object of fear in this case, must be restricted in their movements and expression of their identities (generally through incarceration, institutionalization, and murder) in order to reduce the possibility of fear, thus maintaining an ideology of cisnormativity.

Prompting Fear through Narrative Conventions

The narratives of transgender horror films may seem to be aiming for cheap thrills or scares, but the use of specific conventions sends messages to the audience that the transgender identities of the characters are the sources of their fear. In a variety of ways throughout these films, the characters' transgender identities are positioned as a threat to cisnormativity. The characters are initially positioned outside of cisnormative society and then strike back at the repressive agents of cisnormativity when they are either punished for their deviance from cisnormative standards or forced to reenter cisnormative society. The films end with efforts at containment; these efforts, however, are not aimed at problematizing the violent portrayals of the transgender characters in the films but at assuring cisgender audience members that the transgender characters are no longer a threat.

Positioned as Outsiders by Cisnormative Society

The characters in transgender horror films are positioned as outsiders by cisnormative society. Their outsider status is constructed through physical or interpersonal isolation and separation from society as a whole. Some characters seem to revel in their isolation, such as Norman's frequent assertions in *Psycho* of how happy he is all alone, taking care of the motel and his mother. Whether it is Norman changing the sheets in an empty Bates Motel or Angela in *Sleepaway Camp* being ostracized by the other campers, the characters are all portrayed as having difficulty fitting into society or within certain groups. The transgender characters do not choose lives of isolation but are positioned as outsiders by a cisnormative society that does not accept those who deviate from its standards.

In *Sleepaway Camp*, Angela is labeled as an outsider as soon as she arrives at summer camp with her teenage cousin Ricky. Shy and quiet, lacking the hyperactive energy of the children or intense sexuality of the other teenagers at the camp, Angela is immediately perceived by Meg, her counselor, as a problem upon her arrival at the bunk they will be sharing for the entire summer, with Meg saying sarcastically to another counselor, "Looks like we got a real winner here." From that moment, the film positions Angela as separate from the other girls in the bunk. When Angela refuses to eat her dinner the first night, Ronnie, the head camp counselor, takes her to the kitchen to find her something else to eat. Meg views this as special treatment, saying to Ronnie, "Startin' to spoil the little brat already." In describing Angela as a "little brat," Meg makes it clear that she sees Angela as receiving special treatment through behavior that differs from that of the other campers and intensifies her efforts to make Angela feel isolated from those around her. By narratively positioning Angela as an outsider and then revealing her to be the killer, the film signifies that the turning away of fear is a necessary response by the cisgender audience in order to protect itself.

Norman Bates in *Psycho* is isolated from the rest of society by his living situation, as Norman tells Sam when he comes to the Bates Motel while searching for Marion. "This place happens to be my only world. I grew up in that house up there. I had a very happy childhood. My mother and I were more than happy." Norman is justifying his decision to remain alone at the Bates Motel; as his only world, he would not even know where to begin in trying to start over in a new place. He does not even seem interested in going anywhere else, though his isolation and loneliness are betrayed in his comment to Marion as she eats dinner in the motel's parlor, surrounded by Norman's taxidermy: "A hobby's supposed to pass the time, not fill it." Norman's reluctance to leave the motel is rooted to his attachment to his mother. Norman's isolation is offered as both a product and a cause of his transgender identity.

Bobbie in *Dressed to Kill* is another transgender character positioned as a victim of the bullying and lack of understanding of those around her. While Dr. Elliot appears to be a successful and respected psychiatrist, his alter ego Bobbie is isolated as an outsider, stalking women through the grimy streets of New York in black sunglasses and a black trench coat. She spends her time observing Liz Blake, the only witness to her murder of Kate Miller earlier in the film, through binoculars, while Dr. Elliot continues his work undeterred. In her phone messages to Dr. Elliot, Bobbie identifies the source of her isolation as the refusal of Dr. Elliot and other psychiatrists to approve the sex reassignment surgery she desires. Bobbie's inability to complete her transition is her self-identified cause of her outsider status and the murderous actions she takes to remedy her situation.

Whether they are isolated through physical separation from the rest of society or the bullying of others, the transgender characters in transgender horror films are positioned in some way as outsiders from cisnormative society. Positioning the characters as outsiders performs an important narrative function in these films. As J. Jack Halberstam discusses and Peter Chumo also notes,[15] audience members often reconsider the events of a transgender horror film in light of the revelation toward the end that a character is transgender. By positioning the transgender characters as outsiders, the audience is not as shocked when their transgender identities are revealed. The characters are constructed to highlight their differences, whether it is Norman's physical isolation in a frequently vacant motel or Angela's interpersonal isolation as a quiet loner, and discovering their transgender identities just confirms any lingering suspicions on the part of the audience. The cisnormative aim of positioning the characters as outside of the standards of society is to protect it from the perceived threat of those who deviate from its standards. Cisnormativity refuses to recognize the legitimacy of any individuals who do not conform and must separate those who do not from the rest of society. Positioning the characters as outsiders maintains their distancing as objects of fear rather than raising questions about the treatment they receive from others. The focus remains on the individual identities of the characters rather than larger concerns about the narrative constructions of the characters' transgender identities.

Isolating the transgender characters because of their differences increases the tension and dread experienced by the audience. An affective response of fear is prompted when this isolation is combined with the murders the audience sees on screen. While they may not have connected the murders to the transgender characters or entirely figured out why the characters are so different, the audience is already turning away in fear of contact with the Other. The isolation of the transgender characters is not accidental but is part of the narrative construction of transgender horror films that serves to prepare the audience for the shocking revelation of the characters' transgender identities. Just as the audience can perceive the threat of such characters as Jason Voorhees and Freddy Krueger from only short glimpses, the isolation of the transgender characters plants the idea in the audience's mind that the transgender characters are somehow different from everyone else. This narrative foreshadowing in horror films is necessary to prevent the reveal of the killer from being a complete surprise. After being positioned as outsiders, the transgender characters encounter repressive agents of cisnormativity and strike back with a vengeance.

Kill the Repressive Agents of Cisnormativity

The targets of the often-gruesome violence in transgender horror films are the repressive agents of cisnormativity. These characters either seek to make the transgender characters conform once again to cisnormative standards or punish them for their deviance. The films argue that the violent actions of the characters are located in the intersections of their transgender identities and perceived psychoses; the individual transgender characters are completely at fault while their victims are completely innocent. My reading of their actions focuses instead on the interactions between the characters and cisnormative society. Having accepted their positioning as outsiders, the characters are enraged by the individuals who intrude on their spaces and try to force them to conform once again to cisnormative standards. This focus on the murders as reactions against cisnormativity is not intended to excuse the violent actions of the characters but to provide a fuller picture of why certain characters are chosen as the targets of these violent actions. Focusing solely on the actions of the individual characters ignores the role played by the dominant system of gender behavior in determining who is deviant and who is not. The violent actions of the characters could be avoided if they were either fully accepted by society or left to their own devices. Since neither happens in transgender horror films, I am interested in why the characters choose violence and why certain characters are the targets and victims of violence rather than in laying the blame on the individual identities of the characters.

Psycho features probably the most famous killing in this group of films. Mother's murder of Marion Crane in the shower has been studied in great detail, but Marion is not Mother's only victim in the film; she also kills the private detective Arbogast when he comes upstairs to investigate the Bates home, and she is intent on killing Lila Crane in the fruit cellar until Sam stops her. *Dressed to Kill* is structured in parallel to *Psycho*, with Kate Miller's murder in the elevator coming fairly early in the film while the rest of the film deals with Bobbie trying to contain the aftermath of the initial murder.

Mother's murder of Arbogast and Bobbie's killing of Kate Miller and stalking and attacking of Liz Blake depict the murders as the result of an explosion of rage rather than cold calculation; they are not meticulously planned to account for all contingencies, and the resulting aftermath must be contained by the characters. The shower murder in *Psycho* is "primarily a sexual act, a violent substitute for the rape that Norman dare not carry out."[16] Norman assumes that his mother would be jealous of any sexual attraction on his part, just as he is jealous of her, and so whenever he feels attracted to a woman, his

Mother personality must eliminate her. Norman is content to spend his days tending to the Bates Motel and his mother, but when Marion stops there on that fateful rainy night, his desire for her disrupts the isolated world he had created, and he lashes out violently. Arbogast, Sam, and Lila also become targets for continuing to pressure Norman about his murder of Marion. They do not arouse his desire but are reminders of the way Marion aroused him. As each begins to intrude further into his world, with Arbogast venturing up to Mother's room and Sam and Lila searching the house for her and finding her corpse in the fruit cellar, Norman decides they must each be dealt with so he can return to his peaceful existence prior to their intrusions.

A similar explanation is offered in *Dressed to Kill* for Bobbie's murder of Kate Miller. A psychiatrist argues at the end of the film that Dr. Elliot's attraction to another woman functioned as Bobbie's "red alert": "Elliot's penis became erect, and Bobbie took control, trying to kill anyone that made Elliot masculinely sexual." Bobbie is not a manifestation of Elliot's mother but is in many ways even more jealously vengeful, since she would prefer to be aroused in a feminine manner and is disgusted at the physical evidence of her body's maleness. Dr. Elliot's desire for Kate and its attendant sexual arousal is an unwelcome reminder to Bobbie of efforts to force her to conform to cisnormative standards by denying her request for sex reassignment surgery, so she murders Kate for intruding on her private domain. Bobbie targets Liz because of her witnessing the murder and becomes increasingly concerned as Liz forms connections with Dr. Elliot and Kate Miller's son Peter as all three try to cope with Kate's death. Bobbie's final attack on Liz comes after she seduces Elliot by stripping down to nothing but black lingerie. Liz had hoped to use the seduction to distract Elliot long enough to find evidence to connect him to Kate's murder, but instead, she sets off Bobbie's "red alert." Bobbie sneaks up behind Liz with her razor blade at the ready to slit Liz's throat until she is shot by the policewoman who had been following Liz. While Bobbie initially targeted Liz as a loose end related to Kate's murder, this final attack is the result of Liz arousing Elliot sexually, connecting Bobbie's violence once again to her transgender identity.

We should note that when the violence in transgender horror films is directed at women, as with Marion Crane in *Psycho* and Kate Miller in *Dressed to Kill*, it is often justified as punishment for the characters' sexual promiscuity.[17] Controlling women is another important norm of cisnormativity, so violence as a punishment for women being sexually active reinforces this norm for the audience as well, as it often does in other horror films. It is also important to recognize that, as Linda Williams points out, women are presented in these films not just as the victims but also the monsters committing the crimes.[18] It is generally the female side of the killers that commits the murders,[19] with the emotional instability of women offered as evidence of their violent potential. It is important to be able to recognize how the violence directed at and committed by women in these films reinforces other important norms of cisnormativity without resorting, as the films and many scholars do, to a conception of the male and female sides of a characters' identities as separate and distinct.[20] This is a continuation of the treatment of the characters' transgender identities as nothing more than a manifestation of their psychoses. I resist this tendency by approaching the characters as complete individuals rather than as separate personalities in constant conflict. This perspective offers insight into how these characters are constructed differently for existing outside of cisnormativity rather than treating their actions as the result of individual deficiencies.

Angela's mistreatment at being perceived as different in *Sleepaway Camp* goes beyond just being called names or made fun of. It starts at dinner the first night when one of the cooks tries to sexually assault her when she is left alone with him after refusing to eat. She is rescued by her cousin Ricky but comes back later to get revenge on the cook by dumping an industrial-sized pot of boiling water on him. As a cisgender man, the cook fully bought into the idea that it was his right to have his way sexually with any woman he chose, even a teenage camper, and he tried to force Angela to conform to his beliefs about gender by sexually assaulting her.

The murders in *Sleepaway Camp* follow this pattern of being directed at those who attempt to make Angela conform to the standards of cisnormativity. Angela is particularly mistreated for failing to embody the sociability expected of young women. She does not say a word until thirty minutes into the film when she talks to Ricky's friend Paul after he is nice to her. She continues to talk almost exclusively to Paul and Ricky, completely ignoring frequent taunts by Meg, her camp counselor, and Judy, a fellow camper. While Angela's inability to talk is interpreted by many of the characters as the result of some form of mental handicap, she keeps score of who mistreats her and exacts her revenge in a series of brutal murders. She drops a hornet's nest in the bathroom stall in which she has locked the ringleader of a group of teenage boys who hit her with water balloons, and she drowns another boy in the lake after he made fun of her when she ignored his invitation to join him and his friends skinny-dipping. The visual allusion to *Psycho* that is made by Meg showering alone in an abandoned bunk creates the expectation that Angela will kill her after flinging the shower curtain open, but instead she stabs Meg in the back through the partition between the shower stalls. Angela saves her most gruesome murder for Paul, who she is initially friendly with but with whom she becomes upset after he tries to make a move on her and she subsequently catches him kissing Judy. Angela asks Paul to meet her on the beach by the lake for a late-night rendezvous. When two of the camp counselors find her later, she seems to be cradling Paul's head on her lap while singing to him, but when she stands up, Paul's decapitated head falls to the ground. Angela's relationship with Paul is particularly troubling for her because it brings back memories of catching her father with his male partner in bed. Having been forced to live as a girl by her eccentric aunt (thus having her transgender identity forced on her), Angela sees herself, by kissing Paul, as gay rather than as a straight transgender girl. Reawakening this confusion in her helps to further explain Angela's extreme attack on Paul.

The taunting and bullying Angela endures is rooted in her refusal to conform to the norms of the camp; she does not act like the other kids and is tormented for it. Her violent attacks on the other campers are motivated by the demands that she conform and the bullying she receives for her failure to comply. Judy's taunts are particularly upsetting to Angela, as they hit fairly close to her transgender identity: "Hey, Angela? How come you never take showers when the rest of us do? Oh, I know what it is. You haven't reached puberty yet. Is that it? I bet you don't even have your period!" She saves Judy for next to last among her victims, killing her just before Paul. The only characters to survive her violent rampage are the ones who do not pressure her to conform.

Sleepaway Camp offers an example of an extreme response to the type of abuse many transgender people are forced to endure on an almost daily basis. Verbal harassment and physical attacks are a common, almost daily experience for transgender people in the United

States, particularly transgender people of color. They rarely respond by trying to murder their assailants; unfortunately, a far more common response to bullying and abuse is suicide. However, because of the frequency with which cisgender people harass transgender people, the fictional Angela's murderous response increases the fear of transgender people by the cisgender audience, who, it is implied, may become the next target. Rather than inspiring pity for her mistreatment, Angela's murders only increase the fear the cisgender audience feels toward her and other transgender characters.

The gruesome murders committed by the transgender characters in these films are a response to the pressures to conform to the cisnormative standards placed on them. The fear that is prompted in the audience by these murders is the result of the transgender characters coming too close for comfort. The audience is forced to accompany the characters as they carry out their horrifying deeds, and all they want to do is to turn away and not be part of what is happening on screen any longer. The murders also come too close because the cisnormative ideology that is supported by the audience's identification with the author through their cisgender identities expects them to force transgender people to conform to the standards of cisnormative society just as the repressive agents of cisnormativity do in transgender horror films. Having just seen those characters killed in the films, the audience begins to fear that they might suffer the same fate for their repressive actions. Fear is constructed through the relationship between the one who feels it and the perceived object of it; fear does not simply move from the subject to the object.[21] Fear also does not reside in the object of it but in the relationship that exists between subject and object.[22] The fear the audience feels comes from the relationship that exists between themselves and the transgender characters they have seen on the screen committing murder. Fear also projects into the future as anticipation of injury;[23] the audience's fear comes from anticipation of seeing further murders in the films but also from anticipation of encounters with transgender people outside of the theater. Transgender horror films encourage this fear because the ideology of cisnormativity seeks to punish those who transgress its boundaries. If you learn to fear those whose identities are transgressive, then you will not venture beyond the cisgender norm yourself. The turning away of fear prevents an engagement with what it truly means to be transgender.

The fear produced by the murders in transgender horror films creates problems, though, for cisnormativity. While the audience is prompted to fear the transgender characters, the murders give the appearance that cisnormativity has lost all control in the face of the threat posed by the transgender characters. Recognizing that threat, transgender horror films seek to contain it, assuaging the fears of cisgender audience members that cisnormativity is not still dominant.

Efforts at Containment

Transgender horror films seek to contain the threat constructed around the transgender characters in order to protect the dominant status of cisnormativity. Since the transgender characters are seen violently killing the repressive agents of cisnormativity, the films must find ways to show that cisnormativity is still in control. Most efforts at containment come at the end of a transgender horror film, but in *Sleepaway Camp*, the containment effort comes at the very beginning. The film begins with a series of long tracking shots moving left to right of an abandoned summer camp paired with sounds of children playing heard on the soundtrack, echoes of happier times. As the ominous score builds in the background, the camp buildings show more signs of disrepair (broken doors, mattresses on the lawn) before the camera comes to rest on a notice from the sheriff posted on the front gate and a "For Sale" sign nailed over the Camp Arawak sign at the front entrance. Despite the rampage that Angela is about to embark on, the audience can rest easy knowing that everything is taken care of in the end, though not without requiring the entire camp to be shut down.

The psychiatrist segments at the end of *Psycho* and *Dressed to Kill* are another example of the attempts by these films to explain how the characters are now well under the control of cisnormative society. The psychiatrist in *Psycho* assures Lila, Sam, and the police officers that Norman is not transgender. "A man who dresses in women's clothing in order to achieve a sexual change or satisfaction is a transvestite. But in Norman's case, he was simply doing everything possible to keep alive the illusion of his mother being alive! And when reality came too close, when danger or desire threatened that illusion, he dressed up." The psychiatrist in *Dressed to Kill* confirms that Bobbie is a transsexual woman but still places the source of her murderous rage in Dr. Elliot's refusal to go through with sex reassignment surgery. "The sex change operation was to resolve a conflict. But as much as Bobbie tried to get it, Elliot blocked it. So Bobbie got even." These two films make explicit the claim that the transgender identities of Norman and Bobbie are connected to their psychoses. Through this connection to psychotic breaks, the reality of transgender identity is reduced for the audience. While the potential is there to connect all transgender people to psychosis, the perceived danger posed by transgender people is instead easily contained, explained away by a quick statement by a psychiatrist. My purpose here is not to say that transgender people should be feared as dangerous but to try to understand the purpose of using a psychiatric diagnosis as an effort at containment. Psychosis itself may be frightening to many people, but it is an explanation for the behaviors of the characters. Such explanations are intended narratively to put the audience's minds at ease. The calm demeanor and matter-of-fact explanations from the psychiatrists in these films make the threat that produced the audience's fear seem well under control. While the endings of the films could have been used to make the transgender characters even more frightening (think of Carrie's hand bursting from her grave), fear is also a threat to cisnormativity's power. A little fear is useful to cisnormativity, but too much may lead to the impression that the entire system has collapsed. By making the audience afraid, transgender horror films may go too far and risk bringing down the entire system; a psychiatrist's calm reassurances help to dispel any lingering fears. The audience's fear may be transferred in the future to transgender people outside of the theater (which fits within cisnormativity's goals), but these efforts at containment serve as a reminder that the system can withstand any such threats.

The endings of *Psycho* and *Dressed to Kill* present the lingering possibility that the efforts at containment might fail, but, ultimately, the films conclude that the immediate threat at least has been successfully contained. At the end of *Psycho*, Mother's calm, unbroken stare at the camera and claims that she would not hurt a fly are signs that the menace Mother represents remains. However, she is still locked up and needs cisnormative society's approval to achieve her release and wreak more havoc. In *Dressed to Kill*, after the psychiatrist's explanation of Bobbie's condition and a discussion between Liz and Peter, Kate Miller's son, about what it means to be transsexual, everything seems to be returning to normal until Bobbie escapes from the mental institution in which she is being held by killing a nurse who comes to check on her. In a mirroring of the opening scene of the film in which Kate has an erotic dream in which she is choked by a man in the shower, Liz is showering in the same shower when she sees someone standing just outside the open door wearing a pair of white, patent leather shoes. She tries to get to the medicine cabinet to get a razor to defend herself, but when she opens the door, a hand comes out and slices her throat. At this moment, Liz wakes up screaming, and Peter comes to comfort her from her nightmare. Bobbie's escape was only a dream, and while Liz may continue to be haunted by the events of the film, Bobbie cannot actually hurt her. The films, like many other horror films, want to leave the audience thinking about the possibility of a lingering threat from the transgender characters, about a dangerous killer rather than a peaceful world, but how they do so remains within the efforts at containment that show cisnormativity in control.

The presence of efforts at containment in transgender horror films is evidence that the films recognize the power of the threat constructed around the transgender characters. The efforts at containment work to overcome the threat built up through the other narrative conventions. The transgender characters are presented in these films as violent, unstable individuals, and it might be easy for audience members to decode the messages of the films as applying to transgender people in general. Rather than ending the films by arguing that the transgender characters are not as dangerous as presented, transgender horror films instead communicate the message through the efforts at containment that the transgender characters are well under control by cisnormative society. It is not just the violent tendencies of the transgender characters that are under control but their transgender identities entirely. Cisnormativity may be challenged most directly through the violent actions of the characters in these films, but it emerges unscathed. Audience members can leave the theater reassured that any people who deviate from cisnormativity's standards will likewise be contained. The visual codes of transgender horror films only serve to reinforce this message.

Visual Codes: The Transphobic Gaze

The visual codes of the transphobic gaze work to distance the transgender characters as objects of fear. Transphobia is the fear of transgender people simply because they are transgender. Transphobia is expressed in the anger people have at discovering that a partner, friend, or family member is transgender or the physical or verbal attacks on transgender people by random strangers. The transphobic gaze works to visually construct the characters as objects of this fear in a variety of ways, such as the delayed revelation of the characters' transgender identities in order to intensify the shocking surprise, the forceful unmasking of the characters' identities despite their reluctance to have them revealed, and the modeling of looks of fear in response to the revelation of the characters' transgender identities. These visual codes, along with the narrative conventions, construct the transgender characters as threats to cisnormative society that must be contained. Because a more sympathetic portrayal of the transgender characters might move some audience members to have compassion for them, very particular visual codes such as these are employed to avoid this problem.

Delayed Revelation of the Characters' Transgender Identities

In keeping with the horror tradition of waiting until the end of the film to reveal the identity of the killer, the revelation of the transgender identities of the characters are delayed until the end of transgender horror films. Since it is only at the end of a film that a character's transgender identity is revealed, the audience must "rewind" the events of the film to understand them in light of this new information.[24] The transgender identities of the characters are never fully developed in the narratives of the films but are saved for the end as a shocking twist for the audience. When *Dressed to Kill*'s psychiatrist explains that Bobbie is a transsexual woman, this information is offered not as a sympathetic consideration of Bobbie's identity but only to help the audience process the surprise twist. Because the narratives of transgender horror films want to avoid discussing the transgender identities of the characters, it is up to the visuals of these films to ensure that the big reveal is delayed until later in the film while providing the visual cues necessary so that the twist ending will make sense for audience members who mentally rewind the films later.

One visual code used to delay the reveal is providing the audience with a limited view of the transgender character when they are attacking or killing someone; this is used in *Psycho*, *Dressed to Kill*, and *Sleepaway Camp*. In *Psycho*, Mother is seen a total of seven times before she is revealed to be Norman, including in the upstairs window of the Bates home, in shadow during the shower murder, from an overhead angle while killing Arbogast, and as a corpse in the fruit cellar. Bobbie in *Dressed to Kill* is also seen several times but always wearing black sunglasses and a black trench coat that hide her features. Limiting the amount of visual information available to the audience preserves the revelations of the characters' identities for later in the films.

While Angela's murder spree in *Sleepaway Camp* may be narratively contained, it must first be shown visually for the audience. The film uses a series of point of view shots to obscure Angela's identity as the killer. Many of the murders are seen from Angela's point of view, with the audience watching as Angela pours boiling water on the cook, locks a boy in a bathroom stall before dropping a hornet's nest in with him, and sneaks into the cabin where Meg is showering alone to stab her in the back. The point-of-view shot always cuts away to reveal the aftermath of the murder; the film may want to obscure the identity of the killer but not the gruesomeness of her murders. A recurring device associated with the use of the point-of-view shot is the victims addressing the killer during the murder as "you," demonstrating their knowledge of who the killer is without revealing it to the audience. After the audience gets its first real look at the killer as she comes to kill Judy in a dark cabin, the point-of-view shot is used again and is combined with Judy never saying Angela's name to make the audience doubt their certainty about the identity of the killer.

The fear that is produced by the delayed reveal once again reinforces the audience's turning away from the character. Fear indicates that the Other has gotten too close for comfort,[25] such as seeing a character on a large screen as the focus of a narrative. Delaying the revelation of the killer increases the audience's fear. By combining the revelation of the killer with the revelation of the characters' transgender identities, their transgender identities then become the objects of the audience's fear. Fear often transfers the emotion from the subject who experiences the emotion to the object of the emotion so that the object is then viewed as the cause of the emotion.[26] Once the characters' transgender identities have been revealed, they become the causes of the audience's fear rather than the objects of it.

The delayed revelation of the characters' transgender identities supports the distancing of the characters from the audience as objects of fear because the audience is offered no other way to view the characters. By generally delaying the revelation of the characters' transgender identities until the very end, the films communicate the message that the characters' identities are intended to be shocking, even more shocking than the gruesome murders they commit since the audience sees frequent visual reference to those murders while the revelation of their transgender identities is delayed. If the narratives made more frequent and direct reference to the transgender identities of the characters, the revelations of these identities would lose their shocking impact. Instead, the narratives and visuals work together to present the transgender identities of the characters as shocking. Because cisnormativity treats any gender identity existing outside of its norms as a deviation, any deviant identities must continue to be surprising to those occupying positions as members of cisnormative society. The delayed revelation of the transgender identities of the characters ensures that the transgender characters continue to be viewed this way. The audience's fear at this revelation reinforces cisnormative ideology that positions transgender people as outside the norms and to be feared for existing outside of the norms, removing any possibility of sympathy and understanding for the characters. This lack of understanding is reinforced when it is made clear visually that the revelations of the characters' transgender identities are not by choice.

Forceful Unmasking

In contrast to the characters in transgender comedies who gleefully discard their transgender identities as soon as possible, the characters in transgender horror films do not want their transgender identities to be revealed, so when they are revealed, it is usually done through force and against their wills. The motivations behind this reluctance differ for each character; Norman wants to resist shattering the illusion that his mother is still alive while Angela is still uncomfortable with a transgender identity that was forced on her by her eccentric aunt. When combined with the fact that the characters are killers, this reluctance sends the message that the characters are being will-fully deceitful, hiding part of who they are because they know that the rest of society will not approve. While the transgender identity of a character may be discussed narratively at the end of a film, the actual revelation of that identity is always done visually. There are no scenes of the cisgender characters discussing their off-screen discovery of a character's transgender identity. The forceful, onscreen unmasking of a transgender character generally comes at the climax or end of a film as they are about to kill or are threatening to kill another character. Norman as Mother comes running into the fruit cellar with his knife raised, ready to kill Lila, when Sam tackles him from behind and wrestles him to the ground, knocking off his wig. Bobbie is sneaking up behind Liz ready to kill her with a razor blade when the policewoman who had been watching Liz shoots Bobbie through the window, knocking off her wig and revealing her to be Dr. Elliott. Angela's unmasking comes at the end of her murder spree when the two camp counselors find her naked on the beach cradling Paul's head in her lap. When she stands up, Paul's decapitated head falls to the ground, and she turns to face them, hissing, knife raised, and covered in blood. The camera pulls back to reveal her penis, and Ronnie exclaims, "How can it be? God, she's a boy!" Angela's visual unmasking ensures that her transgender identity cannot be explained away. William Rothman writes of the unmasking of Norman that we "cannot say whether Norman struggles to keep from being stripped of his costume or to be freed from it."[27] My reading of Norman's unmasking is that Norman is straining against Sam pulling on his wig, not attempting to finally escape a compulsion that consumed him against his will. Whether or not Mother is a separate personality created from Norman's psychosis, Norman was willing to kill to preserve his life as it existed. Had these moments of forceful, visual unmasking not occurred, Norman and the other transgender characters in transgender horror films would have continued on with their lives as they had been. The visual unmasking of the characters ensures that their transgender identities can no longer remain hidden or be explained away.

The forceful unmasking of the transgender identities of these characters are all done visually; the audience sees a character's wig coming off or her or his penis. No one holds Norman as Mother at gunpoint and demands that he identify himself, allowing Norman to calmly explain the situation. Instead, he is wrestled to the ground and his wig is ripped off. The forceful, visual unmasking of transgender characters is important for the maintenance of cisnormative control. The forceful manner with which the identities of the transgender characters are revealed is evidence of this need to maintain control; the shocking twist built through the revelation of the characters' transgender identities is not constructed to leave the audience guessing but to provide definitive proof. The fact that the unmasking is visual supports this need for proof. If the audience only learned about the characters' transgender identities through the narrative without ever seeing the proof for themselves, certain members of the audience could choose to disbelieve this information and decode the films in an alternative way. Cisnormative control depends on as few variations from the preferred reading in the decodings of audience members as possible, so visual proof is offered that is more difficult to read against.

Cisnormativity demonstrates its control by not allowing the characters to keep their identities a secret. The forcefulness of the unmasking of the transgender characters' identities can be seen as a counterpoint to the violence the characters enact against the agents of cisnormativity; if the characters respond to cisnormativity through acts of violence, cisnormativity responds by using force to reveal the characters' transgender identities. This exchange of force does nothing to disrupt the status quo; cisnormativity remains in control, and the transgender characters are exposed and violated. This exposure is also a byproduct of the audience's fear. Fear involves anticipation of injury, but it also involves the potential passing by of the object of fear without awareness of it.[28] The fear prompted in the audience demands visual confirmation of the transgender identities of the characters so that the object of fear can be known. The violent actions of the characters may prompt the fear, but the revelation of the characters' transgender identities gives that fear an object.

The violent actions of the transgender characters also do not excuse the forceful unmasking of their identities, but the message communicated in these films is that no change comes from the use of force. If transgender people seek to change cisnormative society, violence does not seem to be the answer. After the characters' transgender identities have been forcefully unmasked, the films model the appropriate cisnormative response to their identities.

Looks of Fear

Just as the trans-misogynistic gaze positions the transgender characters in transgender comedies as objects of ridicule for failing to achieve a cisnormative standard of attractiveness, the transphobic gaze positions the transgender characters in transgender horror films as objects of fear for the deceit that is implied in their transgender identities. By not actively claiming and disclosing their transgender identities, the films argue that the characters open themselves up to forceful unmasking as a result of cisnormative society's fear of those who deviate from the standards of gender behavior. Transgender horror films visually direct this fear toward the transgender characters through the images and reactions that surround the forceful unmasking of the transgender characters' identities discussed in the previous section.

Clear images of transgender characters as objects of fear abound in transgender horror films. These films make use of the visual conventions of the horror genre to present the transgender characters as individuals the cisgender audience is supposed to fear. Norman Bates as Mother running into the fruit cellar dressed in a wig and housecoat over his clothes, a maniacal grin on his face, and a carving knife held high, ready to stab Lila Crane to death, is the classic image of fear in the transphobic gaze. Lila is silent in frozen terror and backs away from Norman's terrifying appearance, a stark contrast to the blood-curdling scream she let out just moments before at discovering Mother's corpse. The disorienting visual effect of the scene is enhanced even further by the light bulb that swings around the room after Lila bumped into it after finding Mother's corpse. The swinging bulb sends light randomly shining over the scene as Norman enters the room, further reinforcing the visual sense of things being off-kilter and out of place for the audience. Audience members may have tried to identify with Norman after Marion is killed, but this identification is shattered as soon as Norman enters the fruit cellar.[29] The Norman seen in the fruit cellar is not a lonely young man who the audience wants to try to understand but an image of pure horror that continues to resonate to this day. The transphobia encoded into images of the transgender characters as monstrous killers raises concerns that audiences may internalize this transphobia and view transgender people they encounter in their daily lives with a similar fear.

At the end of *Sleepaway Camp*, Ronnie and Susie, two camp counselors, discover Angela on the beach where she has killed Paul. She stands up covered in blood, her hair and eyes wild, making a hissing noise, with her bloody knife at the ready. Susie screams and covers her eyes, but Ronnie's gaze keeps alternating between Angela's face and her penis. It is clear from his gaze that he is just as terrified of the fact that Angela has a penis as he is that she has killed Paul and several other people at the camp.

Dressed to Kill contains similar images of looks of fear, including Kate Miller's wide eyes at the elevator door opening to reveal Bobbie waiting for her with a straight razor at the ready and Liz Blake's paralyzed, frozen stare out the window as Bobbie sneaks up behind her in Elliot's office with a razor raised to strike. The reactions in *Dressed to Kill* and other transgender horror films communicate pure terror at the presence of the transgender characters. What is visually terrifying about Norman, Angela, and Bobbie is not just that they are killers, but that they are *trans women* killers. Transgender womanhood becomes, in this sense, just another movie monster costume, with wigs, dresses, and makeup taking the place of the masks of Jason and Michael Myers or the clawed glove of Freddy Krueger.

From these reactions, looks of fear are modeled for the cisgender audience. These are not the looks of ridicule found in transgender comedies that make the characters look ridiculous for adopting transgender identities. Instead, they are looks of pure terror. These looks reinforce the fear that is directed toward transgender people by a cisnormative ideology. They also distance the transgender characters from the audience, who are prompted to back away like Lila or stare in disbelief like Ronnie. After all the buildup in the narrative conventions and other visual codes, the turning away in fear from the transgender characters is complete.

Possible Effects of Transgender Horror Films

Transgender horror films are constructed for an assumed cisgender audience, and fear is the affective and emotional response prompted by these films. Fear is a response from cisgender people that is often on my mind as a transgender woman. The image of Norman Bates dressed as Mother entering the fruit cellar with his knife raised has been burned into my memory. Often when I enter a room, this image flashes in my mind, along with the concern that others might react to my sudden appearance the way the audience reacts to Norman. I have made conscious efforts in the past not to enter a room too suddenly, lest my presence surprise anyone. Public spaces like restrooms and changing rooms are of particular concern. I often delay going in so I can avoid following too closely behind someone and prevent them or anyone observing from having any reason to be afraid of me. Sometimes, though, those preparations are not enough.

On one occasion early in my transition, I was trying on clothes with a friend in a department store changing room. As I exited the stall to show my friend the outfit I had tried on, another woman passed behind her to leave the changing room. I became concerned and wanted to leave immediately, but my friend reassured me that there was nothing to worry about, so I went back in to try on another outfit. While I was changing, an employee came to the door and loudly stated, "If there is a man in the women's changing room, you need to leave immediately!" She approached my friend to ask if there was a man in the stall and left when my friend said no. I was not going to wait around at this point and was hurriedly changing back into my clothes when an announcement came over the store's PA system: "Security to the women's changing room." As my friend and I exited, a group of employees had gathered to watch us leave. While I was fortunate to not be arrested or detained in that moment, I left with the very clear understanding that my presence in the changing room had caused the other woman such fear that she had tried to have me removed by the employees. I had gotten too close by sharing the same space as her, so something had to be done to ensure her safety.

Portraying transgender characters as dangerous, deranged killers plays into the fear that is often directed at transgender people. I understand why people who are members of a marginalized group may find a degree of enjoyment or satisfaction in seeing those who discriminate against and oppress members of their group on the receiving end of violent revenge, but I do not know if this enjoyment is enough to counter the potential negative effects of these representations. I hope it is also clear from my analysis of the films in this chapter that I am not suggesting the films were created with the intention of prompting a sense of pleasure in marginalized members of the audience at seeing a fellow marginalized group member strike back at their oppressors. This sort of pleasure can only be derived through an oppositional reading of the films and not within the texts of the films themselves. This kind of representation is possible for transgender people—the teen vampire thriller *Bit* (2020) serves as a good recent example—but it is important to recognize that while pleasure can be found for transgender people in these films, that pleasure is not their purpose.

The messages communicated by transgender horror films present transgender people as dangerous outsiders whom audience members are justified in fearing. Some people may find positive aspects in the representation of transgender people as dangerous rather than as victims, but the purpose of the image of a transgender woman covered in blood and clutching a knife needs to be considered when analyzing any transgender horror film. Problematic connections are made in these films between transgender identity, mental illness, and violence while limited narrative or visual information is made available to audiences to form their own opinions. The limited information about the embodied experiences of the characters in transgender horror films supports cisnormativity while not providing audience members with an understanding of why the characters are opposed to cisnormativity. More information would not excuse the violent actions of the characters in transgender horror films, but it might assist audience members in better understanding the reasons the characters react the way they do when others try to force them to conform to the standards of cisnormative society.

Figure 2.1. Jerry and Joe's legs seen as they walk down the train platform in *Some Like It Hot*.

Figure 2.2. Joe and Jerry's cross-dressing transformation revealed for the first time in *Some Like It Hot*.

Figure 2.3. Joe manhandles Jerry, dressed as Daphne, after he tries to ruin Joe's date with Sugar in *Some Like It Hot*.

Figure 2.4. Michael Dorsey seen for the first time as Dorothy Michaels while walking down a crowded New York City street in *Tootsie*.

Figure 2.5. One of Daniel's comedic transformations before settling on the final look for Mrs. Doubtfire in *Mrs. Doubtfire*.

Figure 2.6. Daniel, as Mrs. Doubtfire, glares at his ex-wife's new boyfriend Stu as a way to reassert his ownership of the gaze despite his feminine appearance in *Mrs. Doubtfire*.

Figure 2.7. Terri rips open her tuxedo shirt, revealing her naked breasts, in a desperate attempt to convince her friend Rick that she is a woman and that she loves him in *Just One of the Guys*.

Figure 3.1. Norman Bates as Mother enters the root cellar holding a knife in *Psycho*.

Figure 3.2. Angela is briefly seen as the killer in shadow before her big reveal in *Sleepaway Camp*.

Figure 3.3. Angela—naked, covered in blood, and holding a knife—is revealed to be the killer in *Sleepaway Camp*.

Figure 3.4. Ronnie and Susie's reactions to Angela being revealed to be the killer and transgender in *Sleepaway Camp*.

Figure 4.1. Fergus gazes through the window at Dil while she works at a beauty salon in *The Crying Game*.

Figure 4.2. Fergus sees Dil naked for the first time in *The Crying Game*.

Figure 4.3. Fergus vomits in the bathroom sink after seeing Dil's penis while Dil tries to calm herself on the couch in *The Crying Game*.

Figure 4.4. Ace cries in the shower after discovering that Lieutenant Einhorn is transgender—in a parody of the scene from *The Crying Game*—in *Ace Ventura: Pet Detective*.

Figure 4.5. Ace rips Lieutenant Einhorn's close off in an attempt to reveal her to be a transgender woman and the kidnapper in *Ace Ventura: Pet Detective*.

Figure 5.1. Brandon stares at his reflection in the mirror after a shower in *Boys Don't Cry*.

Figure 5.2. Lana and Brandon run out of the jail after she posts bail for him in *Boys Don't Cry*. Note the line of male prisoners in front of the sign for the women's restroom.

Figure 5.3. Brandon stares out into the hallway while being restrained by John and Tom in *Boys Don't Cry*.

Figure 5.4. An apparition of Brandon stares back at him from the hallway in *Boys Don't Cry*.

Figure 5.5. Bree applies lipstick at the end of a montage of her getting ready in the morning in *Transamerica*.

Figure 5.6. Ludovic imagines herself as a bride in *Ma Vie en Rose*.

Figure 5.7. Ludovic fantasizes about flying away while looking down on the real situation where she is being dragged home by her mother to be punished in *Ma Vie en Rose*.

Disgust in Transgender Thrillers

AN INFAMOUS SCENE IN transgender film history is Fergus's discovery in *The Crying Game* (1992) that his romantic interest in the film, Dil, is a transgender woman. As the two make out in Dil's apartment and begin to undress, Fergus sees Dil's penis for the first time and is so repulsed by the discovery that he runs to the bathroom and begins throwing up into the sink. This twist was a major part of the hype that was built up during the film's release. Harvey Weinstein, then cochairman of Miramax Films, is reported to have "called the Associated Press urging the secret remain secret. 'I'm begging,' he said. 'You're not hurting me financially. You're ruining the movie for audiences.' "[1] The salacious manner in which knowledge of Dil's transgender identity was used in the promotion of the film and Fergus's extreme reaction within the film clearly communicate to the audience that Dil's identity is intended to be a shocking surprise, something the audience could not have seen coming. The surprise is intended to be so shocking that, like Fergus, the audience pulls away from Dil in disgust. A similar prompting of disgust is also found in other transgender thrillers like *Myra Breckenridge* (1970), *Ace Ventura: Pet Detective* (1994), *Peacock* (2010), and *Ticked-Off Trannies with Knives* (2010).[2] As with the rethinking of the transgender characters' identities in transgender horror films, transgender thrillers prompt a reexamining of the entire film by audience members. In these films, the audience is unable to engage with a character's transgender identity outside the context of the affective response of disgust. Transgender thrillers support cisnormativity by encouraging audience members to view transgender people and their bodies as objects to be pushed away rather than as people with whom to find connection.

Unlike action-adventure, horror, and other film genres that create worlds in which violence is endemic, thrillers generally "begin in a world that is seemingly free of conflict, at least as far as the main character is concerned."[3] Danger and violence then enter into the protagonist's world, creating "a natural reaction of fear and panic."[4] In response to this dynamic of the thriller, the audience goes through a process in which they become invested in the situation the protagonist finds themselves in, they experience a growing sense of anticipation of surprising plot developments as the protagonist's plans are thwarted, and they are finally satisfied when the narrative comes to a favorable conclusion for the protagonist.[5] The satisfaction or relief felt by the audience at the end of a thriller is dependent, though, on the clarity of the ending. Enjoyment of a thriller is only found "following an unambiguously favorable outcome, but not when the ending was ambiguous."[6] Thus in transgender thrillers, the transgender characters remain at a distance from the audience because their presence introduces for the audience a degree of ambiguity to the ending, as they have to reconsider the events of the film, as they do with horror films.[7] The narratives of the films may be resolved in a way that is satisfying for the protagonists, but inability to resolve the transgender identities of the characters may cause cisgender audience members to find the endings nevertheless unsatisfying.

The need for resolution in thrillers is the result of the suspense that is built up over the course of the films. The goal of thrillers is to "put the reader or audience on edge and keep them there."[8] Putting the audience on edge is a quality of thrillers that is shared with horror films, but Julian Hanich differentiates between the feeling of dread created in thrillers and the horror, or terror, found in horror films.[9] Dread differs from horror in its ability to make the audience afraid not just of the gruesome events that are to come but also for the characters experiencing them.[10] This is another aspect of thrillers that works against the transgender characters. The ability of the audience to feel for the character, dreading what might happen to them, relies upon its identifying with the character.[11] Because of the distance created by transgender thrillers, the audience is unable to identify with the transgender characters, either because they are the antagonist to the main characters or because the suffering they endure is not relatable to a cisgender audience. Instead of feeling for the transgender characters as they seek to endure the danger and violence that enters their worlds, the audience is prompted instead to respond to the characters with disgust.

Transgender characters in transgender thrillers are constructed through the same narrative conventions and visual codes as those in transgender horror films, but instead of the turning away of fear, the affective response the films prompt is the retching of disgust. Disgust "involves a relationship of touch and proximity between the surfaces of bodies and objects" from which "the body recoils [and] pulls away with an intense movement that registers in the pit of the stomach."[12] If fear is the result of the unfamiliar threatening to come too close, disgust is the result of the undesirable being found to be already in close proximity, as when we spit out food that has gone bad as soon as it enters our mouths. Even more so than fear, disgust involves an encounter with the abject, which Julia Kristeva describes as a "massive and sudden emergence of uncanniness, which, familiar as it might have been in an opaque and forgotten life, now harries me as radically separate, loathsome."[13] Susan Stryker encapsulates transgender people's status as abject through a sympathetic analogy between Frankenstein's monster and her life as a transsexual woman.[14] Just as the monster was shunned for his differences by a society that could not understand him, transgender people are frequently rejected for their inability to conform to cisnormativity. Disgust is also a prominent feature of the visual representation of transgender people, and the images of transgender people in media "often rely on prurient, pornographic objectification."[15] The disgust directed toward transgender people is also frequently invoked to defend murders of and attacks on transgender people.[16] Transgender thrillers are constructed narratively and visually to prompt the emotional response of disgust, thus furthering the positioning of transgender people as abject. The narrative and visual construction of transgender thrillers ties the feeling of disgust in the audience to the need to reexamine the films, further distancing the transgender characters from the audience based on the perception that they have been misled into believing the transgender characters are something they are not.

Julia Serano classifies characters such as these as examples of "the 'deceptive transsexual'" whose ability to pass as women successfully provokes disgust in audience members, particularly men.[17] Because of their ability to pass as women, deceptive transsexuals "generally act as unexpected plot twists, or play the role of sexual predators who fool innocent straight guys into falling for other 'men.'"[18] Transgender people exist in a space of being familiar and unfamiliar at the same time to cisnormativity. Accusations of deception extend from this familiar unfamiliarity and are an important aspect of the construction of the characters. The disgust attached to these characters' transgender identities is constructed through the obscuring of these identities; if the characters were only open about their identities, the argument goes, they would not receive the same negative reception. Because the characters are presented as actively hiding their transgender identities from others, they must be trying to deceive others.

The perception of transgender people as trying to deceive others fits within cisnormativity's expectation that everyone fit within the confines of the gender binary. Anyone who exists outside of the binary is positioned as inherently deceptive, by nature of the fact that they do not announce their identities constantly. Transgender thrillers build their tension and the shocking release of it through the uncertain identities of the transgender characters. Disgust is the emotional response prompted in the audience as a result of this tension, because the perceived deception of the transgender characters allows them to get close to others who have no knowledge of their identities. This closeness leads the cisgender characters to reject the transgender characters, often in violent, physical ways that seek to push the unknown and undesired away from them. The transgender characters remain at a distance from the cisgender audience as objects of disgust that the audience members want to eject as far from their bodies as possible. This emotional response is modeled for the audience through the same narrative conventions and visual codes found in horror films. These conventions and codes work together to prompt disgust in the cisgender audience by drawing the audience close to the transgender characters and then pushing the audience away when their identities are revealed.

Prompting Disgust through Narrative Conventions

The narratives of transgender thrillers distance the transgender characters from the cisgender audience by bringing the characters close enough that the audience might be able to form a connection with them before revealing the characters' transgender identities. Once their identities are revealed, the audience responds with disgust, wanting to push the transgender characters away and punish them for getting too close. While wanting to create some space for closeness in order to prompt disgust in the cisgender audience, the narratives of transgender thrillers must also construct the transgender characters as outsiders to cisnormative society so the threat they pose is understandable to the audience once their identities are revealed.

Positioned as Outsiders by Cisnormative Society

The interpersonal or societal isolation experienced by the transgender characters in transgender horror films is also familiar to the characters in transgender thrillers. The transgender characters in these films are generally not the protagonists, so their presence often plays the role of disrupting the peaceful functioning of the protagonist's life that is an important component of thrillers. Some characters are isolated because of their living situations, such as John's efforts in *Peacock* to preserve his life as it was with his deceased mother; others may be isolated because of their role in the workplace, such as Lt. Lois Einhorn being labeled a tough boss who has trouble getting along with her fellow officers in *Ace Ventura: Pet Detective*; and others may be actively working to overcome their isolation, such as Dil flirting with Fergus through the intermediary of Col the bartender in *The Crying Game*. Whatever their attitude about or experience with isolation may be, the transgender characters in transgender thrillers are positioned as outsiders into whose world the cisgender protagonists enter. The transgender and cisgender characters then start to form connections, but the transgender characters remain outsiders at the end of the narratives because of the disgust that is prompted once their transgender identities are revealed. By clearly constructing the transgender characters as outsiders, the narratives of transgender thrillers ensure that no sympathy will be offered to the characters and that they will instead be seen as a threat.

One way that transgender characters seek to deal with their isolation and positioning as outsiders is by creating separate communities. Like Norman Bates in *Psycho*, John's world in *Peacock* revolves around his deceased mother, which is offered as explanation for his decision to continue living in the same house where she died. John's isolation can also be seen in his job as a file clerk at a local bank, where he works in a tiny office in the basement and is pressured by his boss to do more than his fair share of work. Making the choice to remain so focused on his deceased mother and not standing up against his mistreatment at work positions John as outside of the norms for American masculinity. He is presented as strange to the audience, and this strangeness is reinforced once his transgender identity is revealed. John is happy in his isolation at the beginning of the film, but the events of the narrative force him into greater contact with cisnormative society that leads to a rejection of him as a threat.

Interpersonal isolation is also a frequent component of the narratives in transgender thrillers. In *The Crying Game*, Jody, a British soldier, is oblique about the specific nature of his relationship with Dil when discussing her with Fergus, his Irish captor. He denies even finding Fergus's girlfriend Jude attractive, saying "I didn't even fancy her. . . . She's not my type. . . . Now *she's* my type," as he shows Fergus a picture of himself with Dil he keeps in his wallet.

FERGUS: She'd be anybody's type.

JODY: Don't you think of her, you fucker . . . She's mine. Anyway, she wouldn't suit you . . . Absolutely not.

FERGUS: She your wife?

JODY: I guess you could say that.

Jody is hesitant to openly discuss Dil's identity or his relationship with her, exhibiting an element of shame or uncertainty about the reactions of others. He tries to warn Fergus away from pursuing a relationship with Dil, which is what eventually happens, but he never clearly states Dil's transgender identity, either out of his own discomfort or his fear of the reactions he will receive from his Irish captors. This unwillingness to openly discuss the transgender identity of his partner by Jody positions Dil as an outsider who is not spoken of in the same way as those engaged in what are perceived to be more acceptable relationships.

While characters like John and Dil are positioned as outsiders by others, Lois Einhorn in *Ace Ventura* and Myra Breckenridge in *Myra Breckenridge* position themselves as outsiders through their attitudes and interactions with others. The other cops at the station are intimidated by Lieutenant Einhorn, who is less than impressed with Ace's shenanigans. Upon first seeing Einhorn, Ace exclaims, "Holy testicle Tuesday!"—both implying that the male cops feel instinctively protective of their genitals in Einhorn's presence and speaking presciently given the way Einhorn's transgender identity is revealed later in the film. Einhorn is positioned as a no-nonsense leader who makes the men she works with uncomfortable through her unfeminine use of her power and authority. The one opportunity she has to bond with her fellow officers is in her dislike of Ace. At the crime scene where a Miami Dolphins employee seemingly committed suicide, Ace is talking to a dog when Einhorn comes in. She takes one look at Ace and asks, "Who let Dr. Doolittle in?" This joke at Ace's expense elicits hearty laughter from the other cops on the scene, one of the few times Einhorn is positioned on similar ground with the other cops who work for her. Though making fun of Ace endears her a little to her fellow officers, it marks her as an outsider for audience members. While Ace's eccentric behavior would typically mark him as an outsider as well, and he is positioned that way in the film in contrast to the authority figures of the police, the audience has already seen the humorous and actually insightful method to Ace's madness. To the audience, Ace seems to be the only one making progress on the case to find the kidnapped Dolphins mascot Snowflake, while Einhorn and the other cops only serve to stand in his way. And while poking fun at Ace might get a few chuckles from the other cops, Einhorn is still positioned as the cold, heartless ice queen that women are expected to become when occupying positions of authority, completely isolated from the rest of the police force.

Myra Breckenridge sets herself apart from the rest of society in a voiceover monologue that occurs soon after her gender confirmation surgery.

I am Myra Breckenridge, whom no man will ever possess. The new woman whose astonishing history started with a surgeon's scalpel and will end who knows where . . . , Just

as Eve was born from Adam's rib, so Myron died to give
birth to Myra. Did Myron take his own life, you will ask?
Yes and no is my answer. Beyond that, my lips are sealed.
Let it suffice for me to say that Myron is with me and
that I am the fulfillment of all his dreams. Who is Myra
Breckenridge? What is she? Myra Breckenridge is a dish
and don't you ever forget it, you motherfuckers.

By referring to herself as "the new woman," Myra positions herself
outside of dominant society, a position she feels grants her superiority over others. Her goal is "the destruction of the American male
in all its particulars," and she goes to Hollywood to get money from
her uncle, former movie star and acting school owner Buck Loner,
to achieve it. Myra accepts a job teaching at Buck's school while she
waits to collect her money, but her behavior and manner of dress mark
her as different from the other students and teachers. Myra bases her
personality and fashion sense on the movie stars of the 1930s and
1940s, particularly Marlene Dietrich, and attempts to teach etiquette
and elocution to students who have more in common with beatniks
and hippies. Even in a space of outsiders, Myra is seen as different
and is quickly labeled by Buck as "weird." His solution to making her
fit in is sex with him, which would "straighten her up" because "God
knows she wants it." Buck's misogynistic view that sex with a man
would make Myra more submissive to his masculine authority is part
of the male culture Myra is seeking to destroy (though as I discuss
later, her methods do not differ much from what Buck proposes).

The transgender women in *Ticked-Off Trannies with Knives* share
Myra's view that being transgender makes them different, maybe even
better, than other members of society, though this view is framed
more in terms of empowerment than annihilation. Creating a sense
of community is a common practice among transgender people and
members of other marginalized groups to help alleviate the stress
of being ostracized by the dominant society. As the women drink
together at a club, Tipper proposes a toast. "Let's see. Female qualities
and characteristics, male genitalia, straight male mentality, Black girl
attitude . . . um . . . celebrity fashion sense, warrior façade, matriarch
disposition and unparalleled exquisiteness. Isn't it obvious? We're the
solution!" While there are obvious echoes here of Myra's declaration

of herself as the "new woman," Tipper's toast is framed in a spirit of empowerment, building up the positive aspects of being a transgender woman, rather than a spirit of annihilation, seeking to tear down those identified as oppressing them. Tipper's toast is intended to highlight the bond between the group of transgender women, and it is only this bond that helps a few of them survive the savage beating they soon suffer.

Whether they are isolated from others because of their living situations, their interpersonal insecurity, or their attitudes toward others, the transgender characters in transgender thrillers are positioned as outsiders so that the revelation of their transgender identities later in the films is understandable to the audience. As with transgender horror films, transgender thrillers require the audience to reconsider the events of the film in light of the new information about the characters' transgender identities. The cisgender audience may begin to form connections with the characters, but when they reconsider the events of the films, they are not as upset by the revelation because of the outsider status of the characters. The transgender identities of the characters explain why they are outsiders and justifies the disgust felt by audience members. Cisnormativity is reinforced because disgust at the transgender identities of the characters is seen as the proper reaction. Transgender characters are positioned as outside the norms of cisnormative society, so when they or other transgender people get close, disgust is shown to be the proper response. The cisgender audience is being sent the message that disgust is an acceptable, even expected, response to the presence of transgender people, a message that has potentially dangerous implications for transgender people's lives. Positioning the characters as outsiders means cisgender audience members needn't question the disgust that is prompted in them from transgender thrillers. For disgust to be possible, though, the transgender characters in these films cannot be so isolated that they have no contact with the cisgender characters. The cisgender characters and audience members must develop some degree of closeness with the transgender characters or disgust would not be possible as an emotional response. To address this need for closeness, the narratives of transgender thrillers create situations in which the transgender characters come into contact with and must interact with representatives of cisnormativity.

Kill or Threaten the Repressive Agents of Cisnormativity

The narratives of transgender thrillers require that the transgender characters come into contact with cisgender characters who serve as agents of cisnormativity. These encounters allow the cisgender characters and audience members to begin to develop a relationship with the transgender characters, but this is often not a pleasant experience for the transgender characters themselves. Either because they sought isolation or experience rejection after trying to create connection, the transgender characters are generally not treated in positive ways during these interactions. As a result of their mistreatment, the transgender characters seek to strike back against those who try to repress them. This narrative construction of the transgender characters seeking retribution for their mistreatment leads to the cisgender audience being further distanced from these characters. Many cisgender audience members would already feel distanced as a result of not sharing an experience of being an outsider or of not having the same experience of marginalization as the transgender characters, but even more cisgender audience members would not see the actions taken by the transgender characters in response to their mistreatment as appropriate. While the revelation of the characters' transgender identities is accomplished visually in transgender thrillers, as it is in transgender horror films, the extreme and often violent actions taken by the transgender characters keeps the audience at a distance and helps them process the emotional reaction of disgust that is prompted by that revelation.

Depicting an extreme response to cisnormative demands of conformity is the stated goal of the film *Ticked-Off Trannies with Knives*. After surviving an attack by Bubbles' ex-boyfriend Boner and two of his associates who killed two of their friends, Bubbles, Pinky, and Rachel go for secret martial arts training to prepare for their revenge. They set an elaborate trap for Boner and his friends in which Bubbles appears to be home alone unprotected. Boner antagonizes her with a knife before knocking her out and tying her up. In a style typical of a B movie villain, rather than just killing her, he offers her a series of contrived deaths to be chosen through playing cards. Bubbles escapes, and with the help of Pinky and Rachel, she gets the drop on Boner and the others. The three men awaken to find their buttocks wet with some kind of lubricant, and Boner exclaims, "You bitches *raped* us?!" clearly expressing one of the transphobic fears many men hold toward transgender women. Bubbles and her friends did not rape them but instead inserted opened switchblades and a loaded gun into their anuses, set to go off should the three move around too much, thus mocking the elaborately gory schemes typical of grindhouse villains.

An extended fight sequence ensues with the women suffering a number of stab wounds but managing to kill Boner's friends Nacho and Chuy by slitting the throat of one and stabbing the other in the head. Boner manages to remove the gun from his anus and holds it to Bubbles' head, but the women are able to wrestle it away from him. Held at gunpoint by Bubbles, Boner has time for one last grandiose speech.

> She won't do it. She can't. It just ain't in her nature. I mean, look at her. Such a pretty little thing. So insecure. The kinda gal that only feels worthy when you're with a guy like me. The kinda guy that treats you like *shit*. The kinda guy that'll lie to her. Be rude, self-centered cause that's all you think that you deserve. In some strange way, you're attached to me. You can't kill me. If you coulda, you'd already done it. If I were you, I woulda killed me a long-ass time ago! In some strange way, I just don't think you want to. Do you?

This speech is meant to antagonize Bubbles by pointing out the ways she normally conforms to the expectations of a particular kind of heterosexual romance, but it is ultimately ineffective, as Bubbles shoots Boner three times, and Pinky and Rachel finish him off by throwing knives in his chest and mouth before Bubbles delivers the finishing blow.

The film positions itself as an exploitation-style fantasy of transgender women getting revenge on those who frequently abuse and mistreat them, both physically and verbally. While some may feel a sense of satisfaction from this kind of fantasy, violence does not put an end to the pressures to conform to cisnormativity. While Bubbles and her friends may have gotten revenge on a few agents of cisnormativity who killed their friends, violence ultimately causes more problems for transgender people. Pinky recognizes the problematic nature of responding to violence with violence when she asks, "Do you know what the difference is between us and them?" Bubbles and Rachel just shake their heads, and Pinky starts laughing and exclaims, "Me either!," to which Rachel adds, "Cause we killed 'em!" A revenge fantasy may feel empowering, but in the end, it is still violence, the same violence that prompts the revenge fantasy in the first place.

The murders in *The Crying Game* and *Peacock* are more acts of desperation than crimes of passion or revenge. In the former, when Dil ties Fergus to her bed with pantyhose and threatens him with his gun then shoots Jude, it seems to be the actions of a woman who is frustrated by the events swirling around her involving the Irish Republican Army and Jody's death. As a repressive agent of cisnormativity, Jude not only ended Dil's relationship with Jody but she also seeks to end Dil's relationship with Fergus by forcing him to rejoin the IRA. The pressure to conform placed on Dil comes in the form of the removal from her life of those she loves. In *Peacock*, Emma's murder of the man John hires to remove the train car that is attracting attention to their home is a desperate act to hold on to her newfound freedom.[19] She kills the man by taking him to a motel room, bashing him in the head with a shovel, dressing him in John's clothes, and setting the room on fire. Through this, she is able to convince everyone that John is dead. Not only has she removed any need to be John anymore, but she has also prevented the removal of her one point of access to the world outside her home. Had the train car been removed, the attention on Emma's house and her connection with planning the political rally set to take place in her backyard would have gone away. John and Emma would have then returned to their daily routine for the rest of their lives. By killing the man hired to remove the train car and staging John's death, Emma removes the pressures to conform from her life and frees herself to be herself. While these murders may lack the rage found in other transgender thrillers, they reinforce the point that the reasoning behind a target of violence can be found in the pressures to conform placed on the transgender characters.

Where Dil and Emma's actions are desperate and unthinking, Myra's sexual assault of an acting student named Rusty is the height of premeditation. Sex is often identified in *Myra Breckenridge* as a tool to ensure that people fall in line with the standards of cisnormative society. Buck says of Myra, "Bitch! I shoulda put it to her when she first came in. Throwed her on her back and give 'er the ole Buck

Loner Special right there on the rug. Goddamn smart mouth broad."
Sex is apparently all that Myra needs to become an obedient woman.
Her student Rusty also believes that sex defines what it means to be
a man, saying that "a man should ball chicks" in response to Myra's
question about how a man should act.

Myra comes to see Rusty as the epitome of cisnormative masculinity and decides to use sex herself as a tool to break Rusty of his
cisnormative beliefs rather than to reinforce them. She invites Rusty
to her office for special lessons and, on the pretense of giving him
a physical, tells him to strip and then straps him down on a surgical
table, saying "All you men have a lot to learn, and I've taken it upon
myself to teach you." She then straps on a large dildo, the size of
which makes Rusty exclaim "Oh my God, Jesus, you'll kill me!" and
then proceeds to rape him. Myra becomes a parody of how progressive
ideas about sexuality and gender can be just as dangerous as cisnormative ones when force is used to achieve them. The pressures to
conform for Myra come from cisnormative society as a whole, with
Rusty functioning as the most obvious repressive agent of that society.
Myra sees forcing Rusty to conform to her views on gender as the
first step in her destruction of cisnormative masculinity.

The violent actions taken by the transgender characters in
transgender thrillers are in response to efforts to make them conform
to cisnormativity. Whether it is Bubbles, Rachel, and Pinky getting
revenge on the men who killed their friends, Emma removing the
need for her to exist in public as John, or sex being used both against
and by Myra as a means of making someone conform to the beliefs
of another, the transgender characters feel pressure to conform to
cisnormativity, often experiencing violence themselves as a means of
trying to make them conform. Having never experienced the same
pressures to conform to cisnormativity, the intensity and shock of the
violence leads the cisgender audience to distance themselves from the
transgender characters. The distance that is created narratively helps
the audience process the disgust they feel at the revelation of the
characters' transgender identities as the correct response. While disgust
is primarily constructed visually in transgender thrillers, the narratives
in these films play an important role in setting up the possibility for
that emotional response. The violence is constructed for the audience
as out of proportion to the problems experienced by the transgender
characters and as a response they would never choose if they were

in a similar situation. Violence may have led the cisgender audience to feel greater distance from the transgender characters, but it still positions the characters as a threat. As with transgender horror films, transgender thrillers end with efforts to contain the threat posed by the transgender characters.

Efforts at Containment

Transgender thrillers are purposefully constructed as negative representations because the emotional response of disgust to transgender people is shared by the cisgender authors and audience members. The films have shown the transgender characters to be outsiders who do not have a place within cisnormative society and to resort to extreme violence whenever challenged to conform. Any efforts to contain these negative aspects of the narratives are solely for the benefit of the cisgender audience. These efforts are not meant to redeem the transgender characters but to make sure that cisgender audience members can feel comfortable knowing that the threat to cisnormativity posed by the transgender characters is safely contained to the screen. Cisnormative society will be preserved so long as cisgender people take the necessary actions to contain the threat posed by transgender people. Cisnormativity remains dominant, and the peaceful world that existed at the beginning of the transgender thriller has been restored.

Transgender thrillers are not always explicit in their efforts to contain the threat of the transgender characters. *The Crying Game* and *Ticked-Off Trannies with Knives* give the impression that everything has returned to normal. Dil comes to visit Fergus in prison after he took the fall for her in the killing of Jude, again sporting long hair and a clearly feminine style of dress, while Bubbles, Pinky, and Rachel strut into a club dressed to the nines, as if they do not have a care in the world. The transgender characters continue to exist and live their lives, but they are no longer taking clear action to resist cisnormativity as they were last seen doing before the cuts to these scenes of containment. Dil panicking in the hotel room with Fergus after shooting Jude and Bubbles, Pinky, and Rachel sitting on the floor of Bubbles's apartment, covered in blood and laughing about killing Boner and his friends, positioned the characters as threats. While they may be free at the end of the films, they are not still actively attacking cisnormative society, so the threat they represent has been contained.

Emma in *Peacock* seeks to return things to how they were before but is unable to. While initially thrilled with her newfound independence after staging John's death, Emma is nowhere to be found on the day of the rally. Instead of being part of the rally outside, Emma is inside the house taking care of Maggie's son Jake, even posing him for a picture in the dining room. When she realizes the pose is the exact one John's mother posed him in, seen in the black and white picture at the beginning of the film, she suddenly recognizes that her actions have begun to mirror those of John's mother. She gives Maggie the money she had intended to use to adopt Jake and tells them to leave the house and town immediately. She even expresses regret about John's death, telling Maggie that he "shouldn't be dead" and that she blames herself for leaving the house. She resigns herself to never leaving the house again, locking the doors and closing all the curtains. The final image is of Emma watching the world pass her by from her living room window. Emma is now safely contained within the confines of her home, never to leave again.

Myra Breckenridge does not just contain Myra's transgender identity but erases it completely. After failing to seduce Rusty's girlfriend Mary Ann, which would have completed her victory over patriarchal masculinity, Myra walks down a street in downtown Hollywood while Myron drives by in her car. He sees her and circles around to hit her, sending her flying through the air. He gets out of the car and joins a group of people who have gathered around her body only to discover that it is his body lying on the ground instead. At this moment, the film, which has been in color the entire time, switches to black and white. An older man, presumably Uncle Buck, walks through a hospital ward to find Myron lying in bed with his head dressed from a wound. Myron suddenly wakes up and grabs his chest, exclaiming "Where are my tits? Where are my tits?" His transgender identity may still be intact, but his physical transformation has been erased; a picture of Myra on a magazine cover suggests that the black and white sequence is the real world and the preceding story was nothing but a dream, the film having been a bit of transgender wish fulfillment on Myron's part by fulfilling his desire to be an incredibly beautiful woman and put the kind of men who mistreated him in their place. Male members of the audience, however, can heave a sigh of relief, confident that any threat that a beautiful transgender woman might want to destroy their masculinity has been contained.

In *Ace Ventura*, the film is more concerned with showering its masculine hero with the accolades he has earned than on making a clear effort to contain the threat posed by Einhorn's transgender identity. Ace is able to get Dan Marino, who was kidnapped by Einhorn along with Snowflake, back to the stadium in time to play in the second half of the Super Bowl and, of course, gets a kiss from the girl. Victoria Flanagan argues that while the film concludes "by strengthening and confirming Ace's gender identity in accordance with hegemonic masculinity, Einhorn is simultaneously disempowered and dispossessed of her gender identity."[20] For good measure, Ace engages in some final fisticuffs with the opposing team's mascot after the mascot prevents Ace from catching a rare pigeon he has been chasing throughout the film. Cisnormative masculinity is reaffirmed at the end of the film, the transgender woman has been humiliated and arrested, and all is right with the world. The ending of the film works to confirm the cisnormativity inherent in Ace's identity, after repeatedly portraying him as goofy and eccentric, because having Einhorn arrested by a cisnormative character, rather than a goofy outsider, better contains the threat of her transgender identity.

As in transgender horror films, efforts at containment in transgender thrillers reveal transgender people to be seen as real threats to cisnormativity. By choosing not to conform and actively resisting those who would force them to conform, the transgender characters present a viable alternative to cisnormativity. Because the identification in these films is built around the cisgender identities shared between the authors and audience, any alternatives to cisnormativity must be actively rejected. The outsider status and violence in the films are constructed to distance the audience from the transgender characters, and the efforts at containment reassure the audience that the threat has passed. The tension experienced by the audience has been relieved, and they can leave the theater feeling comfortable about the world around them. Enjoyment of thrillers is dependent on whether or not the audience feels that the tension has been unambiguously resolved.[21] Because the transgender identities of the characters may leave the audience feeling unsettled and that new questions have been raised rather than answered, the films must put in extra work to show the audience that things are back to normal. If the films ended on another act of violence by the transgender characters or even just a reminder of the potential for violence—such as Bubbles, Rachel, and

Pinky striking a martial arts pose at the end of *Ticked-Off Trannies with Knives*—the cisgender audience's enjoyment of the films would be diminished. The transgender characters create tension beyond that typically found in a thriller (the audience generally is not surprised by fundamental aspects of the characters' identities in other thrillers, though films like *Chinatown* [1974] represent a rare exception), so containing their identities is an essential component of resolving the narrative tension in transgender thrillers. While the narrative conventions of transgender thrillers are focused on distancing the cisgender audience from the transgender characters, the visual codes of the transphobic gaze are primarily concerned with prompting the emotional response of disgust.

Visual Codes: The Transphobic Gaze

In transgender thrillers, the visual codes of the transphobic gaze work to distance the characters from the audience as objects of disgust. The narrative conventions of these films work to distance the audience by presenting the transgender characters as potentially violent threats to cisnormativity while the visual codes build on this distancing by prompting the emotional response of disgust in the audience. While in transgender horror films, transphobia manifests as fear as the audience turns away from the transgender characters to avoid them coming too close, in transgender thrillers, the transgender characters have already gotten close to the audience through their interactions with the cisgender protagonists, so when their transgender identities are revealed visually, the audience pushes the transgender characters away in disgust. The unknown has gotten too close, so the audience must reject them. Disgust is prompted visually because the visual allows for a visceral reaction to the unexpected closeness of the unknown. Because the transgender identities of the characters are not discussed narratively in the films, the characters are allowed to be closer to the audience than they would otherwise. The unexpected body part or other confirmation of the character's transgender identity is even more shocking when it is disguised and not anticipated by the audience. The disgust felt by the audience is perceived as justified in light of the narrative positioning of the characters as threats. The audience feels that they are in the right by rejecting the transgender characters and wanting to keep their distance from them because they are visually disgusting and narratively threatening. The codes used in transgender thrillers to prompt this emotional response of disgust are the same as those used in transgender horror films. In order to create tension in the audience, the characters' transgender identities must initially be concealed.

Delayed Revelation of the Characters' Transgender Identities

Building tension in the audience is an important component of any thriller. Important information is concealed from the audience or characters in the film until the moment it is dramatically revealed. In transgender thrillers, the tension usually centers on the transgender identities of the characters. Films like *The Crying Game* and *Ace Ventura* build up throughout the films to the dramatic revelation for the audience of the transgender identities of the characters. In films like *Myra Breckenridge* and *Peacock*, the characters' identities may be revealed to the audience early on, but they are not known to the other characters, so the tension comes from how the characters manage the situation and how the other characters respond once the transgender characters' identities are revealed. Because the transgender identities of the characters are the central component of the tension found in the films, their revelation must be delayed as long as possible.

While in transgender horror films, the transgender characters are usually not seen clearly by the audience as a means of delaying the revelation of their identities, the characters in transgender thrillers are generally seen very clearly by the audience, but their transgender identities are not shared openly. Withholding the information that the characters are transgender women is used primarily in *The Crying Game* and *Ace Ventura*. Dil and Lois Einhorn are attractive women whom the audience has no reason to suspect to be transgender. Fergus first sees Dil through the window of the hair salon where she works, and when he enters the salon, the film visually emphasizes Dil's sexy legs by having her sit in the salon chair with her legs crossed and her face turned away from the camera. The use of the voyeuristic and fetishistic gazes in this scene communicates visually to the audience that the characters should be seen as attractive. While the audience may be turned off by Einhorn's dominating authority at work, the film also signals visually that she is supposed to be seen as attractive by depicting, when she is seen for the first time, the fetishistic gaze through the standard slow panning camera movement from her feet up to her face that is generally used to communicate that a woman is attractive. The strategy in this code is to hide the transgender characters in plain sight. The initial visual presentations of Dil and Einhorn make the argument that transgender characters should be free to live as they please and even occupy positions of power, in Einhorn's case, but the overly negative reactions to the revealing of their transgender identities sends the message to the audience that being transgender is not normal, no matter how attractive a person may be.[22]

The construction of these films around the transgender identities of the characters being hidden from the audience raises questions for many scholars about whether the transgender characters reinforce the gender binary, particularly Dil.[23] Scholars are divided along essentialist and performative interpretations of Dil's identity.[24] These analyses of Dil are based in arguments about the essential qualities of the character's identity either in terms of subject position or biology. While I agree that some aspects of Dil's gender identity position are problematic, particularly her submissiveness to men, I am more interested in the ways she and the other transgender characters respond to being positioned outside of cisnormativity. Viewing their identities as positioned outside of cisnormativity opens up a new perspective on the actions of the characters and the ways their identities are constructed in relationship with the audience than is available to analyses more interested in passing judgment on their gender performances.

Other scholars base their analyses in a performative approach to gender that comes closer to the positional approach I use in this book,[25] but I argue that the positional approach I use in my analysis comes closest to understanding how the characters are constructed in these films. While Dil's submissiveness can be viewed as an expression of an essential femininity that supports the gender binary, it can also be viewed as a position Dil takes in a space filled with aggressive men that she begins to reject toward the end of the film. By viewing the identities of the characters as positions they take or are positioned in, no identity is seen as permanent, and no identity is seen as inherently superior to any other. A positional perspective is helpful to understanding the ways the transgender characters are constructed by narrative conventions and visual codes in relation to cisnormativity. The standards of cisnormativity would hold that the characters are being deceptive for withholding information about the supposed truth of their gender identities. By recognizing this as part of construction of the films to prompt an emotional reaction of disgust, we can see how characters like Dil are used to reinforce certain attitudes toward transgender people rather than passing judgment on their gender identities and performances.

The transgender women in *Ticked-Off Trannies with Knives* and *Myra Breckenridge* represent a rupture in this code by the fact that their narratives make their transgender identities explicit fairly early. While in the real world the characters would clearly fit into Serano's deceptive transsexual category, their transgender identities are never in doubt for audience members. The tension comes from how the other characters react once their transgender identities are revealed. A more significant rupture of this code can be found in *Peacock*. As the film begins, the audience sees Emma going about her daily chores, doing the laundry and making breakfast, when she heads upstairs and sits down at a vanity in the bedroom. Emma is then clearly seen taking off her makeup, wig, and dress and changing into John's clothes, leaving no doubt of her transgender identity. Rather than hinging on the big reveal of a character's transgender identity, the film reveals Emma's identity in the first five minutes and becomes, instead, an exploration of how the character deals with no one else knowing that she is transgender. The message sent by the film could almost be positive if it were not for the fact that its exploration of transgender identity is built on the fact that Emma and John are distinct split personalities.

The delayed revelation of the transgender identities of the characters in transgender thrillers, either to the audience or to the other characters in the films, further reinforces the distance between the audience and the characters. The audience may feel an initial connection with the characters, but when their transgender identities are revealed, the audience pushes the characters away as they reassess everything that happened in the films. The delayed revelation also sets up the disgust the audience feels when the characters' transgender identities are revealed. Because the audience forms initial connections with the characters, they are allowed to come closer than the ridiculous characters in transgender comedies or the shadowy killers in transgender horror films. When their transgender identities are revealed, though, the audience responds with disgust, pushing away the now unknown characters for getting too close to them. The emotional response of disgust is prompted by the forced revelation of the characters' transgender identities.

Forceful Unmasking

As with the characters in transgender horror films, the characters in transgender thrillers do not necessarily want their transgender identities to be revealed. Some characters may be actively trying to hide their transgender identities, such as Lois Einhorn in *Ace Ventura* using her identity as a transgender woman as a part of her revenge plot or Emma in *Peacock* hiding her transgender identity as part of her split personality as John, but many of the characters in these films, particularly Dil, do not share their identities with the audience or with other characters because they either assume the knowledge is already known or that it is not information the other person deserves to know. These characters, including Einhorn and Emma, are not hiding their transgender identities in order to deceive others but because they do not feel this is information that must be shared with everyone. As the films reach their climax, though, the characters' transgender identities are revealed whether they like it or not.

The revelation of the characters transgender identities is all done visually. For a film like *The Crying Game*, the visual revealing of Dil's transgender identity at the climax of the film is one of its main draws. Visual unmasking ensures that there is no doubt in the minds of the audience or the other characters about the gender identity of the characters. The characters' reluctance or refusal to reveal their identities often means that the revelation must occur using force. Even the less violent unmasking in *Myra Breckenridge* is still accomplished visually. Myra's transgender identity is well known to the audience, but it is not known to the other characters in the film. Buck brings in two of his lawyers to refute Myra's claim to part of Buck's estate by virtue of being Myron's wife. When it becomes clear that Myra will be unable to talk her way out of the situation, she declares herself to be Myron Breckenridge and stands up on Buck's desk so he and the lawyers can look up her skirt and confirm her claim. All that is seen on screen is a medium shot of the lower half of Myra's body, cut off at the waist, while Buck and one of his lawyers lean back in their chairs to look up her raised skirt, a big grin on the lawyer's face. The scene then cuts to another shot of the other lawyer cocking his head to the side in order to look up Myra's spread legs, through which the camera shoots. Numerous shots fill this scene of Myra's legs cut off at the waist, and she is usually shot from behind, so even in full-body shots, her face is not seen, reducing her identity to her genitals. Even in the more verbal arena of a legal proceeding, visual proof is still required of a character's transgender identity.

Dil's unmasking comes not in a moment of violence but in one of intimacy. After Dil returns from the bathroom after making out with Fergus, Fergus begins to remove her robe as the camera moves down her body from her face to her flat chest before stopping at her penis, at which point the music that had been playing in the background stops as well. Dil's reaction to Fergus's surprise—"You did know, didn't you?"—reveals her belief that disclosing her transgender identity was unnecessary since she assumed everyone, Fergus included, already knew about it. Fergus's reaction to the unmasking, to be discussed in the next section, is a clear example of the reason many transgender people choose to keep their gender identity a secret to all but close friends and family.

The most forceful unmasking of a transgender character in a transgender thriller is found in *Ace Ventura*. Ace tracks Einhorn to a marina in Miami where she is keeping hostage quarterback Dan Marino and the Miami Dolphins mascot Snowflake. The two begin to fight, and when nearly the entire police force arrives on the scene, Einhorn orders them to shoot Ace, whom she plans to frame for the kidnappings. Ace counters by asserting that Einhorn is actually Ray Finkle, the disgraced former kicker for the team who blames Marino for missing a field goal, and to prove it, Ace proceeds to strip her in front of everyone. He first grabs her by the hair and tries to yank off her supposed wig, only to find that her hair is very real. He then asks if a "real woman" would be "missing these" and rips open her blouse to reveal a very real pair of breasts. At this point, even Ace's friends are beginning to doubt him, as shown by the exasperated glances they share with each other. In a last-ditch effort, Ace rips off her skirt, exclaiming, "I doubt he could find the time in his busy schedule to get rid of big ole Mr. Kanesh!" He appears at first to be wrong on this point as well, since Einhorn shows no visible evidence of a penis beneath her panties. A visibly shaken and humiliated Einhorn stands nearly naked in front of the members of her force until Marino whispers a hint to Ace. Ace then grabs Einhorn by the shoulders and spins her around, exclaiming, "But if I am mistaken, if the lieutenant is indeed a woman as she claims to be, then, my friend, she is suffering from the worst case of hemorrhoids I have ever seen!" Einhorn's tucked-back penis and testicles are now clearly visible her underwear to the other cops and to the audience, providing incontrovertible proof that Einhorn is a transgender woman. While the scene plays out initially as a humiliation of Ace because of his hubris, it ends with him having confidently caught a criminal while Einhorn has been publicly violated. Einhorn could have been taken in for questioning with her dignity intact, but her position of power required a visual confirmation of her transgender identity that could only be accomplished through having a man pull her by the hair and forcefully rip her clothes off.

As with the delayed revelation, the rupture of this visual code can be found in *Peacock*. As discussed in the previous section, the audience sees Emma change into John's clothes in the first five minutes of the film, so they already know that Emma is a transgender woman. This initial knowledge on the part of the audience is generally followed by an unmasking for the other characters, as in *Myra Breckenridge*, but this never happens in *Peacock*. No other characters ever find out that Emma and John are the same person. The neighbors who find Emma after the train derails do not recognize her as John, and the sheriff, who often checks up on John ever since his mother died, does not recognize Emma as John either. Even Maggie, when she comes to ask John for money, does not recognize Emma when she comes downstairs, even though she had been talking with John just a few minutes earlier. When John is assumed to be dead in the motel room fire, no one ever questions it, and Emma locks herself in her house at the end of the film, never to leave again. While an element of deceit is present, Emma could confess that she is John and remove her wig at the end of the film; the fact that she chooses not to do this sends the message that it is at least possible for transgender people to be accepted but only if they completely erase their past.

The forceful unmasking of the characters' transgender identities represents another means by which cisnormativity asserts its control. Cisnormativity demands that everyone adhere to a strict gender binary in which one's gender identity and expression conform to the sex assigned at birth. By refusing to allow the transgender characters to keep their gender identities private or to at least decide to share their identities of their own volition, the films send the message that a person's transgender identity is always public knowledge. Cisnormativity maintains its control by making it clear that anyone who deviates from the gender binary can expect to be publicly outed and shamed.

The cisgender audience is often shocked and surprised at the revelation of a character's transgender identity; this is why these revelation scenes usually form the climax of transgender thrillers. As the audience searches for ways to process this new information, they often turn to the narrative positioning of the characters as threatening outsiders as a means of understanding how to respond. Instead of feeling sorry for the transgender characters for having their identities forcefully revealed, the audience now feels that the characters somehow deserved what happened to them and should have behaved differently if they did not want to be publicly exposed and violated. The films provide further evidence of how the audience should respond through their modeling of reactions of disgust.

Looks of Disgust

Disgust as an emotional response involves forcefully expelling the unknown when it has come too close. The affective responses to this expelling involve spitting or vomiting, as the body tries to remove the invading material, as when we spit out rotten meat or vomit as a result of food poisoning from eating spoiled or undercooked food. These affective responses are then processed into the emotion of disgust. In transgender thrillers, there is a lot of spitting and vomiting in response to the revelation of the characters' transgender identities. The cisgender audience is being shown in these films how they should respond when a transgender person's identity is revealed to them. Any potential connection the audience members may have to a transgender character are undermined by modeling disgust as the proper response. The emotional response of disgust is intensified when combined with the delayed revelation and forceful unmasking of the characters' transgender identities. These visual codes allow the characters to get close to the audience, and the films then show the audience how they should respond when they discover that a transgender character or person has gotten too close.

The prime example of this visual code is found in *The Crying Game*. After the camera moves down Dil's nude body revealing her penis, Fergus slaps her hand away when she tries to touch him and says, "It's, just, I feel sick." He pushes her down on the bed, bloodying her nose, as he runs to the bathroom and throws up. She comments on the way he pushed her down, "It's alright, Jimmy. I can take it. Just not on the face," and he slams the door to the bathroom so he cannot hear her anymore. The scene is shot with Dil in the foreground barely covering her chest with her hands and robe and Fergus in the background throwing up in the bathroom sink. Dil is placed in the foreground to remind the audience of the reason Fergus is throwing up. After he finishes being sick, he comes out of the bathroom and says "I'm sorry" before leaving without saying another word. Visually, the image of Fergus throwing up in the bathroom sink has come to define the way cisgender men are expected to react upon learning the transgender identity of a woman to whom they are attracted.

Ace Ventura parodies the scene from *The Crying Game* twice in another example of modeling the emotional response of disgust. In the longer of the two sequences, Ace discovers that Lois Einhorn is Ray Finkle when the fur of one of his dogs lies on Finkle's photo in such a way to make it appear that he has long hair. It does not take Ace long to make the connection: "Finkle is Einhorn! Einhorn is Finkle! Einhorn is a man! Oh my *God*, Einhorn is a man!" Ace is disgusted at having been aggressively kissed by Einhorn earlier in the film, and he rushes to the bathroom, like Fergus, to try to deal with this new knowledge. While Fergus threw up in the sink, Ace's reaction is more over the top, consisting of brushing his teeth, pouring a whole tube of toothpaste down his mouth, using a plunger on his lips, burning the clothes he had on (even thought they were not the clothes he was wearing when Einhorn kissed him), and ending with him sobbing in the shower. The reference to *The Crying Game* is repeated at the end of the film when Ace reveals Einhorn's penis and all the cops present spit on the ground in unison. To ensure that no one misses the reference, the song "The Crying Game," which, in the eponymous movie, Dil sings at the bar but is not the song that plays during the big reveal, plays during both *Ace Ventura* scenes. While the latter film's scenes may be read as parodies of those of the former, the length of the first *Ace Ventura* scene, in particular, implies that *The Crying Game*'s Fergus was not wrong to be disgusted upon the revelation of Dil's transgender identity; indeed, his expression of disgust was insufficiently intense. The message from both films is clear: audience members should be disgusted by transgender bodies.

Myra Breckenridge provides another example of a similar visual reaction to the revealing of a character's transgender identity. After Myra declares herself to be Myron, she stands up on Buck's desk in a short pink skirt so that Buck and his lawyers can confirm her claim. One of the lawyers takes one look up her skirt and faints. The audience never gets to see up Myra's skirt and is left to speculate on what could have been so disgusting that it would cause a grown man to faint. The narrative conventions and visual codes of the transgender thriller would suggest that he sees a penis on what he has believed up to this point to be a female body, but the film begins with Myron having gender confirmation surgery in which his penis would have been turned into a vagina. It is possible that seeing a vagina on what had purportedly been a male body was enough to make the lawyer faint. All that can be said for sure is that something about Myra's transgender body was disgusting and disturbing enough to make a man faint. The image of the lawyer's eyes rolling back and seeing him fall to the floor is of a kind with the images seen in *The Crying Game* and *Ace Ventura*.

Finally, the transphobic gaze gains some of its power by working in conjunction with a trans-misogynistic gaze. *Ace Ventura*, *Myra Breckenridge*, and *Ticked-Off Trannies with Knives* feature numerous shots of the breasts and legs of the transgender characters and multiple instances of the camera panning up and down their bodies. *The Crying Game* features an extended long shot of Dil walking across a rugby field to the hoots and hollers of construction workers. An extended tracking shot at the beginning of *Ticked-Off Trannies with Knives* focuses on Bubbles's legs as she walks down the street in heels and a short skirt; her face is not seen until she gets to the dressing room of the club where she performs. Lois Einhorn is introduced via a camera panning from her feet to her face as she exits an elevator. It is important for transgender thrillers to visually establish the transgender characters as attractive, so the same techniques that are used in film to make a woman into a sex object are used in these cases. If cisgender, heterosexual men did not find the characters attractive, there would be no need for them to be disgusted upon finding out that the characters are transgender women. This is a key element of transphobia—not just the fear of transgender people as different but the fear that a cisgender person may find a transgender person attractive. For cisgender, heterosexual men, this is tantamount to being attracted to another man, an attraction that cannot be tolerated in the system of cisnormativity.

The transphobic gaze demonstrates for cisgender people how to react when a transgender person's identity has been revealed. The camera movement down Dil's body is the clearest example of the combination of the transphobic and trans-misogynistic gazes. The camera begins to move down Dil's body, and the audience expects to see the usual pleasurable sights of the female body but instead finds a flat chest and a penis. The use of the techniques of trans-misogyny work to undermine the audience's expectations. Fergus's actions, though, end up modeling a transphobic response to the situation, missing a chance to undermine trans-misogyny and transphobia by having him react in a supportive manner. Cisnormative standards of gender are supported by the inability of Fergus, Ace, and others to accept the transgender identities of their partners.

Disgust is the emotional response modeled for the cisgender audience in transgender thrillers. When the transgender identities of the characters are revealed to the cisgender characters, they respond by spitting, vomiting, and fainting. The effect of seeing a transgender person's body prompts an immediate physical reaction. These reactions send the message to the audience that the transgender characters are unknown and unknowable and should be violently expelled from the presence of cisgender people. The transgender characters get close to the cisgender characters in the films as objects of affection or lust, and it is this closeness that prompts the emotional response of disgust. The transgender characters in these films are not threatening to get close, as in transgender horror films, but are already close by. By prompting an emotional response of disgust, transgender thrillers send the message to the cisgender audience that they are justified for keeping transgender characters—and, by extension, real transgender people—at a distance. Transgender people will always be unknowable, so any attempt to get closer will only be seen as disgusting.

Possible Effects of Transgender Thrillers

Transgender thrillers continue efforts to distance the transgender characters from the cisgender audience. Disgust is a reaction that is familiar to transgender people. As a transgender woman, I have often been the recipient of sneers of disgust, often when moving through public spaces. Disgust reactions are different than fear reactions in these spaces, in that fear reactions are about perceiving me as a threat that must be punished whereas disgust reactions often manifest as treating me as an intruder whose presence must be managed by others in order to maintain the illusion of control over their lives. My perceived abnormality means that I should not exist within their spaces, so they have to do something in order to prove they are still in control. For example, a man in a grocery store once angrily yelled at me as I walked away after denying his request to take my picture with his smartphone. He viewed me in that moment as an oddity that he had the right to record, and his anger was the result of me denying his assertion of power and control over the situation. An odd experience with this kind of disgust reaction happened when I walked into a Walmart in Muskogee, Oklahoma, to use the restroom while on a road trip. As I walked by, a mother stopped her young daughter, bent down to her, pointed at me, and asked her, "Is that a boy or a girl?" I walked on by without acknowledging her comment, but it stuck with me because it is usually children who ask that question out of (hopefully) innocent confusion. For a mother to ask her daughter the question instead demonstrates that she intended it to serve as a means of controlling the situation by highlighting my perceived incongruity. Restaurants are another space in which this reaction has often manifested, and a particular version of this reaction was repeated attempts to render my name masculine. On several occasions, cashiers or servers have changed the name assigned to my order to Lucian or Lucius as a means of asserting control over the situation by refiguring me as a man.

A particularly hurtful example of this kind of reaction involved a former colleague who I thought of at the time as a friend. We'd had classes together as graduate students and even taught public speaking next door to each other, so we had many opportunities to chat and grow closer. I felt like we were friends, so when I had a dentist appointment that required sedation, I did not hesitate to ask her if she would drive me. She agreed, and on the morning of the appointment, she arrived to pick me up with a friend, saying that she needed her friend's help in case she had any trouble physically helping me after the procedure. I did not mind, but I quickly noticed that her friend was calling me by my former name. I did not say anything in the moment because the dentist appointment was important, but I asked my colleague about it afterward. What resulted was a more than three hour debate at a nearby coffee shop in which she made it clear that she did not accept or respect my transgender identity (even though I had been out for most of the time she had known me). She invoked biblical teaching as immutable evidence that I was wrong (even after I provided the examples of slavery and women's rights as evidence of the fact that the church's position had changed on issues over time), and her ultimate conclusion was that going forward she would only refer to me as "L," since saying my name would be tacitly acknowledging my identity. I have very rarely in my life felt further away from someone who I had grown close to than I did in that moment. It was honestly shocking to me that she had harbored such disgust for who I am even as she maintained a façade of friendship. Disgust reactions may not always manifest as a sneer of the lips or a gag, but they do clearly communicate that a person views himself or herself as separate from the person they are directed toward.

Transgender thrillers contribute to this feeling of disgust directed toward transgender people by presenting the transgender characters as unknowable deceivers who the cisgender audience is justified in being disgusted by. The transgender characters are seen as deceptively hiding their gender identities in order to get close to the cisgender characters. When these characters then discover the transgender identities of the transgender characters, their disgust is positioned as appropriate because they did not have access to full knowledge of the transgender characters' identities. The message being sent to transgender people is if they want to be included is cisnormative society, they either must conform to the standards or at least openly communicate their transgender identities at all times and with everyone they meet, regardless of the fact that cisgender people are not expected to perform this level of public self-disclosure. This is framed as the only way transgender people can keep themselves safe. The message provided for the cisgender audience is that they are justified in being disgusted by transgender people and that they should keep their distance from transgender people in order to protect themselves from being deceived. More contact with transgender people may help to overcome these feelings of disgust, but contact that demands public disclosure by transgender people of all aspects of their gender identities just conforms to the standards of cisnormativity. Working to undo the association of transgender people with deception, along with a dismantling of the cisnormative expectation that everyone clearly adhere to a strict gender binary, may be a more productive means of overcoming the messages communicated through transgender thrillers.

5

Sympathy in Transgender Dramas

TRANSGENDER CHARACTERS IN transgender dramas like *Different for Girls* (1996), *Ma Vie en Rose* (1997), *Boys Don't Cry* (1999), and *Transamerica* (2005) differ from the other characters analyzed so far in that they all personally identify as transgender.[1] Their transgender identities are not a temporary disguise adopted to escape a crisis or a secret revealed at the end of the film. Reflecting on the lack of acceptance most transgender people face in their everyday lives, transgender dramas prompt an emotional response of sympathy in the audience. Suzanne Keen distinguishes between sympathy and empathy, noting that empathy is "a vicarious, spontaneous sharing of affect" while sympathy is "the more complex, differentiated feeling for another."[2] For Keen, empathy is the affective response while sympathy is the emotional response. For example, you are walking through the supermarket, and you see a mother trying to comfort her toddler, who is having a meltdown in the frozen food section. As your gaze meets the mother's and you see the exhaustion in her eyes, an affective response of empathy may be prompted in you as you recall similar experiences raising your own children. If you do not have children, you may feel sorry for what the mother is going through in an emotional response of sympathy, but you will not have that immediate, affective response of empathy because you do not share similar experiences. Sympathy involves "feeling for" another person as compared to the "feeling with" of empathy.[3] Feelings of empathy on the part of audience members also lead to more positive attitudes toward marginalized groups.[4] The audience is prompted to feel sympathy for the transgender characters in these films out of recognition that the cisgender audience to whom these films are directed may be becoming more aware of the experiences of transgender people, but because these experiences are ones that the audience still will never share, they are unable to fully experience empathy for the transgender characters.

Audience members who are experiencing tender feelings like sympathy and kindness may be drawn to dramas and other sad films out of "eudaimonic concerns—ones in which meaningfulness and insight are the desired outcomes rather than necessarily pleasure or positive affect."[5] The emotional response of sympathy that is prompted by these films may not seem to produce the same visceral, affective response as the loud guffawing of a comedy or the cathartic jumps of a horror film, but this feeling for another that is sympathy can be appealing. It is important to recognize that audience members may have more reasons to watch dramas and other sad films beyond just feeling sad themselves. The sense of meaning and insight that is gained from these films is not just a result of audience members being in the proper mood for a drama but is also the result of stylistic norms. In the case of transgender dramas, the stylistic norms are found in the narrative conventions and visual codes of independent drama.[6] One of the conventions of independent films in general is that they "tell stories about fairly ordinary people in recognizable places and situations."[7] The films in this chapter fit this focus on ordinary people and situations; though I argue that some of the situations are more contrived than would be expected of the genre, the distancing of the audience from the characters is a product of a particular mode of realism.

Many indie films are presented as if they are merely capturing events as they would happen in the real world. Much of contemporary indie drama is typified by an almost clinical documentary style of representation (in contrast to the hyperkinetic style of most big-budget Hollywood fare), with a strong trend in indie film toward "the creation of a greater impression of reality or authenticity than is associated with the glossier style typical of the Hollywood mainstream."[8] One of the few stylistic flourishes present in indie film is the use of form to create "*expressive*" effects "designed to create effects other than those of an ersatz documentary-realist nature."[9] The main motivation for using expressive effects is to present a "*subjective* realism that seeks to create an impression of individual experience, as it might seem from the inside, as opposed to an impression of events seen more objectively."[10] Examples of the use of expressive effects in transgender dramas include the flights of fancy to the Barbie-like world of Pam in *Ma Vie in Rose* and Brandon's disembodied experience in *Boys Don't Cry* as John and Tom forcibly expose his genitals and force his girlfriend Lana to look at them. These moments allow audience members access to the perspectives of the transgender characters in ways that are not possible through the typical stylistic choices made in indie dramas.

For many viewers, indie films bring attention to characters and situations that are less familiar to them, and while this can help make a wider community more familiar with transgender people and other marginalized groups, the audience comes from a position that is already distanced from the lives of the characters shown on screen and is only distanced further by the narrative conventions and visual codes in these films. Though indie films may claim to reflect the unvarnished truth of the characters' situations, they are still playing to an audience generally unfamiliar with the lived experiences presented on screen in ways that tend toward exoticization. When combined with the trend in many indie films toward ironic detachment, the characters are still presented to the audience as the distanced Other.

The films in this chapter situate the audience in a position of sympathy, rather than empathy, for the characters; audience members feel *for* the characters, recognizing the difficulty of the situations the characters experience while remaining unable to feel *with* the characters, not only because of a lack of personal understanding of what the characters are experiencing but also because the films are unwilling to convey the level of intimate knowledge necessary to connect with the characters at a deeper level. Transgender representations take an important step forward in transgender dramas by presenting the characters as objects of sympathy rather than of ridicule or fear, but it is important to recognize that sympathy does not equal unconditional acceptance of the characters' transgender identities. Because the films resist the kinds of intimate knowledge that would allow for deeper connections with the characters—in part because of their common tendency toward an ironic or detached indie sensibility—the characters remain at a distance from the audience. Audience members may feel sorry for the characters, but as the characters are constructed by the films, they are unable to fully bridge the gap that separates them.

The inability of these films to bridge that gap reinforces an ideology of cisnormativity. Audience members are not forced to think beyond their cisgender identities and actually try to understand the experiences of transgender people. They are prompted to feel sympathy for the transgender characters, but they are provided with few opportunities to really feel with the transgender characters. Their identification remains firmly with the cisgender authors of these films as they are invited to share in an opportunity to become more aware of the struggles of a marginalized group of people with whom they will never fully be able to identify. The distancing of the characters from the audience through the narrative conventions and visual codes of transgender dramas encourages the audience to view the, admittedly sad, difficulties the characters face as, to some degree, the product of their own decisions. While in no way excusing the pain the transgender characters suffer, the audience can remain confident that they will never be placed in a similar position. The audience may no longer cheer at the transgender monster being killed as they do in transgender horror films, but this does not mean that they feel any deeper connection with the transgender characters.

In contrast to characters in movies of the genres considered in previous chapters, the characters in transgender dramas actively claim a transgender identity. Instead of focusing on the discovery or revelation of a character's transgender identity, the films make particular narrative and visual arguments about the gender identities of the characters in a cisnormative society. The narrative conventions and visual codes work together to portray the struggles the characters endure in a cisnormative society while distancing the audience from the characters through feelings of sympathy for their plights.

Prompting Sympathy through Narrative Conventions

The narrative conventions of transgender dramas construct the characters as struggling to find a place in society, which their transgender identities make difficult. By constructing the characters' lives as a struggle, the films present the characters' identities as continually challenged by cisnormative standards of gender. The characters must then decide how to respond, only prompting further challenges. After an initial claim to a transgender identity is made, the characters face constraints on their identities by those around them, primarily family and friends. These constraints are the first expression of a lack of acceptance of the characters' transgender identities. The characters respond to these constraints by trying to prove their gender identities through their actions, as if all that prevented their acceptance by others is definitive proof of their claims. So far, the characters are not that different from the characters in transgender comedies, horror films, and thrillers; the characters occupy specific gender positions and make claims to certain identities that are either accepted or rejected by cisnormative society. What differentiates the characters in transgender dramas and leads to the feelings of sympathy from the audience is the harsh, often violent, reprisals the characters suffer for refusing to conform to cisnormative standards. The characters do not want to discard their transgender identities or violently strike back at repressive cisnormativity, so their struggles evoke feelings of sympathy rather than ridicule, fear, or disgust. Though the characters are positioned outside of cisnormative society and, therefore, distanced from the assumed cisnormative audience, transgender dramas come closest to a connection between the characters and the audience through the feelings of sympathy for the struggles of the characters in the face of repressive actions.

Constraints on Gender Identity

Constraints on gender identity in transgender dramas include words and actions directed at transgender characters for the purpose of correcting their (perceived) deviant behavior or expressing disapproval about their behavior. Constraints, for my purposes, stop short of physical or verbal attacks to punish transgender characters for disregarding cisnormative rules of behavior and are meant more as a corrective to that behavior before cisnormative violence, to be discussed in the third part of this section, becomes necessary. Rather than being able to assert their gender identities and have them accepted by those around them, transgender people are constantly judged in relation to the standards of cisnormativity, whether or not their gender expressions conform to cisnormativity. These constraints play a major role in the lived experiences of many transgender people and in the narratives of transgender dramas.

One type of a constraint on gender identity can be found in *Boys Don't Cry*, in several comments made by Lonny to his cousin Brandon

Teena. After Brandon finishes getting dressed for a night of picking up women at a skating rink, Lonny says, "If you was a guy, I might even wanna fuck you!" With just a subtle turn of phrase, Lonny makes it clear that he does not accept Brandon's gender identity. Though he makes no attempts to forcefully change Brandon's behavior, Lonny clearly refuses to acknowledge Brandon's masculine gender identity as legitimate. Later in the film, Brandon runs back to Lonny's trailer with a group of men, angry that he had sex with one of their sisters, chasing after him. Brandon seems bewildered by why the other men are so upset, and Lonny suggests that the problem stems as much from Brandon's misunderstanding of an issue of sexual orientation as one of gender identity.

> LONNY: You are not a boy! That is what went wrong!

> BRANDON: Tell them that. They say that I'm the best boy-friend they ever had.

Brandon's argument is based on his view that as a man, there should be no issue with him sleeping with women, but Lonny still refuses to accept Brandon's gender identity.

> LONNY: Why don't you just admit that you're a dyke?!

> BRANDON: Because I'm not a dyke.

Brandon's refusal to accept or abide by the constraints Lonny places on his gender identity leads to Lonny kicking him out for attracting trouble.

Constraints like these from close friends and family are fairly common in transgender dramas. Not all the constraints on gender identity are as direct as those directed at Brandon by Lonny. Constraints can include a casual remark or a thoughtless comment in a moment of anger, such as Paul, in *Different for Girls*, yelling Kim's former male name in an attempt to stop her from leaving the pub while they are having dinner. Paul's use of Kim's male name, even in a moment of anger, is a sign that he does not completely accept her transgender identity. Another constraint on transgender identities can be found in references to biology, such as in Bree's dinner with her parents in *Transamerica*. When Bree states that her argumentativeness with her family is the result of her hormone cycles, her mother angrily responds, "You don't have cycles!" Bree retorts, "Hormones are hormones. Yours and mine just happen to come in a little purple pill." Constraints on gender identity in transgender dramas not only try to limit the behaviors of transgender people but also point out the limitations inherent in their own bodies.

Looks, nasty remarks, and questions are other forms of constraints on gender identity experienced by the characters in transgender dramas. Throughout her trip from New York to Los Angeles with her son Toby, Bree is constantly aware of the looks she receives from others, particularly as groups of men watch her pumping gas in West Virginia and Kentucky. Bree's consciousness of their presence stems from a fear of being read while performing a typically masculine action (filling up with gas) in a masculine space (the gas station).[11]

The constraints on transgender women entering traditionally masculine spaces are also felt by Kim upon entering the masculine space of the police station. After Paul is arrested for exposing himself in public and Kim is arrested along with him for arguing with the police, they are brought to the station for booking. Kim is told that she may have to share a cell with another person and when she asks who, the officer replies, "It's the great unknown. Kinda like yourself," making it clear that she should not expect fair or equal treatment. The officer's comment informs Kim that, even though she has lived as a woman for several years and completed gender confirmation surgery, her transgender identity and gender expression are treated as a mystery rather than as legitimate. It is no surprise that Kim flees to the relative safety of her sister's house after the ordeal rather than testify on Paul's behalf.

While Kim is read by the booking officer at a police station, Bree's parents barely recognize her when she arrives at their house looking for help. Her father opens the door and asks, "Can I help you, young lady?" Bree responds simply "Dad, it's me." Her mother gasps and slams the door in her face, leaving Bree to bang on the door until her mother opens it again and says, "Get in here before the neighbors see you." It is clear that Bree's father barely recognizes her, calling into question her mother's concern about her being recognized by the neighbors and the negative implications this apparently will have for her parents. As Bree makes a sandwich, her father says,

"We're gonna need more time with that. We both love you . . ." before her mother interrupts.

> BREE'S MOTHER: But we don't respect you! I'll never understand why you're doing this to me.

> BREE: I'm not doing anything to you. I'm gender dysphoric. It's a genetic condition.

> BREE'S MOTHER: Don't try to blame your father and me for this.

Bree's mother makes it clear that she does not accept Bree's transgender identity. Even Bree's attempt at offering an explanation is met with the accusation that she is trying to blame her parents for her situation. Their refusal to recognize her transgender identity is an attempt to shame her into conforming to cisnormative standards.

While the constraints discussed so far are very real, the most direct pressure to conform to cisnormative standards is placed on transgender children, particularly *Ma Vie en Rose*'s Ludovic Fabre. Seven-year-old Ludovic's dependence on her parents prevents her from just leaving when up against the constraints on her gender identity. As the youngest character analyzed in this book, Ludovic faces the most direct control on her gender identity and expression. Ludovic faces constraints from her parents from the very beginning of the film, when she comes outside at her family's housewarming party in a pink princess dress, heels, and makeup. Her mother takes her in to change and as she wipes the lipstick from Ludovic's lips tells her, "You're seven, Ludo. Too old to dress up as a girl even if you think it's funny." Ludovic's mother tries to play the entire incident off as a joke, an extension of her husband referring to Ludovic as a "joker" to their guests, but the message is clear that this behavior will no longer be tolerated, implying that it has been tolerated for a while. Ludovic's father is more direct; he asks Ludovic why she was dressed the way she was. "I wanted to be pretty," Ludovic replies, to which her father responds with a clear, "Never again."

Ludovic faces several different constraints on her gender identity. While her mother is initially the more supportive parent, having read that it is natural for children to take seven years to search for their identity (which is conveniently Ludovic's current age), she soon becomes exasperated. After Ludovic tells her grandmother that she wants to marry her neighbor Jerome, her mother tells her, "You know, Ludo, boys don't marry other boys." Ludovic sighs and rolls her eyes, saying "I know that!" Her mother seems content until Ludovic says she will be a girl when she marries Jerome; her mother then loses her cool: "Cut it out! You're a boy, and you'll be a boy all your life! You're so stubborn! Just like your mother." She then smiles at Ludovic and is able to coax a smile out of her in response, but her message of disapproval has been sent loud and clear.

Ludovic also faces constraints at school. She is made fun of by the other students for bringing Pam and Ben dolls (the film's equivalents to Barbie and Ken) for show and tell, with one boy exclaiming, "He plays with dollies!" The teacher tries to smooth over the situation by saying that Ludovic and Sophie, another student who brought a Pam doll, would make a good couple and that Ludovic wants to be like Ben, moving on despite Ludovic shaking her head no. Later at school, Jerome, the boy Ludovic has a crush on, asks to sit anywhere but next to Ludovic; when the teacher asks why, Jerome answers, "Otherwise, I'll go to Hell," a message he received from his conservative Christian parents. Ludovic is crushed, and at recess, she runs crying to her sister Zoe, begging her to promise that she will not go to Hell, which Zoe does while hugging Ludovic. Zoe also brings biology into the constraints on Ludovic's gender identity.

> ZOE: We learned in biology what makes boys and girls. XY, you're a boy. XX, you're a girl. It's like playing poker. Get it?

> LUDOVIC: Doesn't God decide?

> ZOE: Of course He does.

Rather than accepting Zoe's explanation, Ludovic imagines God holding a list with her name on it: "Ludovic Fabre—*fille*." God tosses two X chromosomes and a Y down the Fabre's chimney, but one of the Xs bounces off and falls into the trash. Ludovic then exclaims, "I know what happened to my X." Through her active imagination, Ludovic is able to avoid Zoe's attempt at constraining her gender identity and devise her own explanation for her transgender identity.

Though Ludovic refuses to compromise on her claim of a transgender identity, she does express regret to her grandmother at the tension that exists between herself and her parents.

LUDOVIC: They say I refuse to change, and I only bring them trouble.

GRANDMOTHER: They have a point.

LUDOVIC: I don't want to change, but I do want them to love me.

GRANDMOTHER: They do but they still think they know what's best for you.

LUDOVIC: It's not best for me!

In *Transamerica*, Bree expresses a similar sentiment to her son Toby while sitting by her parents' pool. "I wish just once they'd look at me and see me. That's all. Really see me." In response to the constraints on their gender identities faced by transgender people both in film and in real life, transgender people often respond with a sincere desire to be recognized for who they are. This lack of recognition, an inability to or lack of desire to understand what it means to be a transgender person, is offered by Ludovic and Bree as an explanation for the tension and struggle they experience when dealing with their families and others in their lives.

Comments and conversations that are similar to all of the examples discussed here so far might be overheard while walking down any American street, but *Transamerica* provides an example of the way the narrative construction of the film itself works as a constraint on the character's gender identity. After receiving a call from her newly discovered son, who is living in a juvenile detention center in New York, Bree goes to see her therapist to make the final preparations for her gender confirmation surgery. Bree has an appointment the following week for her surgery and tells the therapist that nothing will stop her from checking into the hospital, not even her son's problems. The therapist responds, "Bree, this is a part of your body that cannot be discarded. I don't want you to go through this metamorphosis only to find out you're still incomplete." The therapist then refuses to sign the paperwork for Bree's surgery until she deals with her son. Bree is desperate and begins to panic because the hospital where she is having her surgery is booked a year in advance, and with just a week to go before her appointment, she will have to wait another year if she misses it.

The therapist's refusal to approve Bree's surgery is an unnecessary constraint intended to set up the main action of the film: Bree going to New York, bailing out her son Toby, and the two of them driving back to Los Angeles. While it is an effective set up for a film, it is a blatant disregard on the part of the therapist for her patient's well-being. Making her signature conditional puts an undue psychological burden on Bree, causing her an unnecessary amount of stress right before major surgery. It is also a decision that fails to take into account the economic realities of Bree's life; given the exorbitant out-of-pocket costs of gender confirmation surgery and the fact that Bree earns a living as a dishwasher at a Mexican restaurant and as a telemarketer, flying from Los Angeles to New York and then driving back with a teenager puts undue strain on Bree's finances. This decision is couched in concern for Bree, wanting to ensure that she does not feel "incomplete" after her surgery, but it only serves the film and is not an accurate representation of concern for a transgender patient. There is no reason Bree could not have gone to help her son after recovering from her surgery, but apparently that would not have made for as interesting of a plot.

Transamerica also features an important rupture in the constraints on gender identity when Bree constrains the gender identities of a group of transgender people she meets in Dallas. After being read by a young girl at a restaurant in Arkansas, Bree complains to her therapist about her problems with Toby, so her therapist connects her with a transgender woman in Dallas who is willing to open up her home to them. Upon arriving, Bree is a little put off that her host and a group of transgender women and men, who are there to plan a "Gender Pride" cruise, are passing around pictures of one member's "new vagina." Bree says to her host, "Margaret [the therapist] said you were stealth," meaning she does not tell people she is a transgender woman. Her host replies, "I am in public, but this *is* the privacy of my own home."

Bree is uncomfortable with the openness and frank sexuality of the women at the party and sits away from the group. When she tells

Toby they have to leave, Toby replies, "Why do you have to be so uptight? It's a party." Bree is out of her element, having spent the last few years trying to hide her transgender identity rather than celebrate it. Later that evening, Toby goes looking for Bree and startles her as she comes out of the bathroom in her underwear. After putting on a robe, she apologizes to Toby for "those ersatz women," defining the term as "phony. Something pretending to be something it's not." To this constraint by Bree of the gender identities of the other women, Toby replies, "I thought they were nice." While Bree faces a number of her own constraints, from her parents belittling her to her therapist requiring her to travel across the country before signing her paperwork, she demonstrates how transgender people can be as constraining of each other as anyone. Being a transgender person does not free anyone from the pressures to conform to cisnormativity.

Constraints on gender identity are cisnormativity's first line of defense against those who would claim an identity outside of its purview. By trying to curtail behavior that is seen as undesirable, constraints work to change behavior before more drastic actions become necessary. For cisgender audience members, these constraints provoke the beginnings of an emotional response of sympathy. They may recognize the earnestness with which the transgender characters assert their gender identities, but the characters' experiences are unfamiliar to them, having most likely never questioned their gender identities or had someone deny their avowed identity. The unfamiliarity of the characters' experiences prevents sympathy from fully developing at this point. While the audience may recognize that the transgender characters are chafing at the constraints placed on their gender identities, the constraints alone do not seem serious enough to warrant the intense emotional reactions of the characters. The transgender characters are going to have to suffer much more for sympathy to truly be prompted in the audience. In order to attempt to avoid this suffering, the characters in transgender dramas work to overcome the constraints by proving their transgender identities through their actions.

Proving Gender Identity through Actions

Lacking constant voiceovers of their internal monologues, the characters in transgender dramas must demonstrate their gender identities, both to the other characters in the films and to the audience, through their actions. While this reliance on action to prove gender identity represents a limitation in the realistic style found in indie dramas, the narratives of the films also provide the characters with numerous situations in which to prove their gender identities. These actions are attempts by the transgender characters to find a place within cisnormative society. Having had their identities constrained by others and fearing reprisals should they continue to act outside of cisnormative standards, transgender characters seek to prove they belong in a society often hostile to their avowed identities. While the actions and behaviors of the transgender characters are often used to justify constraining their identities, the response by these characters is to work to prove their identities as definitively as possible.

Brandon's actions in *Boys Don't Cry* are about finding his place in an often-hostile world. Brandon learns his lesson after being chased back to Lonny's trailer by a group of angry men, and when he makes a new group of friends, he does whatever it takes to perform traditional masculinity in order to be accepted, regardless of the danger. While out drinking one night, Brandon agrees to be pulled around a field by a pickup truck while holding on to a rope as a test of courage. Lana, with whom Brandon is smitten at first sight, questions his need to prove himself with such risky behavior.

BRANDON: I've been bored my whole life.

LANA: Yeah? Is that why you let John tie you to the back of a truck and drag you around like a dog?

BRANDON: No. I just thought that's what guys do around here.

Brandon attributes his behavior to boredom that must be relieved through risky actions, but Lana offers him a way out by questioning his use of John as a measuring stick for what it means to be a man. Brandon soon becomes disillusioned with John and focuses on proving his gender identity by wooing Lana.

Brandon is not shy in his performance of gender and clearly wants to be seen by others and to have them validate his performance of masculinity. Bree's actions at the beginning of *Transamerica*, in contrast, express a desire to *not* be seen. As she waits at a bus stop to go to an appointment with a psychiatrist, she tries to avoid letting people see her face by standing apart from them and turning her head whenever they look in her direction. She also crouches down and stoops her shoulders to make herself appear shorter than the man standing next to her. Transgender people are often represented in film as overly flamboyant attention seekers, but Bree's actions are an example of her attempt to prove her gender to others by fitting in and not standing out. Ludovic, like Brandon, is constantly seeking the approval of her gender performance from others in *Ma Vie en Rose*, particularly Jerome. One day at school, as she and Jerome wash their hands after using the restroom, she offers her ability to urinate while sitting down as proof of her girlhood, an action which Jerome points out is not impossible for boys; Ludovic then declares herself a "girlboy" merely waiting for God to deliver her missing X chromosome. For Ludovic, she already is a girl and is waiting for nothing more than the outward confirmation of her inner feelings, an experience common for many transgender people. She asks Jerome if he will like her once she has received her missing X.

> LUDOVIC: But God'll fix it. He'll send me my X, and we can get married, okay?
>
> JEROME: It depends on what kind of girl you are.

Jerome confirms the importance of actions in establishing gender. It is not enough for Ludovic to physically become a girl. Instead, the deciding factor for Jerome is how she acts as a girl, what kind of girl she will be. While he will later give in to his parent's conservative beliefs and reject Ludovic, it is surprising to hear Jerome base Ludovic's identity upon such positional and performative aspects of her personhood, rather than on essentialist notions of attraction and behavior.

While the behavior of the transgender characters may be questioned or essentialized, one of the clearest ways the characters demonstrate their claimed gender identities is through their romantic relationships. In *Different for Girls*, Kim and Paul flirt with each other while dancing together in his apartment after going to a rock club, and Kim is encouraged enough by the connection between them to ask Paul to come up to her place for a cup of coffee after he takes her home. He turns down the offer, but she is not ready to give up yet, so she leans in to kiss him. He backs away, offering his hand to shake instead.

PAUL: I am straight, you know?

KIM: So am I.

At this point, Paul is unable to separate Kim's gender identity from his memories of the boy he went to school with, though he will later overcome his hesitations and fall in love with Kim.

Kim actively pursues Paul as a way of demonstrating her claim to womanhood, though Paul might have found this unappealing, since the initiation of relationships by women remains taboo in some circles of Western society. Brandon does not face this issue in his relationship with Lana since, as a man, he would be expected to initiate a relationship and so has more initial success than Kim has with Paul. After returning from a court date in Lincoln, Nebraska, Brandon watches Lana as she takes a smoke break at the factory where she works and even takes Polaroid pictures of her, an action that Lana treats as charming (though she'll treat similar behavior by John later in the film as creepy). Brandon's romantic gesture is successful, and he and Lana make out on a hill near the factory. During this initial romantic encounter, Brandon takes Lana's bra off and performs oral sex on her, which she enjoys immensely, but she does not reciprocate by performing a similar sex act on him, which ignores the usual masculine demand for sexual satisfaction. Brandon's greater interest in Lana's pleasure than his own offers a view of masculinity that differs from the heteronormative standard but is still generally accepted as masculine. This alternative masculinity may explain why Brandon successfully pursues multiple women in the film while more overtly masculine characters like John and Tom are shunned.

The most chaste relationship among the transgender dramas we consider here, between Ludovic and Jerome, also provides the clearest example of the lengths to which a character in such a film will go to show their love for another character. Beyond telling her grandmother that she will marry Jerome in the future, Ludovic also has two opportunities to demonstrate her love for him. The first comes while she plays with Jerome at his house. She sneaks into the bedroom of Jerome's dead sister, which has a very feminine character to it, and finding a pink dress in the closet, she decides to put it on and enact a pretend wedding with Jerome. All is going smoothly until Jerome's mom catches them just as they are about to kiss, which causes her to faint. Ludovic's second opportunity also involves trying to kiss Jerome. Dissatisfied at school with her role as a dwarf in her class's production of *Snow White*, Ludovic locks the girl who is playing Snow White in the restroom and take her place on stage in time to be kissed by Jerome, who is playing Prince Charming. Jerome recognizes Ludovic as he bends down to kiss her, and he freezes and backs away, pulling off the veil and headband covering Ludovic's face and revealing her to everyone. Ludovic is too young at seven years old for any relationship that would go beyond a kiss, but she tries to replicate the experiences that she hopes to have in the future with Jerome or a man like him. Though her fantasies of getting married and being kissed are fairly conservative, the attraction that they seek to fulfill brings her as much negative attention, if not more, than her claim to a feminine gender identity.

Those in these films who disapprove of the transgender characters' actions and the gender identities they express also make claims to cisnormative gender identities through their own actions. These actions can be as simple as Ludovic's father yelling at the entire family during dinner after finding out about Ludovic's pretend wedding with Jerome and then going out to the garden and doing pull-ups. The physical exertion is not only a way to release anger but also a typically masculine action; Ludovic's father is demonstrating to her the way a man should act. Paul must also reassert his claim to masculinity after he gets turned on during dinner at Kim's apartment by her flirtatious description of her physical transformation while undergoing hormone treatment and gender confirmation surgery. When he heads for the door rather than admit his attraction, Kim responds, "Now you know what it's like to be confused about your cock." The two begin to argue, and Paul unzips his pants and pulls out his penis as a demonstration of society's obsession with it. Being arrested for public indecency, for Paul, just proves his point. Paul gets in a shouting match and exposes himself to prove his masculinity after feeling that it was called into question because of his attraction to Kim. Cisnormative gender identities must be clearly established in the face of transgender identities, particularly those that arouse desires that are seen as outside the norm.

The actions of Paul and Ludovic's father assert and build up their own masculine identities. By raping Brandon, John and Tom seek to assert their own masculinity by diminishing his. After forcefully exposing Brandon's transgender identity, John and Tom wait for him outside Lana's house, force him into their car, and take him to an abandoned meat-packing plant. Brandon begs them not to do anything after John tells him to take his shirt off, and John responds, "You know you brought this on yourself," before punching him twice in the mouth and shoving him in the backseat of the car.

After John rapes Brandon, Tom rips Brandon's clothes off, pushes him onto the trunk of the car, and rapes him a second time. After Tom finishes, John punches Brandon again as the two celebrate, leaving Brandon naked and curled into a fetal position. When Brandon asks to be taken home, John tells him to keep their "little secret."

> TOM: Cause if you don't, we'll have to silence you permanently.

> BRANDON: Yeah, of course. This is all my fault, I know.

Brandon is able to escape out a window at John's house while the other two men think he is taking a shower. He goes to Lana's house, but when Lana's mom sees him, she says, "I don't want *it* in my house." Lana convinces Brandon to report his rape to the police, who prove to be less than helpful.

> OFFICER: Why do you run around with *guys* bein' you're a girl? Why do you go around kissin' every girl?

> BRANDON: I don't know what this has to do with what happened last night.

> OFFICER: Cause I'm tryin' to get some answers so I can know exactly what the fuck's goin' on.

Like John and Tom, the officer suggests that because Brandon is a transgender man, he brought the attack on himself. In doing this, the officer implicitly supports John and Tom's cisnormative actions. Rape is often implicitly supported through the blaming of victims and the ignoring of cases and accusations, because it is seen as an assertion of cisnormative masculinity, which includes as one of its central features the (often forceful) sexual domination of women.

John and Tom rape Brandon to diminish his masculinity and assert the dominance of their own. Brandon cannot be a masculine person, because a truly masculine person would never allow himself to be raped. Likewise, John and Tom are truly masculine because of the ease with which they are able to rape Brandon. It is important for John and Tom's claims to a masculine identity that their rape of Brandon was preceded by their forceful exposure of his transgender identity. By exposing Brandon's transgender identity, John and Tom are able to view him, and force their friends to view him as well, as a woman instead of as a man, thus preventing their rape from being read as undermining their own masculinity. The implications of Lana's refusal to look at Brandon's exposed genitals in this moment will be discussed in a later section.

The assertions of cisnormativity by John, Tom, Paul, and Ludovic's father are all in response to being challenged by the transgender identity of another character. Ludovic's father is disturbed that she is transgender and that she fantasizes about marrying Jerome; Paul is disturbed by his physical attraction to Kim; and John and Tom are disturbed by the women in their lives being attracted to Brandon. When challenged, cisnormative masculinity in these films responds through actions, ranging from pull-ups to public exposure to rape, that reassert its dominance and control. Even a seemingly benign action like Ludovic's father doing pull-ups sends a clear message that cisnormative masculinity is expressed physically and those who challenge it should expect to be the target of that physicality.

Transgender characters seek to prove their gender identities through actions as a way of pushing back against those who would deny the legitimacy of their identities. These actions face their own pushback as cisnormativity seeks to reassert its dominance, often through repressive physical force. Asserting their identities through their actions also leads the audience to have less sympathy for the transgender characters. While the audience may recognize the earnestness with which the characters bristle against the constraints placed on their gender identities, asserting their identities through their actions makes the transgender characters seem like the aggressive ones. From the cisnormative perspective, gender identity is something that one is simply supposed to have, without being questioned or scrutinized by others rather than a claim that must be accepted by others. For cisgender audience members unfamiliar with having to make claims to a true gender identity, such claims by the transgender characters seem inappropriate; transgender characters should just quietly be themselves and hope to one day be recognized for who they are. The audience's sympathy for the characters is reduced because their actions seem unwarranted. If transgender dramas are constructed to prompt the emotional response of sympathy in the cisgender audience, why would the narratives of these films include elements that make the audience less sympathetic? By reducing the audience's sympathy for the characters through their actions, the films increase the impact of the violent, repressive responses to these actions. The audience's sympathies for the characters may have waned as a result of their actions, but even so, the audience does not believe that the characters deserve the violent response to their actions depicted in the films. The films prompt sympathy from the audience as they watch the characters suffer. Just as horror films and thrillers must build up the tension, dramas must first lower the audience's sympathy so that the narrative moments intended to inspire that sympathy are able to be more impactful. In transgender dramas, these narrative moments take the form of the transgender characters becoming the objects of violent, repressive actions in response to their failure to conform to cisnormative standards.

Repressive Actions of Cisnormativity

Having endured constraints placed on their gender identities and tried, in response, to demonstrate their identities through their actions, the characters in transgender dramas then face the full force of the cisnormative drive to repress their identities for deviating from the norm. I have chosen to separate these instances from the examples discussed above (involving Ludovic's father, Paul, John, and Tom) because while their actions in the previous section were about reasserting their masculinity when confronted with a transgender person, the examples we now turn to involve direct action to repress the gender identities of the transgender characters and to punish them for deviating from the norms set by cisnormativity. The repressive actions discussed in this section include verbal abuse, intimidation, physical violence, and murder. It is worth noting that Brandon Teena's murder at the hands of John and Tom, the discussion of which ends this section, is the only major death of a transgender character that occurs in any of the films under analysis.[12] Even with the monstrous portrayals of such characters as Norman Bates in *Psycho* and Angela in *Sleepaway Camp* or the near-death experiences of comedic characters like Joe and Jerry in *Some Like it Hot*, the characters survive until the end of the films, the former to return in later sequels and the latter because the danger is meant for laughs, not fear. Not so for Brandon Teena. While the representations of transgender characters in transgender dramas are generally more accepting of transgender identity as legitimate, Brandon's murder sends the message that this acceptance may make the characters in transgender dramas more of a threat to cisnormativity than the frivolous and frightening representations seen in previous chapters.

A clear example of a social group turning against a transgender character can be found in *Ma Vie en Rose*. After Ludovic takes Sophie's place as Snow White in the school play in an attempt to kiss Jerome, the Fabres exit the auditorium to find the entire audience, including all of their neighbors, waiting for them. No sound is heard, except for crying children, as the adults stare disapprovingly at the family as they make their way to their car. What had been discussed before in joking or hushed tones is now treated openly with grave importance. The town has made it clear that they stand united in their disapproval of Ludovic's behavior and of her family for tolerating it. Not only does this disapproval weigh heavily on Ludovic's young shoulders, but it also begins to tear her family apart.

As we have noted is the case in other genres, the recurring theme of transgender characters as liars is also an element in transgender dramas. In *Boys Don't Cry*, John is very direct in his accusations of Brandon. After learning from Candace that Brandon was put in a women's cell after being arrested for forging checks, John goes to Lana's house and tells her mom, "He's got her brainwashed. That's what they do." Not only is lying the only way that Brandon could have possibly convinced Lana to go out with him, but it is also part and parcel with being transgender (rather than simply a personality flaw). When John finds a book on gender identity disorder among Brandon's belongings, he tosses it aside, exclaiming, "Get this sick shit away from me!"

When Lana and Brandon return home, she gets mad at John for going through Brandon's belongings. When John locks the front door behind Brandon, Lana realizes what is going on and tries to warn Brandon, saying "Brandon, turn around and walk out that door, right now. This is a nuthouse!" Brandon is slow to heed the warning, so John has his opportunity to confront Brandon directly. "You've been spouting nothing but lies from the minute you came into town." Lana's mother then accuses Brandon of exposing Lana to the idea of being attracted to someone like him.

> LANA'S MOM: I can't believe I invited you into my home, and you exposed my daughter to your sickness.
>
> JOHN: You know, Lana, if you are a lesbian, you just need to tell me.
>
> BRANDON: It's not Lana, it's me.

Brandon does not shy away from taking the full brunt of their accusations, hoping to spare Lana their wrath. This noble act is lost on John, who decides to confront Brandon with the main thrust of his accusations: "You fucking pervert. Are you a girl or are you not? Are you a girl or are you not?!" John essentializes Brandon's identity, reducing the complexity of gender identity formation and performance to a simple yes or no question. For John, the question of whether Brandon has lied can be solved with a simple analysis of his genitalia because, as Tom says, there is "a real easy way to solve this problem."

Lying has been one of the central accusations leveled against transgender characters in all the films analyzed in this book. Transgender characters are accused of lying for claiming a gender identity that differs from the standards imposed by cisnormativity. Even if the gender performance of the character falls within these norms, they are accused of deceit and experience the distrust and disgust that others direct toward those whose gender identities do not match the gender they were assigned at birth. In *Transamerica*, after seeing Bree's penis while she urinates on the side of the road, Toby outs her to a roadside vendor, who tells him to obey his mother. As she follows him back to the car, Toby yells, "You're a fucking lying freak!" He goes on the offensive when she tries to share her reasons for withholding the information from him.

> TOBY: Whaddaya want outta me?

> BREE: Just because a person doesn't go blabbing her entire biological history when she meets someone doesn't make her a liar.

> TOBY: Why didn't you just tell me the truth?

> BREE: So you could humiliate me in public even sooner?

> TOBY: You knew all about me!

Bree expresses the fear, experienced by many transgender people, that the information they share about their gender identities will be used to attack them rather than used to understand them better. To their accusers, Bree and Brandon are liars for not openly sharing their gender identity; they are seen as withholding the information for nefarious purposes rather than for self-preservation. The solution would seem to be for the transgender characters never to withhold their gender identities, but even a character like Ludovic, who is open nearly to a fault, faces cisnormative repression for not conforming to society's standards.

Ludovic is the victim of both direct and indirect repression. Ludovic's father comes home drunk one night after his boss, Jerome's father, fires him as an indirect way of punishing Ludovic for her gender transgressions and her family for tolerating her behavior.

> LUDOVIC: Is it my fault?

> LUDOVIC'S FATHER: No. People are shit.

Ludovic's mother, though, is not as sympathetic to Ludovic's feelings. Saying she is tired of all of the hypocrisy, she tells Ludovic, "Yes, it's all your fault! Everything!" Ludovic is also the victim of direct repression when a group of twenty parents sign a petition demanding that Ludovic be removed from school. The principal caves, saying that

Ludovic's "behaviors" and "tastes" are "too eccentric" for the school. Her mother again directs her anger at Ludovic, complaining about the hour-long bus ride Ludovic must now take to get to school.

This form of repression (catcalls, snide remarks, firing people, and so on) is meant to hurt the transgender people against whom it is directed but go unnoticed by others. When the transgender characters still refuse to conform to societal standards, the verbal and physical repression becomes more violent and more visible to the rest of the community. After Ludovic's father is fired, her parents wake up one morning to find that someone has written the message "Bent Boys Out," a slang term for a gay man in France, on their garage door. In response, Ludovic's mother angrily grabs her, drags her into the kitchen, and shaves her head. After she finishes, her eyes dart frantically back and forth over Ludovic's face, desperately searching for the boy she wants Ludovic to be. She then refuses to allow Ludovic's father to take her to school, instead walking her to the bus stop in full view of the neighbors to make clear that she has forced Ludovic to conform. Making Ludovic walk to the bus stop is a response meant to be seen by the entire neighborhood, just as the graffiti's disapproving message was meant to be seen by all. Ludovic's mother ensures that her repressive action is just as visible as the one to which she responds.

While Ludovic's mother is forceful in shaving her head, she is not yet violent in her repression of Ludovic. The first instance of violence against Ludovic comes when the boys on her soccer team gang up on her in the locker room after a game. The bullies begin by calling her "fancy-pants" and questioning why she never takes off her shirt in front of them. One bully then says, referring to her penis, "Do we pull it off? Make you a real girl?" Jerome leaves as the bullying begins, and the youngest of Ludovic's brothers wants to help when the soccer team begins beating her up, but her oldest brother stops him. Following the assault and her abandonment by her siblings, Ludovic runs away from home. The entire family starts looking for her, but in a blatant disregard for her child's wellbeing, her mother goes to the garage to have a secret smoke instead of searching. While in the garage, she discovers Ludovic in the freezer clutching a crucifix. Ludovic's father downplays her obvious attempt at suicide in response to the constant bullying and harassment as a joke, her "freezer trick," as a way of ignoring the repressive cisnormative behavior their entire family has engaged in and supported. Ludovic's family ignores their own role in repressing her. Unfortunately, this will not be the last act of repression that Ludovic must endure at their hands.

Ludovic also suffers a rage-induced act of physical violence. After the Fabre family moves to a smaller house in a new city for her father's new job, Ludovic's mother stops her as she runs outside to play with her siblings to remind her that "it's not our fault we're here." It is clear that Ludovic's mother has drilled into her head that her transgender identity is the cause of all of her family's problems. When Ludovic is invited to her new friend Christine's birthday costume party, she dutifully attends dressed as a musketeer. The tomboyish Christine, who is dressed as a princess, likes Ludovic's costume better and demands that she trade. In contrast to her first appearance at the housewarming party, Ludovic refuses to trade, but Christine is able to force her to switch costumes. Ludovic's mother sees Christine wearing the musketeer costume and goes looking for Ludovic. She tries to run away, but her mother catches her and scolds her: "I warned you! You're bent on ruining our lives! Give us a break!" She violently shakes and slaps Ludovic in the face multiple times, stopping only when the other mothers at the party physically restrain her, yelling, "Stop it! You'll kill him. Calm down!" A visibly shaken Ludovic can do nothing in response but run away.

While Ludovic manages to survive, Brandon is not as fortunate. After threatening Lana's mother with a gun for information on Brandon's whereabouts, John and Tom head to Candace's to get their revenge on Brandon for going to the police about the rape. Tom asks John, "Think they'd recognize her if we chopped off her head and her hands?" Lana goes to Candace's house as well and tries to stop John. She tells Brandon that the two of them can still leave and go to Lincoln together, but John shoots Brandon in the head, dropping his gun after firing. Tom picks up the gun and shoots Candace in the chest, with her baby at her feet, and then turns the gun on Lana, but John grabs him at the last second, causing him to miss. Tom then grabs Brandon's lifeless body as it slumps against the wall and stabs him in the gut with a knife. Lana screams and pulls Tom from Brandon's body. John tries to get Lana to go with them, but she refuses. He fires one last shot in Brandon's direction as the two run out the door of Candace's house. Brandon pays the ultimate price for daring to go against cisnormative standards for gender identity and expression. Though the other characters endure their own share of repressive verbal and physical attacks, the films conclude with their lives continuing on, while Brandon's does not.

The repressive actions directed at the transgender characters evoke feelings of sympathy from the audience. After seeing Ludovic being hit by her mother and Brandon being shot by John, the audience feels sorry for the characters for everything they have endured, even though the characters still refuse to conform to cisnormative standards. The direct acts of violence the characters suffer are presented as a step beyond mere disapproval of the characters' transgender identities. Just as transgender horror films evoke feelings of fear at the violent actions of the characters, transgender dramas open up the possibility that this level of violence could be seen by audience members as an extreme response to the pressures to conform to cisnormativity, though the characters' transgender identities prevent the audience from fully connecting with them. They may feel sorry for the struggles the characters go through and may not want them to be violently attacked, but their transgender identities still exist outside of cisnormative standards and cannot be fully embraced.

The ending of *Ma Vie en Rose* provides a model for this sympathetic distance. Ludovic runs away after being hit by her mother, and after getting the full story of the change in costumes from Christine, her mother follows after her. Her mother climbs up onto a billboard for the *Pam's World* TV show that Ludovic loves and hallucinates/dreams that Ludovic goes to join Pam in her Technicolor world so as to not ruin their lives anymore. When she tries to follow her daughter into this fantasy world, she falls through the ground, her anger and intolerance not accepted there. When she comes to, she finds Ludovic safe and sound with the rest of the family, still wearing Christine's torn princess dress. Ludovic asks if she should take the dress off.

LUDOVIC'S FATHER: Do whatever feels best.

LUDOVIC'S MOTHER: Whatever happens, you'll always be my child. Our child. I've tended to forget it lately but not anymore.

This is a complete change of attitude by Ludovic's parents and gives the film a happy ending as Ludovic runs off to play with the other children.

The end of *Ma Vie en Rose* works to define the narrative as one of family bonding and togetherness, but this ending, in which the family accepts Ludovic after her mother hits her at a birthday party, is a "rushed attempt" to wrap up the story in a satisfying conclusion.[13] The ending ignores the abusive treatment Ludovic has suffered at the hands of her family and other cisnormative members of her community by presenting her family as finally accepting her transgender identity. The family's acceptance of Ludovic "is actually a *rejection* dressed up as acceptance of [her] difference."[14] By resorting to the tolerance of Ludovic's differences and individualist concepts of personal freedom, the family avoids any real acceptance of Ludovic's transgender identity.[15] The family is comfortable in feeling sorry for everything Ludovic has suffered at their hands but is not interested in a deeper understanding of her. While Ludovic's family feeling sorry for her is a more positive ending than either her abandoning her identity or others containing the threat that it presents, she is still kept at a distance from her family and, by extension, from the audience. The narrative construction of the character allows the audience to get only so close to Ludovic while preventing a deeper connection with her.

Ludovic's parents adopt an attitude of distanced sympathy in response to her transgender identity. They have recognized the danger of their repressive actions and offer Ludovic space to express her identity but fall short of completely embracing her. Her mother's last statement that Ludovic will always be their child "whatever happens" suggests that she still holds out some hope that Ludovic will ultimately conform to cisnormative standards. She does not say that she accepts Ludovic for who she is or even call her "my daughter." Either of those would have been a clear indication of acceptance of Ludovic's transgender identity. Instead, her parents feel sorry for everything she has been through and will no longer actively try to stop her from expressing her transgender identity, but their sympathy implies a lack of full acceptance of her and a hope that she will ultimately conform to cisnormative standards. The reaction of Ludovic's parents is constructed as a model for the audience's own distanced sympathy, feeling sorry for what has happened to the characters but still not fully accepting their transgender identities.

An anecdote from a colleague may help to illustrate this point. When she taught *Boys Don't Cry* in a Gender Studies class, a student commented that Brandon should not have been murdered but should have gone to jail. When pressed to identify what crime Brandon had committed, the student could not name one but still strongly felt that jail was appropriate. The student felt sympathy for Brandon but still was uncomfortable with his transgender identity, seeing it as comparable to a crime. It is important that transgender dramas open up the possibility for audiences to fear the actions of cisnormative society, but overcoming the distance between the transgender characters and the audience remains an important step that few transgender films have yet accomplished.

The narrative conventions of transgender dramas encode a sympathetic view of transgender people based on the struggles they endure. The visual codes continue this sympathetic project by situating the daily lives of the characters as objects to be looked at. The positive aspects of sympathy are emphasized through the way the characters are looked at by others, but this is not enough to completely bridge the distance between the characters and the audience.

Visual Codes: The Trans-Pathetic Gaze

The visual codes of the trans-pathetic gaze work to distance the transgender characters as objects of sympathy. The trans-pathetic gaze visually presents the characters as people the audience should feel sorry for rather than connect with. For Julia Serano, the pathetic transsexual differs from the deceptive transsexual by being unable to deceive others about their gender identity, even though they may want to.[16] The transgender characters in transgender dramas embrace their transgender identities, but they are still expected to conform to cisnormative standards of appearance. The visual codes in these films render the transgender characters somewhat pathetic to the audience in their efforts to conform to these standards. The characters are distanced from the audience based on the perception that their efforts to conform will never be fully successful. The audience is sympathetic to the plight of the transgender characters, but they are unable to fully erase the distance that exists between themselves and the transgender characters because of the visual codes of the trans-pathetic gaze.

Attention to Dressing

Transgender dramas share an interest with other media, particularly news media, in the processes transgender people go through when getting dressed. Film and other media "tend not to be satisfied with merely showing trans women wearing feminine clothes and makeup. Rather, it is their intent to capture trans women *in the act* of putting on lipstick, dresses, and high heels, thereby giving the audience the impression that the trans woman's femaleness is an artificial mask or costume."[17] Getting dressed is not a behavior often depicted in popular film, except in comedic moments when a character rushes to get ready for an appointment they are late for or dramatic moments as a character nervously prepares for an important first date or job interview. The audience generally only sees characters looking their best, with no consideration of the time and effort it took for them to look that good.

For characters in transgender dramas, a lot of visual attention is given to the process and effort they go through to get dressed every day. The characters are seen applying makeup, shaving, putting on various undergarments, and looking at their reflections in the mirror to check the results. In contrast, the characters in transgender comedies, horror films, and thrillers are rarely seen going through the process of dressing in order to maintain the comedic impact of their initial transformations or the mystery of their identities, respectively. The message sent by this attention to dressing is that these characters are the most threatening to the stability of cisnormativity and must be somehow exposed; if audiences just look closely enough at the amount of effort a transgender character must go through to be perceived as the gender they claim, then the character will appear pitiful and worthy of sympathy rather than respect and acceptance. More information, in this case, does not lead to greater levels of respect; rather, a trans-pathetic gaze prompts sympathy for everything the transgender characters put themselves through to go against the gender identity they were assigned at birth. More information might be useful in transgender comedies, horror films, and thrillers to better understand the characters' transgender identities, since they either privilege their cisnormative identities or hide their transgender identities for a shocking revelation, but in transgender dramas more information only functions to expose the characters as somehow less than who they appear to be.

Transgender dramas frequently feature extended sequences of characters dressing and putting on makeup. *Transamerica* begins with a close-up of Bree following along with a video of a woman demonstrating vocal delivery by putting her fingers down her throat to learn about mouth movement. Bree's face is never clearly seen as she practices speaking or as she goes about the rest of her morning routine. Wearing a pink robe, she pulls a pair of white stockings up her legs, pulls on a pair of white shapewear, puts a pair of breast forms in her bra to supplement her own breasts, and tucks back her penis. Throughout this routine, the camera focuses on her legs, breasts, and crotch, never showing her face or a full view of her body. This reduction of Bree to her body parts, while also trans-misogynistic, emphasizes the effort and equipment that constitutes her appearance. She is not a woman getting dressed but a pair of legs in white stockings, a penis tucked and constrained with shapewear, and a pair of breasts supplemented by silicone breast forms. The trans-misogynistic gaze highlights the transgender identities of the characters by focusing on the individual parts of their bodies in a parody of the sex appeal and desirability of the female body, while the trans-pathetic gaze frames Bree as a sympathetic figure the audience should feel sorry for because of the effort she has to expend to be comfortable in her everyday life, implying that all of the parts the audience has seen do not completely add up to a woman.

After putting on her undergarments, Bree puts on a pink suit and begins applying her makeup. While hints of Bree's face can be seen in the mirror as she applies foundation, eyeliner, mascara, and blush, the focus remains on the makeup, and it is only as she applies her lipstick that the audience finally sees Bree's face in focus. She looks at herself in the mirror, having completed her daily routine, and smiles wanly. This smile signals that Bree has the same opinion of herself—disappointment with the fact that she will never fully be the woman she wants to be—that the trans-pathetic gaze has directed the audience to have of her. Her wan smile communicates the message that despite the great lengths she has just gone through to be who she is, she is not completely satisfied with the results.

This scene clearly demonstrates the different decodings possible of any scene or film and the widely differing messages communicated based on the decoding. It is entirely possible to decode the previous scene in an empathetic way, based on a shared experience with Bree of the difficulty and dissatisfaction in adopting a position as a woman. Her wan smile that concludes the scene would not communicate dissatisfaction with her transgender body but the exhaustion inherent in the performance of femininity in a misogynistic society. I argue that the contextual information in this scene, such as the transgender voice tape Bree follows along with at the beginning and her actions at the bus stop after getting dressed, constrain this empathetic reading, but this scene remains an important reminder of the different decodings that are possible.

This pattern of attention to the process of dressing for a transgender character through the use of close-ups of individual body parts is used to similar effect in *Ma Vie en Rose*. As the Fabres prepare for their housewarming party, the camera tilts up to an upstairs bedroom window where Ludovic's hands, again not her entire body, are seen playing with a Pam doll. She is wearing a pair of red heels that are obviously too big for her (after we heard her mother complaining moments earlier about being unable to find her red heels) and a pink dress. As Ludovic puts on lipstick in a mirror, her brown hair is seen in the shot but not her face, and as she puts on a pair of earrings, only the back of her head is shown. As their neighbors begin to arrive, a shot focuses on the white shoes that Ludovic's mother is wearing, emphasizing again that the red heels Ludovic has on were not given to her with her mother's permission. Ludovic's father begins introducing the family, and the audience sees Ludovic's feet coming down the stairs in the red heels; Ludovic stumbles on her way down, as a result of the shoes being too big and her inexperience wearing them. As her father calls for her sister Zoe, Ludovic walks through the screen door into the backyard, and the audience sees her face for the first time.

The focus on Ludovic's individual body parts without seeing her face is intended to have a similar effect as the scenes of Bree dressing in *Transamerica*. Unlike Bree, though, Ludovic is portrayed as sympathetic more for her naiveté regarding cisnormative gender roles than for the effort that goes into her getting dressed and doing her makeup. The neighbors clap at first, thinking she is Zoe, then stop clapping and look at each other in confusion after finding out she is Ludovic. The reactions of the adults in this situation give the audience a clue about how to decode seeing Ludovic in a dress. Ludovic should be viewed with sympathy as a child who does not know or understand that she should not wear a dress, heels, earrings, and lipstick. Like Bree, she should be pitied for her failure to fit into cisnormative society.

To these two extended sequences of transgender characters dressing, we might mention shorter scenes in other films, such as Kim checking her makeup while waiting for Paul in *Different for Girls* and Brandon wrapping his breasts with a bandage in *Boys Don't Cry*. The attention to dressing in transgender dramas focuses audience attention on getting dressed as a process for transgender characters. Audience sympathy is evoked through the lengthy process that transgender characters go through in getting dressed. Cisgender people are positioned as having a simple dressing process to go through compared to what transgender people must endure. The audience is distanced from the characters by all the attention they pay to something that comes naturally for cisgender people. The audience is also distanced from the transgender characters through the frequent visual reminders of the characters' bodies.

Reminders of the Body

Frequent visual attention is given in transgender dramas to the bodies of the characters. Having spent a significant amount of time on the characters getting dressed, the films remind the audience of the aspects of their anatomy that the characters work to manage. It is not enough that the characters claim a transgender identity or that the narratives position them as transgender people. Transgender dramas must confirm the transgender identities of the characters by presenting undeniable visual proof of their bodies' subversion of cisnormativity by showing incongruous pairings of body parts, such as a woman's penis or a man's breasts. The characters are distanced from the audience through these visual reminders that their bodies exist outside of the norm.

The first visual reminder of Brandon's body in *Boys Don't Cry* actually concerns his menstrual cycle rather than his genitals or breasts. Brandon's pained expression as he inserts a tampon into his vagina while getting dressed at Candace's house makes clear his dislike and dissatisfaction in having to use a tampon; he then hides the wrapper under his mattress, continuing the pattern of hiding any evidence of tampon use that began at the convenience store when he stole them rather than have Lana find out he needs to use them. The scene is shot in a medium close-up that focuses attention on Brandon's face while cutting him off at the waist, thus not showing his vagina. The framing of this scene emphasizes the bodily pain and displeasure Brandon experiences rather than a visual presentation of his body. Despite the focus on his face instead of his vagina, Brandon's tampon use is meant to reinforce the material reality of his body. Though he may claim a masculine gender identity, he is unable to escape the need to use tampons to absorb the monthly flow of menstrual blood. The purpose of showing him using a tampon is to subtly undermine his masculine gender identity. To people who have difficulty separating gender and biological sex, the incongruity of a man using a tampon does not make sense. A similar situation would be seeing a woman going to her doctor to be checked for prostate cancer. In cases like these, gender is usually essentialized in terms of biological sex, so a man like Brandon who needs to use a tampon is seen as a woman pretending to be a man. It could be argued that visually presenting a man who needs to use tampons could serve to break down cisnormative conceptions of gendered behavior, but given the social context in which this visual representation exists, these scenes are intended to confirm an essentialized understanding of Brandon's identity. In spite of his claims to a masculine identity, he is seen by cisnormative society as really just a woman.

While Brandon provides a clear example of the way reminders of the body of a transgender character can be presented visually without reference to genitals, the visual presentation of genitals and other secondary sex characteristics is the primary way that transgender dramas remind the audience of the bodies of the transgender characters. In the opening scene of *Different for Girls*, it is the clear lack of genitals that is most striking. A teenage Kim stands naked in a locker room shower, her legs crossed to keep her penis tucked back. She looks down at her body, clearly relishing its apparent femaleness. The scene uses a full shot of Kim's body to capture her flat chest and tucked penis in one image, highlighting the incongruity. A series of tighter shots would not have allowed the audience to have as full an understanding of Kim's body. This use of the full shot to frame Kim's body is repeated when she allows Paul to see her naked toward the end of the film.

While a young Kim is pleased with her feminine appearance, Bree and Brandon express dissatisfaction with their bodies, centering on their genitals and breasts. After her visit with a psychiatrist to be approved for gender confirmation surgery, Bree checks out her reflection in a mirror before going to bed. She is mostly satisfied except for the bulge under her nightgown, which she tries to tuck back. This scene, like Kim's, uses a full shot to focus attention on the apparent contradiction of Bree's feminine body and penis. Dissatisfied with the still-present bulge, she straightens a picture on her wall before getting in bed. While a seemingly innocuous action, straightening the picture reveals a need for Bree to have everything in her life in its right place, including her body. This small moment reveals a wealth of information about how Bree interacts with the world. Brandon also expresses dissatisfaction while looking at his reflection in a mirror. After getting out of the shower at Candace's house, Brandon comes back into his room and catches a glimpse of himself in the mirror with a towel wrapped around his chest in a very feminine manner. While it may be a practical way to cover his body, having a towel wrapped around his chest once again draws attention to the femaleness of Brandon's body by focusing on his breasts. Less attention would have been drawn to Brandon's breasts had he come into the room naked or with a towel around his waist because of the femininity of the action of wrapping a towel around his chest. In this shot, Brandon is presented not only as a person with a female body but also as a person who is inherently feminine, only pretending to be a man.

Other than the violent exposure of Brandon's genitals when he is raped by John and Tom, Bree is the only other character considered here whose genitals are seen by others. While driving across the New Mexico desert at night with Toby, Bree stops by the side of the road to use the restroom. She is startled by a coyote howling and jumps up from her crouched position, exposing her penis. Toby discovers her transgender identity when he sees her penis in the car's rearview mirror, and his attitude toward Bree becomes extremely hostile. Beyond just complicating Bree's relationship with Toby, showing her penis clearly on screen also serves as confirmation for the audience of the realities of her body. The image Bree had worked to construct for herself is undone, and she must work to regain Toby's trust and the audience's sympathy.

Since her penis was shown during her road trip with Toby, Bree's vagina must also be seen in order to visually confirm the success of her gender confirmation surgery. As she recovers from her surgery in the hospital, Bree feels her crotch and when her therapist asks how she feels, she says, "I feel like a Medieval heretic impaled on a very large stake. With splinters." Though her vagina is not seen in this scene, the joy and pleasure on Bree's face as she feels her crotch signals that the surgery was a success. Later, when Bree is at home taking a bath, she lifts her waist and crotch out of the water so her vagina is clearly visible. Lifting her body out of the water in this way is a purposeful decision to unequivocally show Bree's vagina. While this decision could work to downplay concerns that a transgender woman's vagina would be deformed or in some way not real, it once again reduces a transgender woman to her genitals.

The multiple exposures of Bree's genitals reveal how transgender characters are often reduced to their genitals or other physical traits. This reflects the concern of transgender people in general that they are being judged based on their physical appearance rather than as people. Focusing on the genitals, breasts, or other physical characteristics of transgender characters reinforces the cisnormative belief that any mismatch between gender and the body is undesirable. The visual reminders of the bodies of the characters also help assuage any fears on the part of cisgender people who can do away with any concerns that they might be transgender, since they do not feel any disconnect between their gender and their physical bodies. Ultimately, this reinforces the essentialist notion that gender and biological sex are one and the same, thus distancing the transgender characters from the audience for claiming identities that exist outside this norm. While facing reminders of their physical bodies, the characters in transgender dramas also receive sympathetic recognition of their gender identities from others.

Sympathetic Recognition

J. Jack Halberstam argues that *Boys Don't Cry* "establishes the legitimacy and durability of Brandon's gender not simply by telling the tragic tale of his death by murder but by forcing spectators to adopt, if only provisionally, Brandon's gaze, a transgender look."[18] His argument is primarily based on the out-of-body experience Brandon has while John and Tom are stripping off his clothes to expose his genitals. Stripped down to nothing but his white T-shirt, with Tom holding him by the arms while John forces Lana to look at his genitals, Brandon looks up from his assault and out of the bathroom door, a bright, nondiegetic light illuminating his face. Behind the others who have gathered at the door, Brandon sees himself standing there still fully clothed and still in full control of himself. The bright light shines on the face of the other Brandon in the hallway, and no sound is heard. The other Brandon straightens up and stares directly into Brandon's eyes. The camera cuts between the other Brandon's gaze and the reality of his situation as Tom and John now hold him up, revealing his exposed lower body. The scene only lasts a few seconds. As the others at the door turn away, the audience gets one last glimpse of the other Brandon looking into Brandon's eyes.

Halberstam argues that this scene places audience members in the position of a transgender character.[19] This brief respite from the terror Brandon is experiencing at the hands of Tom and John is meant to place the audience firmly in Brandon's shoes as he struggles to maintain his sense of himself as a transgender man. He seeks to escape the current situation in full control of himself. When he imagines himself this way, he does not look away from what is actually happening to him, but his look is one of sympathy rather than of total understanding. In this moment, Brandon is sympathizing with himself. The threats of violence that have followed him throughout the film have come to fruition, and like the others peering in through the bathroom doorway, Brandon feels sorry for himself. He cannot empathize with himself because he does not understand how he ended up in the position he is in. The other Brandon is able to maintain his masculine dignity by standing apart from the situation and feeling sorry for everything Brandon has to endure. When the other Brandon leaves and the scene unfreezes, Brandon's confidence and self-image are shattered, and all he can do is try to survive John and Tom's constant assaults.

While this one brief moment may attempt to place the audience in the point of view of a transgender person, it is still brief. The transgender gaze is not sustained throughout the entire film; the director, Kimberly Peirce, ultimately abandons it during Brandon's sexual encounter with Lana toward the end, a move that is framed, visually and through dialogue, in a way that supports lesbian readings of Brandon's identity.[20] For Halberstam, this abandonment of the transgender gaze "opens up a set of questions about the inevitability and dominance of both the male/female and the hetero/homo binary in narrative cinema."[21] Cisnormative society remains uncomfortable with those people whose gender is indistinct or does not match up with expectations. A film like *Boys Don't Cry* "simultaneously generates sympathy for the gender-confused Brandon (whom the narrative turns into a tragic victim) while reassuring the audience that their own sex/gender identities remain intact."[22] Adopting a more traditional gaze, even one that looks at a queer couple, allows space for the audience to feel sorry for Brandon but remain confident in the certainty that the issues plaguing his life will not affect their own.

The sympathy that is dominant in this film and other transgender dramas marks the visual representation as part of the trans-pathetic gaze. Instead of encouraging audience members to identify with the transgender characters, the trans-pathetic gaze evokes sympathy for the struggles the characters must endure to live as the gender they claim. Sympathy may be a more positive feeling than the ridicule, fear, and disgust discussed in previous chapters, but it still distances the audience from the characters by encoding messages of feeling sorry for the characters rather than helping the audience truly understand what the characters are going through.

Halberstam is on the right track when discussing Brandon's return to Lincoln to deal with a court summons. Before leaving, Brandon kisses Lana a couple of times, and she licks her lips as she watches him go. Halberstam argues that the film "makes the transgender subject dependent upon the recognition of a woman."[23] The transgender characters in transgender dramas are dependent on the recognition of other characters. While enduring constraints on their gender identities, repressive cisnormative actions, and essentialist reminders of their bodies, the one source of positive recognition the characters receive comes from individual characters who are able to accept the gender identities they claim. This acceptance is initially based on feelings of sympathy, feeling sorry for the characters for all they have had to endure, but it does, in certain circumstances, develop into a deeper understanding. While this recognition is unable to completely span the distance created through the other narrative conventions and visual codes, the recognition of the legitimacy of the transgender characters' identities models a possible positive response to transgender people for audience members.

Another example from *Boys Don't Cry* involves Brandon's trip to Dallas with Lana and her friends. While in their hotel room, Lana tells her friends Candace and Kate about being with Brandon. In a flashback, Brandon is seen taking off his pants and penetrating her with the dildo seen earlier in his bag, definitively answering the question of how Brandon and Lana had sex. The scene then switches to a point-of-view shot from Lana's perspective as she looks down Brandon's shirt and sees a close-up of his bound cleavage. She does not immediately say anything but is freaked out enough that they stop. The scene then cuts to a close-up shot of Lana's hand as she reaches for Brandon's pants and then stops as the scene cuts again to a shot of her looking at his face. Though initially turned off by the material reality of Brandon's body, Lana sympathizes with Brandon and chooses to look at him as the man she is attracted to rather than someone whose body could problematize that attraction.

In *Transamerica*, Bree receives a similar sympathetic look from her sister Sydney, who exclaims "Holy shit!" upon seeing Bree for the first time. Unlike Bree's mother, who either wants to kick her out or refuses to even look at her, Sydney attempts to actually look at Bree as the person she is rather than the person she wanted or expected her to be. A medium shot frames the sisters as Sydney looks at Bree for the first time in several years. "This is so bizarre. I can still see Stanley in you, but it's like you put yourself through a wringer and got rid of all the boy pulp." The two women are framed by the large mirror in their mother's bathroom, visually connecting them and helping them span the years of separation. Sydney's willingness to actually look at Bree and try to see her for who she really is, even if tempered by sympathy for how she has been treated by their parents, is an important gesture of recognition and acceptance that any transgender person would value.

While familial acceptance is important to many transgender people, it is love of a more romantic nature that motivates many of the looks of sympathetic recognition in transgender dramas. After Brandon is arrested for check fraud, he is placed in a women's cell. As Brandon and Lana talk through the bars of the cell in a series of close-ups when Lana comes to visit him, he tries to explain that he is a hermaphrodite and was put in a women's cell for that reason. Lana responds, "Shut up! It's your business. Look, I don't care if you're half-monkey or half-ape, I'm getting you outta here." Lana's frequent refusal to question Brandon's gender identity, as numerous others do, is an important act of recognition of the legitimacy of his identity. The tensions between Brandon's identity and his body are nicely encapsulated as he and Lana run down a hallway in the jail after she bails him out. On the left side of the hallway as they run toward the open door is a row of orange-jumpsuit-clad male prisoners while on the wall is a sign with an arrow pointing to the left that reads "Ladies' Room." Brandon and Lana are framed in the light of the open doorway while the question is raised about whether Brandon belongs in the line with the men or in the restroom with other women. Lana's sympathetic recognition of Brandon's identity, though, is not enough to overcome cisnormative society's demand for clear, uncomplicated answers.

Sympathetic recognition from another person helps Bree and Toby out of a financial predicament when their car is stolen. They make their way to a diner where Bree meets Calvin. Calvin not only offers to pay for their food but also gives them a place to stay for the night and a ride to her parent's house in Phoenix. It is soon apparent that Calvin sees more in Bree than just sympathy for her situation. At his house that night, he serenades Bree on the back porch with his rendition of "Beautiful Dreamer." The next day, they stop for lunch on the way to Phoenix. While eating in the bed of Calvin's pickup truck, Bree says she needs to go to the restroom, and Calvin helps her down. As Calvin and Toby talk in the back of the truck, Bree can be seen in a long shot walking into the brush in a very feminine manner with her hands held high above her chest, her hips swaying back and forth, and taking very short, careful steps; Bree is going to be certain a second mishap while going to the restroom does not happen on this trip! This image of Bree is contrasted with the conversation in the foreground of the shot taking place between Calvin and Toby as Toby tries to hint that Bree has been less than truthful with Calvin.

TOBY: Dude, there's things about her she's not telling you.

CALVIN: Well, every woman has a right to a little mystery, *dude*.

TOBY: You know she's a Jesus freak? She's probably waiting to convert you.

CALVIN: She can convert me anytime she wants to.

Like Lana, Calvin is not swayed by those who would try to force him to see the person he cares for in a negative light. He also displays the easiest, most unconditional acceptance of a transgender character seen in any of the films in this book. Calvin serves as a model of the positive acceptance that is possible not just for transgender characters but for transgender people in general.

When transgender characters do not receive the recognition from others they desire, they often turn inward to private fantasies that allow them to provide their own sympathetic recognition. In *Ma Vie in Rose*, Ludovic uses fantasy to create a world in which she is accepted by others. Ludovic's numerous fantasies in the film revolve around Pam and the magical world she inhabits. After her pretend wedding with Jerome turns disastrous, Ludovic imagines Pam showing up and flying her away from her troubles. She even looks down and, in a long shot, sees herself, no longer in the pink dress she is still wearing while flying but in shorts and a flannel shirt, being dragged back home by her mother. The use of a long shot in this scene communicates the distance Ludovic feels between her identity as a girl and the everyday world she inhabits. Ludovic's fantasies generally function as an escape from the problems of the world around her. Her most significant fantasy in terms of sympathetic recognition comes after finding out that her family will be moving away in order for her father to start a new job. After a cut from her family's living room, Ludovic finds herself in Pam's world wearing a white dress, white gloves, a white veil, and the earrings she wore at the housewarming party, as voices from outside yell "The bride! The bride!" After opening the door, she finds her family waiting for her with faces beaming and at the end of a long pink carpet is her groom, Jerome, in a white tuxedo. The entire neighborhood is there to watch the two of them get married, and the fantasy ends with everyone present doing a dance from the *Pam's World* TV series that Ludovic loves so much. In this fantasy, Ludovic is creating a world that she believes is no longer possible because of the anger of her family and her neighbors. Since they are unable to accept her for who she is, Ludovic imagines a world in which they do. The film once again reinforces the distance between her desires and the real world with a cut to a "For Sale" sign being hammered into her family's front yard. Ludovic's fantasies are not enough to allow her to completely escape the cisnormative world in which she lives.

Moving out of the realm of fantasy, in *Different for Girls*, Paul decides to focus on the reality of Kim's body rather than any ill-conceived notions that may exist in his head. After Kim testifies on Paul's behalf and the charges against him for his indecent exposure are dropped, the two go back to her place to celebrate. Paul asks Kim if he can see how her body has changed, to see "what all the fuss is about."

PAUL: I'd like to *see* everything more clearly. Could I?

KIM: No one else has ever asked.

It is clear that Kim has learned from experience that while many people talk about the bodies of people like her, few are actually interested in dealing with them. They move to Kim's bedroom, and she slowly unbuttons her blouse. After taking off her bra, she stands with her back to Paul and says, "It's funny, I went to all this trouble, and I can't even bring myself to turn around." She then turns to face him, and all the audience can initially see is her back as Paul looks her up and down. The camera then cuts to a reverse shot of Kim from the front, her breasts bare, as she removes her skirt and panties and stands completely naked in front of Paul. Emblematic of sympathetic recognition, Kim's disrobing after the reverse shot is filmed as one long shot without the typical close ups of her individual body parts or a camera movement up her body from her feet to head. This is not a big reveal meant to shock the audience but an intimate moment that Kim shares with someone she cares deeply about.

After Kim finishes undressing, Paul slowly approaches her, saying, "You said your mind could never accept your body before. Well, I don't want to struggle with it either." He then reaches out and takes her hand before pulling her into an embrace and kissing her. The pair then moves to the bed, and Kim quickly moves on top. While Paul expresses some initial surprise—"It fits. It bloody fits"—he shows no sign of regretting his decision. The scene then cuts to a tracking shot of their clothes strewn about the floor, the disheveled sheets and bedspread, and then to an overhead shot of the couple lying naked on their backs in post-coital pleasure, with Kim's head laying on Paul's chest and his arm wrapped around her—a shot familiar to audience members from numerous sexual pairings throughout film history. The composition of this scene reinforces not only Paul's recognition of Kim as a woman and as a person worthy of respect but also argues that this couple is no different than any other couple seen in film. By treating the couple the same as any other, the film sends the message that transgender people are no different than anyone else and are just as deserving of love and life. All of this is communicated through the visuals in contrast to the cisnormative messages often communicated through the narratives of transgender dramas.

Finally, an errant piece of clothing in *Ma Vie en Rose* leaves the audience with hope that people will ultimately be able to overcome the cisnormative pressures weighing down on them and offer the transgender people in their lives the recognition they deserve. As the Fabres drive away to their new home, their neighbors stand on their lawns to watch disapprovingly as they go. The pink princess dress that Ludovic wore to the housewarming party comes loose from the luggage strapped to the roof of their car. The dress is isolated in a medium close-up against a bright blue sky as it floats through the air before landing at Jerome's feet. Jerome can do nothing but stare at the dress, implying that there might be more to his initial sympathetic recognition of Ludovic, before his father comes and kicks the dress away. While the forces of cisnormativity may still be in control for now, Jerome's fixation on the dress and longing stare as Ludovic's car recedes into the distance send a message of hope that sometime in the future, Jerome might be able to accept Ludovic for who she is or at least not treat any other transgender people he meets as poorly as he treated her.

While the trans-pathetic gaze may initially support cisnormativity through the attention to dressing and reminders of the body, sympathetic recognition of the transgender characters by others opens up the possibility of real acceptance. While the initial attention given to the characters may be motivated by sympathy for their struggles, which would keep the audience at a distance, some characters, particularly Calvin and Paul, are able to overcome their misgivings to reach a point of complete acceptance of the transgender people in their lives. The mise-en-scène and shot choices discussed in this section support this modeling of positive acceptance by treating the characters as equals to any other characters in film, cisgender or not. This visual equating of transgender people and cisgender people may be the best way to counteract the cisnormative messages communicated through the narratives of the films.

Possible Effects of Transgender Dramas

I have been the beneficiary of sympathetic reactions throughout the more than a decade since I publicly came out as a transgender woman. Since sympathy is a positive emotion, it is nice to receive support from friends and colleagues, and some of my closest relationships with the people I trust most have developed since I came out. I do not doubt the sincerity of anyone's feelings, and my closest friends have repeatedly demonstrated to me how their feelings go much deeper than surface-level sympathy. I want to address, though, how sympathy can still lead to feelings of distance from my perspective.

When I first came out publicly, the difficulties I had with my family and the process of adjusting to what it meant to exist as a transgender woman in a Texas college town consumed my life. It was all I wanted to talk about, and while most people were sympathetic to what I was going through and wanted to listen, as time went on I began to notice a growing distance between us. They never stopped being supportive, but I began to notice an increasing disinterest in listening to me once again complain about something negative my family had said to me. So to avoid creating even more distance, I stopped talking about my experiences. Even as I began to develop friendships with new people, I did not share too much about being a transgender woman, often out of fear that I would push them away again. It was only after years had passed that I realized how little they knew of what my transition experience had been like. I only talked about my experiences in moments of crisis, and these moments helped me to understand that my closest friends were not going anywhere. I began to slowly open up more, sharing the occasional story, and now the fear is mostly gone. I do not know if I could have done anything differently in those early days, since transitioning was such an all-consuming experience for me, but it comforts me to know that I have the support of the wonderful friends in my life now. The distancing that results from sympathy does not mean that someone does not care for you, but recognizing that it exists help us to understand the challenge that is present in maintaining close, emotionally expressive relationships.

Transgender dramas are constructed to prompt an emotional reaction of sympathy in the audience. Sympathy implies feeling sorry

for someone as compared to empathy's implications of truly understanding what the other is going through. The identification built
around transgender dramas is still focused on a cisgender identity. The
audience, by definition, cannot truly understand what the transgender
characters are going through. Attempts are made to place the audience in the perspective of a transgender character, particularly in *Boys
Don't Cry* when Brandon searches for anyone to see him as he truly
is while he is being assaulted by John and Tom in the bathroom and
is only able to find his gaze returned by another Brandon standing
in the hallway, but these scenes are generally brief while the majority
of the films are built around a feeling of sympathy. Sympathy keeps
the audience at a distance by reinforcing the fact that they can never
truly understand the experiences of transgender people. But some
characters in transgender dramas, particularly Calvin in *Transamerica*
and Paul in *Different for Girls*, are able to model acceptance of transgender people for who they really are. While these positive looks do
offer some hope for the future, sympathy still generally leads to the
distancing of the audience from the transgender characters. More
films must begin to work on helping the audience truly understand
the lives of transgender people if more progress is going to be made.

One final point about the reactions of the transgender characters
to the lack of acceptance they face. Transgender dramas are filled
with images of freedom. At the beginning of *Boys Don't Cry*, Brandon
drives down the road alone in a car, and as he passes another car, his
eyes light up as he looks back at it in his rearview mirror. Brandon
experiences a sense of freedom in his car that he is unable to find
in the rest of his life. The film ends with Lana driving down a road
alone, possibly to Memphis as she discussed with Brandon, escaping
the repressive environment that killed the man she loves. At the end
of *Ma Vie en Rose*, Pam flies across the screen and sprinkles some
pixie dust over the scene, providing some hope that all the magic is
not gone from Ludovic's life. Hopefully, her fantasies in the future
will be positive rather than an escape from an abusive home life. I
highlight these images of freedom to show that even in the face of
cisnormative pressure, the transgender characters still dream of a
better, more accepting life.

6

Improving Transgender Representation in Film

POPULAR TRANSGENDER FILMS are not made for a transgender audience; they are made for a cisgender audience. The narrative and visual construction of the films reflect that cisgender people are the primary audience for transgender films. In transgender comedies, the transgender characters choose to adopt transgender identities to escape outlandish situations and only reveal their cisgender identities in a big reveal at the climax of the films. In transgender horror films and thrillers, they are positioned as threatening outsiders who strike back against those who would compel them to conform to cisnormativity and have their transgender identities revealed through the use of force. And in transgender dramas, they face constraints on their gender identities that push them to try to prove their identities through their actions and have repeated attention brought to the disparities between their claimed gender identities and the realities of their bodies. These are not the stories transgender people would tell about themselves, so they are not the intended audience for these films. As I conclude my analysis, I want to begin with a few suggestions on how to improve transgender representation in film, then offer some brief considerations of possible uses of the approach used in this book for the analysis of other genres of film, and end with some final thoughts on my experience with transgender representations in film.

Suggestions for Improving
Transgender Representation in Film

These suggestions are made within the context of previous academic research and activism on the subject of representation. Since film and other media have embraced a diversity of representations only as far as they are profitable,[1] it is not surprising that film producers approach transgender representations through a cisgender point of identification. Audience members often feel more comfortable with media representations than with the marginalized groups they present.[2] The continued popularity of transgender representations may be partially explained through this distanced approach to difference; it is more comfortable for a cisgender audience to watch a man wearing a dress on screen than to interact with an actual transgender person. Because of this tendency in audience members to only want to see marginalized groups represented in limited ways, marginalized groups often have to accept the dominant group's rules in order to be represented at all. Media studies scholar Larry Gross has described the arrangement well:

> The great American bargain offered to successive minorities continues to be: assimilate, but on our terms. By all means, add your flavoring to the national stew, but keep it subtle enough not to threaten the dominance of white, middle-class, Christian, hetero-normativity. We welcome any style that can be repackaged and sold to other markets . . . but we do insist on inspecting all goods at the border and we reserve the right to demonize and marginalize those who refuse to play by our rules.[3]

Part of the limits placed on any representation is the pressure to cater to the demands of the dominant groups in society. The following suggestions are offered with these limitations on representation in mind.

Increasing the Number of Transgender People On-screen and behind the Scenes

This first suggestion is an institutional one, and it has been made in similar ways in the past by such advocacy groups as the National

Association for the Advancement of Colored People (NAACP) and GLAAD (formerly the Gay & Lesbian Alliance Against Defamation).[4] The authors who have a hand in creating a film play an important role in shaping the identification with the audience. By increasing the number of transgender actors in the film industry and film executives in studio boardrooms, the chances increase that a transgender voice will help to shape transgender representations. Kathryn Montgomery, in her analysis of the relationship between advocacy groups and television networks, found that the "most effective groups were those whose strategies were compatible with the network TV system, and whose strategies were fashioned with a keen awareness of how that system functioned."[5] Rather than trying to work outside the system, any effort to address the lack of representation of transgender people within the industry must acknowledge the structure of media institutional production and work within that context.

One of the difficulties transgender people and advocacy groups face in gaining access to the media is that "in an institutional sense, non-transsexual individuals have the first and final word on the matter."[6] The only film analyzed in this project to include transgender actors is *Ticked-Off Trannies with Knives*, and none of the directors identify as transgender people. It has primarily been cisgender people in control of creating transgender representations. In his discussion of the misrepresentation of transgender and Hispanic people in the 2012 ABC comedy *Work It*, in which two unemployed, cisgender men dress up as women in an attempt to get jobs as pharmaceutical sales reps, artist and activist Jack Tomas argues that it is not enough to bring members of marginalized groups only into creative roles, such as actors and directors; they must also fill executive positions if any significant progress is to be made in improving representation.[7] The businesspeople making financial decisions play just as great a role, if not greater, in shaping what appears on screen. Increasing the number of transgender voices in the boardroom is just as important as increasing the number of transgender faces on screen.

Work It provides a useful example of the importance of a transgender presence at the executive level. In an *Entertainment Weekly* article, Lynette Rice discusses the reaction by the head of ABC to the uproar from the transgender community over the show's trivialization of their lives and struggles. "ABC Entertainment Chief Paul Lee told reporters last week that he didn't understand the response from the advocacy groups. He has said in the past that, as a Brit, he appreciates the cheeky humor that comes with cross-dressing comedies like the Dustin Hoffman movie *Tootsie*."[8] Since transgender representation generally supports cisnormativity, it is not surprising that a prominent executive would not understand why a show like *Work It* would upset transgender people. What Lee considered to be done all in good fun was seen by many transgender people as a serious misrepresentation of their everyday lives. Having a transgender voice in the boardroom might have ensured that a show like *Work It* never saw the light of day.

A more recent example shows that there are still limits to the positive benefits of more involvement by transgender creators. *Adam* (2019) is a coming-of-age story about a teenage cisgender man who spends his summer after high school hanging out with his sister and her LGBTQ+ friends in New York City. When he meets a young woman named Gillian at a party, who assumes he is a transgender man because of his group of friends, Adam does not disabuse her of her misunderstanding until much later in the film because of his attraction to her. The film has been the subject of a boycott campaign for perceptions of the plot as transphobic,[9] and the director Rhys Ernst, who is a transgender man himself, has defended his decision to make the film by noting the changes he made to the story in the process of adapting it from Ariel Schrag's 2014 novel of the same name and by appealing to "the power of trans art and storytelling, even when it is challenging or uncomfortable."[10] Defenders of the film have claimed that the detractors are misguided because the purpose of the film is Adam's journey of increased engagement with the LGBTQ+ community in which his "trans-ignorant and cis-centric ideas evolve to the point that he becomes the kind of well-informed queer ally this world so desperately needs."[11] How can people criticize this film and call for a boycott rather than celebrate the work of a transgender creator? From my perspective, a main issue is the continued centering of cisgender identity as the point of identification with the film. A cisgender audience is asked to identify with a cisgender character in order to experience LGBTQ+ life from a cisgender perspective. The film's authors and defenders may be correct that the film deserves a more nuanced reading than critics have offered and that it can open a cisgender audience up to learning more about LGBTQ+ lives, but as my analysis of transgender representations in this book has shown, centering a cisgender perspective on transgender lives and experiences often leads to the transgender characters being distanced from the audience rather than brought closer. Roland Emmerich's *Stonewall* (2015) was similarly criticized for its use of a White, cisgender protagonist in its depiction of a historical event that is widely understood to have been led by transgender and LGBTQ+ women of color.[12] Another possible reason for the criticism of *Adam* is its use of deception, with Adam deceiving Gillian by omission into believing that he is a transgender man. Ernst tried to address this concern by arguing that the main character is "trapped in a lie, but he is ultimately culpable."[13] But given the violence and abuse that transgender people have received for being perceived as deceiving others, both on-screen and in real life, it should be clear why people would be upset with a film that presents deception on the part of a cisgender man as a profound lesson in growth and understanding. The film may be more nuanced and may provide a more progressive perspective on LGBTQ+ life than its detractors give it credit for, but the controversy around the film is a good reminder that films and media produced by transgender authors are not immune from or undeserving of criticism because of the identities of their creators.

Transgender people have made greater inroads into the world of acting, with actress Laverne Cox arguing that "more films are being written and produced with transgender characters and that there is a willingness to hire trans actors to play these roles,"[14] but transgender actors still face an uphill struggle. A few transgender performers have appeared in film and television, including Divine in a number of Jon Waters's films, Lady Chablis in Clint Eastwood's *Midnight in the Garden of Good and Evil* (1997), and Candis Cayne in *Dirty Sexy Money* (2007–2009). But most transgender performers have been relegated to supporting parts while the most prominent transgender roles are played by cisgender performers. When able to secure acting roles, transgender performers still face varying levels of acceptance. William Keck discusses the casting of transgender actress Jamie Clayton as a preoperative transgender woman in HBO's *Hung* (2009–2011), in which Thomas Jane plays a male prostitute named Ray: "When Thomas first got wind of Ray's new adventures, 'the idea of kissing a man was not a comfortable one for him, but he did great,' says creator Colette Burson, who is exploring the possibility of making Kyla Ray's full-time girlfriend in season four. 'They had to kiss for hours. After his initial shyness, she became a woman for him.'"[15] Jamie Clayton, Burson implies, was initially not "a woman" for Thomas Jane but she "became" one through their interactions. Keck reported: "Any insecurities Tom had disappeared when he arrived on set. 'I asked, "So where's the guy?" and was told, "That's her!"' he told me at the 2011 Saturn awards. 'There was this beautiful girl who blew me away.'"[16] Jane's reference to Clayton as "the guy" is illustrative of the perceptions that transgender performers, and transgender people in general, must overcome. This perception is part of the reason cisgender performers are usually cast in transgender roles.

Jamie Clayton's role as the transgender character Nomi Marks on the Netflix series *Sense8* (2015–2018) and the transgender cast members on FX's *Pose* (2018–2021) represent increasing opportunities for transgender performers on screen. The indie film *Tangerine* (2015) provides an example of what is possible narratively and visually when transgender perspectives and performers are centered. Where some recent films like *The Danish Girl* (2015) still have cisgender performers playing transgender characters (Eddie Redmayne in this case) and feature narratives that involve external forces creating the characters' transgender identities, transgender actresses Kitana Kiki Rodriguez and Mya Taylor, as Sin-Dee and Alexandra, respectively, are narratively positioned in *Tangerine* as the protagonists, since they are the ones with agency, when Sin-Dee sets off to find the woman her boyfriend cheated on her with while she was in prison. The characters initiate the plot instead of having events happen to them, as in a crisis that forces them to cross-dress or repressive agents of cisnormativity that enter and disrupt their lives. Visually, the film also positions the transgender characters as central, favoring over-the-shoulder medium shots that give Sin-Dee and Alexandra a sense of purpose in their movement. The narrative conventions and visual codes of the film reduce the distance for the audience by offering no other point of identification so that when a car full of faceless strangers dumps a cup of urine on Sin-Dee at the end of the film, the audience is by her side with Alexandra comforting her in the laundromat, which produces an emotional response closer to the feeling of empathy. Films like *Tangerine* and *A Fantastic Woman* (2017) demonstrate the potential for transgender representations when transgender lives and experiences are centered.

Increasing the number of transgender creative personnel, including performers, writers, and directors, and executives will increase the number of transgender voices speaking up for improved representations of transgender people, but this alone will not improve transgender representations (and given the difficulty with which many marginalized groups have had breaking into the upper echelons of the entertainment industry, it will probably be a long time in coming). The number of transgender voices does not matter if the media texts being discussed maintain a cisnormative view of transgender identity. With transgender people in positions of power, narratives can be repositioned to center transgender experiences rather than distancing them.

Humor Found in Characters Rather than Directed at Them

Transgender characters feature prominently in several film narratives, but as we have seen above, the events of the narratives generally happen *to* the characters rather than presenting the characters as active subjects taking control of their situations. Whether it is Joe and Jerry having to join a girls band and travel to Florida to avoid being killed by mobsters or Bree having to travel across the country because of an ultimatum from her therapist, the characters are generally not in control of the events swirling around them. This communicates a lack of agency on the part of transgender people. A second suggestion for improving transgender representations, then, is to make transgender characters more active participants in their own narratives. It is the difference between having things happen *to* the characters rather than because of their own actions. I will use comedy here to illustrate this point, but this principle applies to dramas, horror films, thrillers, and any other film genre.

Comedy is one of the trickiest genres for members of any marginalized group; no one wants to see members of their group being made fun of for who they are. One of the keys to respectful comedy is to locate the humor in the experiences of the characters rather than directing it at the characters for some perceived deviation from social norms. An example of how not to be respectful is the implicit transphobia running through the television sitcom *How I Met Your Mother* (2005–2014), particularly in the character of Ted Mosby. Ted is presented in the series as the hopeless romantic searching for the woman of his dreams, but he seems to be terrified by the idea of falling in love with a woman only to discover that she is transgender. In season six, Ted dates a woman named Zoe whom he meets protesting outside an abandoned hotel that is about to be torn down. Because of the seedy neighborhood where he meets her, one of the first questions Ted asks Zoe is whether she is a drag queen, since he would not be interested in a relationship with her if she were. In season seven, Ted goes on a date with a woman after they both agree not to look up any information about each other online. As the date progresses, Ted grows increasingly nervous about the potentially horrible secrets this woman might have. His worst fear—that he will go into the men's restroom and she will walk in behind him, step up to the urinal, pull up her dress, and begin to urinate—finally prompts him to look her up on his phone, revealing her big secret to be her amazing accomplishments. Ted is entitled to his choice of romantic partners and to not date transgender women, but the problem is that the show never balances Ted's irrational fears of transgender people with any alternative representations. Instead, the show portrays transgender women as romantic bogeymen rather than as real people and, for some, potential romantic partners.

How I Met Your Mother, like *Friends* and numerous other shows before it, is an ensemble comedy focusing on a group of friends living in New York City. In his examination of gay and lesbian representations on television, Ron Becker argues that many TV series featuring gay characters in the early 2000s, such as *Queer Eye for the Straight Guy* (2003–2007) and *Boy Meets Boy* (2003), "put straight men in the heterosexual closet and helped them establish a progressive straight male identity forged from the anxieties of straight guilt rather than the anxieties of homosexual panic."[17] Transgender representations could be improved through a similar positioning of concerns within cisnormativity rather than on the marginalization of transgender people. There is no reason that a transgender person could not be part of a film or TV ensemble. Having a transgender person in that position would present them as equal to the other characters and would open up opportunities for humor about the character's experiences because they would not be merely a sight gag or one-off character that the audience has no chance to connect with. For example, one might imagine an ensemble comedy that features a transgender woman named Brenda sharing an apartment with a cisgender man named Joel and the ridiculous shenanigans and romantic flirtation they get into with their group of friends. A recurring storyline could be Brenda's unlucky attempts at finding love, from her bad choice of a Tinder profile pic that shows more of her cat than her face to her repeatedly sticking her foot in her mouth when trying to flirt with the barista at the group's favorite coffee shop. Finding humor in the experiences of a transgender person also does not mean treating the transgender characters with kid gloves where everything works out perfectly for them. A common plotline on ensemble comedies is that members of the friend group fall in love with one another. If Brenda confessed her love to Joel, he would have every right to consider whether he wants to date her and even to turn her down, just as he would with any other woman. The transphobic choice would be for him to laugh and say, "I don't date dudes, dude!" This would not only fail to acknowledge Brenda's identity as a woman but would deny the relationship the two have shared as friends and roommates throughout the show. Improving transgender representations does not involve putting transgender people on a pedestal where they can never be touched but starts from a place of respect for their identities.

Continuing to consider how our imaginary show might play out, if Joel turned down Brenda, a simple way to show that he still respects her and thinks of her as a woman would be to have him stand up for her. After turning Brenda down, Joel goes to their regular bar and sees Brenda sitting alone, but he decides to keep his distance because of the awkwardness between them. As he drinks his beer, he overhears Brenda talking to a handsome man. The man says, "I don't date dudes, dude!" and he turns to his group of friends who begin to laugh in her face. Joel then walks up to them, says, "Not cool, *dude*," and dumps his beer on the guy's head before grabbing Brenda's hand as they run out of the bar. Joel would not have to change his decision about having a romantic relationship with Brenda in order to show that he still respects and cares for her. In an ensemble comedy, much of the humor and audience connection comes from the love and support between a group of friends. Including a transgender person as an equal would demonstrate to the audience that transgender people in general are deserving of the same love and support. Centering transgender characters within the action is an important suggestion, but another important way to improve transgender representations is to remove the exclusive focus on the transgender identities of the characters.

Recognizing the Multiple Aspects of a Transgender Person's Identity Position

When a transgender character is featured prominently in a film, the narrative generally revolves around their transgender identity and what it means to be transgender. While this has been and will continue to be an important project in raising awareness about the experiences of transgender people, it also sends the message that the only interesting thing about a transgender person is their transgender identity. It is time for films and other media to feature transgender characters in a way that acknowledges that there is more to their lives than just being transgender.

In most films, the gender identities and sexual orientations of the characters are not the focus. A police drama is not about the police officers as cisgender men and women who also happen to solve crimes. Even in a romance, the focus is on the relationship between the characters, not the fact that they are heterosexual. In films featuring transgender characters, everything about the characters is secondary to their transgender identities. Joe and Jerry are musicians only so they can escape to Florida; Robert is a psychologist only so his attraction to Kate Miller will enrage Bobbie; and Brandon is never seen at work, though he is wearing coveralls when he is arrested for check fraud. A person's occupation does not define them, but it is telling that the transgender characters are only seen at work in order to move the plot in a direction toward the characters' gender identities. Even in their other relationships, the gender identities of the characters are placed in the forefront; Bree is presented as a transgender woman traveling with her son rather than as a parent who also happens to be transgender. It is the second way of thinking about the characters that I am suggesting.

For example, if a romantic drama wanted to feature a transgender woman as part of its central couple, it could turn the focus away from the transgender identity of the character by focusing on the developing relationship between the couple. This is not about hiding the transgender identity of the character; her identity is important, but it does not have to be the whole focus of the film. A woman agonizing over when to tell her partner about her gender identity or her partner searching their feelings to determine how they feel about dating a transgender person is not the same as focusing on the transgender character's gender identity. If the climactic moment of your supposed romance is a character telling their partner about their gender identity instead of the two characters confessing their love for each other, you are doing it wrong.

The short-lived CBS legal drama *Doubt* (2017), which was cancelled after two episodes, provides an example of offering the audience another point of identification with a transgender character. In the show, Laverne Cox plays a defense attorney named Cameron Wirth. Cameron is a transgender woman, but as an ensemble drama, the point of identification for the audience with Cameron lies in the lawyer identity she shares with her fellow attorneys rather than in her transgender identity. She does not hide or deny her transgender identity, but the audience is able to see her as more than just a transgender woman. In the first episode, for example, when a client of Cameron's, who was diagnosed with schizophrenia, asks her bluntly if she is a man or woman, she takes the question in stride and explains her transgender identity to him, to which he responds that he was uncertain if her transgender identity was real or all in his head. By addressing her identity matter-of-factly, Cameron is allowed space to acknowledge it and then shift the focus back to being a lawyer. By moving the point of identification away from gender identity, the audience is able to identify with Cameron as similar to the thousands of other lawyers they have seen on TV. This raises the possibility of the audience being able to see transgender characters in terms of the numerous other identities (worker, parent, sibling, friend, lover) they embody. The emotional response to the scene described above also changes with this shift in the point of identification. Instead of responding to Cameron's discussion of her transgender identity with disgust or ridicule, the audience responds with the frustration many professionals experience when dealing with challenging clients. Shifting the point of identification reduces the distance between the audience and the transgender characters without denying or ignoring the characters' transgender identities.

Reality TV provides a few more examples of this suggestion in action. Competition programs have been a dominant force in reality TV over the past decade, and transgender people have been featured in a number of programs. VH1's *TRANSform Me* (2010) featured three transgender women, Laverne Cox, Jamie Clayton, and Nina Poon, conducting fashion makeovers on other women in the vein of *Queer*

Eye for the Straight Guy (2003–2007). Isis King was a contestant on The CW's *America's Next Top Model* (2003–2015) and proved popular enough that she participated in a 2011 all-star season. Logo's *Transamerican Love Story* (2008) was a dating competition in the style of *The Bachelor*, featuring transsexual artist Calpernia Adams choosing from eight men who were aware of her gender identity, removing the shock element. These series are notable for prominently featuring transgender participants but keeping the focus on the goals of the series, whether it is fashion or dating. It would not be inconceivable to have a transgender person participate on such competitions as Bravo's *Top Chef* (2006–present) or CBS's *The Amazing Race* (2001–present) with little or no objection from audience members.

Implementing this suggestion would be an important step in showing that transgender people are a part of the fabric of everyday life. The goal here is not to ignore the transgender identities of people, in a transgender equivalent to colorblindness, but to simply acknowledge that transgender people cannot be defined solely by their transgender identities. We are teachers, chefs, cashiers, and engineers. We are sisters, brothers, friends, lovers, and neighbors. As long as the focus of transgender representation remains solely fixed on the gender identities of transgender people and not the fact that they are people with friends, families, and jobs, cisnormative society will continue to define transgender people by their deviations from the norm rather than trying to relate to them as people.

All of these suggestions are merely intended to start a discussion about how to improve transgender representation. They are not the final or authoritative word on improving transgender representation, and they each have their own flaws. My hope is that they will spur discussion about how to improve transgender representations rather than continuing to focus solely on what is wrong with transgender representations. Along with improving transgender representation, I also hope my approach to identification and affect will be applied to other films.

Identification and Affect in Film

The use of a combination of a rhetorical approach to identification and an understanding of how affective and emotional responses are prompted in the audience are a major contribution of the present work to the analysis of representation in film and media. This approach is not limited to transgender representations. Every film makes an appeal across certain similarities between the author and audience that serves as the point of identification. A film is then constructed narratively and visually in line with the identification between author and audience. For example, Hollywood summer blockbusters have long been constructed to appeal to teenage boys and the men who still reminisce about being teenage boys. The author finds similarity with the audience through the shared experience of growing up in a particular context (nowadays, this is mostly the films and other media of the late 1970s to late 1990s) and constructs a film to appeal to the audience, often featuring such elements as frequent explosions, underdog characters saving the day, fast cutting of action scenes, and copious use of the male gaze when presenting female characters. The audience, likewise, feels a sense of identification with the author through the text and is persuaded to come to the theater and enjoy the film. Disappointment, frustration, and anger may result for an audience when the expected point of identification is not present, either before (for example, a trailer that suggests radical changes to a beloved character's backstory or appearance) or after viewing the film. More recent blockbusters—*Star Wars: The Force Awakens* (2015), *Mad Max: Fury Road* (2015), the *Ghostbusters* (2016) remake featuring female leads, *Star Wars: The Last Jedi* (2017), and *Captain Marvel* (2019), to name a few—have signaled a desire to not appeal exclusively to this audience, seeking to build identification around a broader enjoyment of action, adventure, and comedy. To some degree, this shift in identification helps to explain the savage attacks on these films by adolescent male moviegoers, who seem to equate a movie not identifying with them exclusively with failure to identify with them at all. The identification between author and audience, in this case, has worked so well for so long that any shift in perceived identification is cause for abandoning the shared connection entirely.

The superhero film *Black Panther* (2019) provides an example of how identification and affect can be used to reduce the distance between the audience and a marginalized group. The film's narrative and visual construction signals a direct appeal to a Black audience. Many of the prominent creators involved as authors of the film are Black, including director and cowriter Ryan Coogler, cowriter Joe

Robert Cole, and soundtrack artist Kendrick Lamar. The cast—including Chadwick Boseman as T'Challa, Michael B. Jordan as his nemesis Killmonger, Lupita Nyong'o as undercover spy Nakia, Danai Gurira as special forces leader Okoye, and Letitia Wright as scientific genius Shuri—is also primarily Black. The predominantly Black authors of the film brought an approach to its narrative and visual construction that centered a Black perspective and sought to appeal to the audience using that perspective as the point of identification. This was clearly signaled in the sidelining of White characters, such as Martin Freeman as CIA operative Everett Ross, much as Black characters are often sidelined into supporting roles in similar films. Ross attempts to assert control over the plot early in the film by taking charge of the villain Klaue after he is captured in a heist of Wakandan artifacts. By the end of the film, Ross is taking orders from Shuri as he risks his life to prevent Wakanda's secrets from being revealed to the rest of the world. The affective and emotional responses prompted by the film also support Blackness as the point of identification. Whether it is Killmonger's anger at Wakanda's isolation and obliviousness to the suffering of Black people around the world or T'Challa's pride at Wakanda's value as a Black nation that can take a leading role on the world stage, both responses remain centered in Black experiences. The film does not present a White perspective on Black lives in order to appeal to a wider audience. Instead, it centers the experiences of a marginalized group, and the result is that the audience members, both those who are part of the group and those who are not, are able to learn more about the lives of Black people and feel a greater connection to them. Films that instead center a dominant perspective, as is found in the transgender films we have discussed, lead to a distancing from the marginalized group as dominant beliefs are maintained. Distancing does not have to be the only way that marginalized groups are represented, but this book reveals that distancing is found in transgender representations because of the centering of a cisnormative perspective.

Final Thoughts

What stands out to me as I bring this work to a close is the importance of legitimacy in the representations of marginalized groups. The problems

I have discussed in these chapters could be solved if the transgender identities of the characters were merely treated as legitimate. No character would be the object of ridicule, fear, disgust, or sympathy simply for being transgender if the films treated their identities as legitimate. Cisgender characters, particularly White men, are generally not treated as objects, because the legitimacy of their identities is never questioned. Audience members would find it odd if the same techniques used to hold the identities of transgender characters up to cisnormative scrutiny were also used on cisgender characters since their identities are never in question. Until transgender characters are able to appear on screen with the same degree of self-assurance as their cisgender counterparts, the legitimacy of their identities will remain in doubt.

Legitimacy is the main connection I see between my analysis of transgender representation and research on the representation of other marginalized groups. To delegitimize the identities of a marginalized group is to say they have no place in society. The distancing effects I have discussed throughout this project are rooted in the delegitimization of the characters' identities; it is hard to identify with a character who is not seen as an equal. Whether it is in terms of race, class, ethnicity, gender identity and expression, sexual orientation, religious affiliation, or immigration status, accepting and embracing the legitimacy of every person is the first step in improving representation. All the problems with representation stem from this lack of legitimacy, and all the solutions flow from taking this first step. The main failing of cisnormativity is not that it tries to impose its standards on all others but that it fails even to recognize possible alternatives. Many people and groups have sought to separate themselves entirely from cisnormative society for this very reason. By forcing the issue of legitimacy, this flaw in cisnormativity can be exposed and true conversation can begin.

This work is far from the last word on transgender representation, nor should it be. It has several limitations that open up space for future research. First, by choosing to focus on representations across groups of films, the high level of detail possible through close textual analysis became impossible. A detailed analysis of each individual text included in this project might reveal more about the functioning of the narrative conventions and visual codes in an individual text.

Second, notable works of transgender representation, including *To Wong Foo Thanks for Everything, Julie Newmar* (1995), *Hedwig and the*

Angry Inch (2001), and Tyler Perry's Madea films (2005–2019), were not included in this project. Some of these films share connections and could be developed into new categories of transgender representation. *To Wong Foo* and *Hedwig* share the narrative convention of transgender characters entering a hostile place and making it more welcoming. Tyler Perry's films would be interesting to analyze along with other films, such as *Hairspray* (1988, 2007) and *Jack and Jill* (2011), in which the performer is meant to be seen by the audience as a member of the gender they are presenting as. Numerous other films, such as *Charley's Aunt* (1941), *Just Like a Woman* (1992), and *She's the Man* (2006), could be analyzed to confirm or refute the narrative conventions and visual codes I argue for in this book.

Third, I was unable to include foreign films and other visual media to the degree I would have liked. Transgender representations are prominent in the film traditions of Japan, China, Spain, India, and numerous other countries. Each national cinema is deserving of its own analysis. Transgender representations also figure prominently in the history of television, including such shows and characters as *M*A*S*H* (1972–1983), *Bosom Buddies* (1980–1982), Zoe on *All My Children* from 2006–2007, *Degrassi* (2001–2015), and *Work It* (2012). Transgender representations also feature prominently in Japanese anime and manga, including such series as *Ranma ½* (1989–1992), *Otoboku* (2006), and *Princess Princess* (2006). Transgender representation in different national cinemas and media formats deserve attention for the narrative conventions and visual codes unique to them.

Finally, I made use of Stuart Hall's encoding/decoding model in order to understand the messages encoded into the films using certain narrative conventions and visual codes to be decoded by audience members to communicate certain messages about transgender people. This method was useful for accomplishing the goal for this project of analyzing the messages about transgender people contained in popular films, but it did not allow me to make any claims about how audience members would actually decode these messages beyond my own decodings. A thorough analysis of how audiences process the messages sent by these films would be a useful addition to the research on transgender representation. This analysis could be conducted through quantitative surveys in order to understand how large numbers of people respond to transgender representations in general, or through qualitative questionnaires after film screenings to better understand how specific audiences process the messages in particular films. This type of in-depth audience analysis is necessary before any claims can be made about how audiences respond to these films as opposed to the implied audience found within the films' texts.

My experience with transgender representations in film began a long time ago, in that theater in 1993 watching *Mrs. Doubtfire* for the first time. Though I was initially fascinated just by seeing a transgender character on the screen, I quickly realized that most people in the audience did not respond to the character in such a positive way. My desire to understand what it was about this film and other transgender representations that led other audience members to distance themselves from the transgender characters instead of wanting to know more about them eventually led me to this book. There is still a long way to go in improving the representation of transgender people in film. The affective and emotional responses to the transgender characters of ridicule, fear, disgust, and sympathy are the result of narrative and visual constructions that reflect an identification between author and audience rooted in a cisnormative ideology. Reducing the distance this identification creates and changing the affective and emotional responses that are shaped by it are key to improving the representation of transgender people in film.

Notes

Introduction

1. Stuart Hall, "Encoding/Decoding," in *Media and Cultural Studies: KeyWorks*, rev. ed., ed. Meenakshi Gigi Durham and Douglas M. Kellner (Malden, MA: Blackwell, 2006), 172–173.

2. The texts I analyze in this book are primarily mainstream, commercial films released by major Hollywood studios. More potential for positive messages about transgender lives can currently be found in the art and indie films being made by transgender creators, but analyzing these films goes beyond the scope of this book.

3. Stuart Hall, "The Work of Representation," in *Representation: Cultural Representations and Signifying Practices*, ed. Stuart Hall (London: Sage, 1997), 25–26; Jen Webb, *Understanding Representation* (Thousand Oaks, CA: Sage, 2009), 11.

4. Stuart Hall, "Culture, the Media and the 'Ideological Effect,'" in *Mass Communication and Society*, ed. James Curran, Michael Gurevitch, and Janet Woollacott (Beverly Hills, CA: Sage, 1979), 343; emphasis in original.

5. Stephen Heath, *Questions of Cinema* (Bloomington: Indiana University Press, 1981), 115.

6. Heath, *Questions of Cinema*, 115.

7. Julia Serano, *Whipping Girl: A Transsexual Woman on Sexism and the Scapegoating of Femininity* (Emeryville, CA: Seal Press, 2007), 35; Kay Siebler, "Transqueer Representations and How We Educate," *Journal of LGBT Youth* 7, no. 4 (2010): 330.

8. Serano, *Whipping Girl*, 35.

9. Siebler, "Transqueer Representations," 330.

10. Siebler, "Transqueer Representations," 342.

11. Judith Butler, *Bodies that Matter: On the Discursive Limits of "Sex"* (New York: Routledge, 1993), 126.

12. Marjorie Garber, *Vested Interests: Cross-Dressing & Cultural Anxiety* (New York: Routledge, 1992), 69–70.

13. Garber, *Vested Interests*, 70.

14. John Phillips, *Transgender on Screen* (New York: Palgrave Macmillan, 2006), 53.

15. Serano, *Whipping Girl*, 36.

16. Serano, *Whipping Girl*, 37.

17. Annette Kuhn, *The Power of the Image: Essays on Representation and Sexuality* (London: Routledge, 1985), 56–57.

18. Chris Straayer, *Deviant Eyes, Deviant Bodies: Sexual Re-Orientations in Film and Video* (New York: Columbia University Press, 1996), 42–43.

19. Rebecca Bell-Metereau, *Hollywood Androgyny*, 2nd ed. (New York: Columbia University Press, 1993), 237.

20. Bell-Metereau, *Hollywood Androgyny*, 58–59.

21. Rebecca Bell-Metereau, *Transgender Cinema* (New Brunswick, NJ: Rutgers University Press, 2019), 12.

22. Sandra Meiri and Odeya Kohen-Raz, *Traversing the Fantasy: The Dialectic of Desire/Fantasy and the Ethics of Narrative Cinema* (New York: Bloomsbury Academic, 2020), 168.

23. Meiri and Kohen-Raz, *Traversing the Fantasy*, 170.

24. Meiri and Kohen-Raz, *Traversing the Fantasy*, 197.

25. Meiri and Kohen-Raz, *Traversing the Fantasy*, 171.

26. Joelle Ruby Ryan, "Reel Gender: Examining the Politics of Trans Images in Film and Media" (PhD diss., Bowling Green State University, 2009), 18.

27. Linda Alcoff, "Cultural Feminism versus Post-Structuralism: The Identity Crisis in Feminist Theory," in *The Second Wave: A Reader in Feminist Theory*, ed. Linda Nicholson (New York: Routledge, 1997), 349–355.

28. Susan Stryker, *Transgender History* (Berkeley, CA: Seal Press, 2008), 19.

29. Lucy J. Miller, "Becoming One of the Girls/Guys: Distancing Transgender Representations in Popular Film Comedies," in *Transgender Communication Studies: Histories, Trends, and Trajectories*, ed. Leland G. Spencer and Jamie C. Capuzza (Lanham, MD: Lexington Books, 2015), 127.

30. Michael Warner, "Introduction: Fear of a Queer Planet," *Social Text* 29 (1991): 16.

31. Kate Bornstein, "Gender Terror, Gender Rage," in *The Transgender Studies Reader*, ed. Susan Stryker and Stephen Whittle (New York: Routledge, 2006), 241.

32. Christian Metz, "Identification, Mirror," in *Film Theory and Criticism: Introductory Readings*, 7th ed., ed. Leo Braudy and Marshall Cohen (Oxford: Oxford University Press, 2009), 696–699.

33. Kenneth Burke, *A Rhetoric of Motives* (Berkeley, CA: University of California Press, 1969), 22.

34. Burke, *A Rhetoric of Motives*, 21.

35. Edwin Black, "The Second Persona," in *Readings in Rhetorical Criticism*, 2nd ed., ed. Carl R. Burgchardt (State College, PA: Strata, 2000), 192.

36. Reference to the author here should not be conflated with the auteur in auteur theory, since the author being discussed is the implied author in the text and not an actual person able to adopt a personal style.

37. Edward W. Said, *Orientalism* (New York: Random House, 1979; New York: Vintage Books, 1994), 21.

38. Aristotle, *On Rhetoric: A Theory of Civic Discourse*, trans. George A. Kennedy (Oxford: Oxford University Press, 1991), 38–39.

39. Silvan S. Tomkins, *Affect, Imagery, Consciousness*, Vol. I, *The Positive Affects* (New York: Springer, 1962), 22.

40. Tomkins, *Affect, Imagery, Consciousness*, 126.

41. Julian Hanich, *Cinematic Emotion in Horror Films and Thrillers: The Aesthetic Paradox of Pleasurable Fear* (New York: Routledge, 2010), 62–63.

42. Herman Gray, "The Feel of Life: Resonance, Race, and Representation," *International Journal of Communication* 9 (2015): 1112–1113.

43. Sara Ahmed, *The Cultural Politics of Emotion*, 2nd ed. (New York: Routledge, 2015), 12.

44. Ahmed, *The Cultural Politics*, 10.

45. Jasmine Rault, "White Noise, White Affects: Filtering the Sameness of Queer Suffering," *Feminist Media Studies* 17, no. 4 (2017): 593.

46. Dana L. Cloud and Kathleen Eaton Feyh, "Reason in Revolt: Emotional Fidelity and Working Class Standpoint in the 'Internationale,'" *Rhetoric Society Quarterly* 45, no. 4 (2015): 303.

47. Brigitte Bargetz, "Mapping Affect: Challenges of (Un)timely Politics," in *Timing of Affect: Epistemologies, Aesthetics, Politics*, ed. Marie-Luise Angerer, Bernd Bösel, and Michaela Ott (Zurich: Diaphanes, 2014), 293; emphasis in original.

48. Bargetz, "Mapping Affect," 299.

49. Bargetz, "Mapping Affect," 299.

50. In research with transgender audiences, media studies scholar Andre Cavalcante found that many of the texts analyzed in this book functioned for transgender audience members as "breakout texts" that have offered "'first of its kind' visibility" for the transgender community and "generate three definitive breaks: (a) a break into the cultural mainstream, (b) a break with historical representational paradigms, and (c) a breaking into the everyday lives of the audiences they purport to represent." While transgender audience members have found usefulness in these texts, this does not refute the

argument made in this book that the films were constructed for a cisgender audience. Andre Cavalcante, "Breaking Into Transgender Life: Transgender Audiences' Experiences with 'First of Its Kind' Visibility in Popular Media," *Communication, Culture & Critique* 10, no. 3 (2017): 539.

51. Elspeth Probyn, "Writing Shame," in *The Affect Theory Reader*, ed. Melissa Gregg and Gregory J. Seigworth (Durham, NC: Duke University Press, 2010), 74.

52. Probyn, "Writing Shame," 74.

53. Alan McKee, *Textual Analysis: A Beginner's Guide* (Thousand Oaks, CA: Sage, 2003), 17.

54. Franco Moretti, *Graphs, Maps, Trees: Abstract Models for Literary History* (New York: Verso, 2007), 1.

55. Hall, "Culture," 343–344.

56. David Bordwell, *Making Meaning: Inference and Rhetoric in the Interpretation of Cinema* (Cambridge, MA: Harvard University Press, 1989), 3.

57. Hall, "Culture," 344.

58. John Downing and Charles Husband, *Representing "Race": Racisms, Ethnicities and Media* (Thousand Oaks, CA: Sage, 2005), 43.

59. Donald Bogle, *Toms, Coons, Mulattoes, Mammies, and Bucks: An Interpretive History of Blacks in American Films*, 4th ed. (New York: Continuum, 2001), 4.

60. Herman Gray, *Watching Race: Television and the Struggle for "Blackness"* (Minneapolis: University of Minnesota Press, 1995), 84.

61. Larry Gross, *Up from Invisibility: Lesbians, Gay Men, and the Media in America* (New York: Columbia University Press, 2001), 12–17.

62. Audre Lorde, "Age, Race, Class, and Sex: Women Redefining Difference," in *Out There: Marginalization and Contemporary Cultures*, ed. Russell Ferguson, Martha Gever, Trinh T. Minh-ha, and Cornel West (Cambridge, MA: The MIT Press, 1990), 281.

63. Lorde, "Age, Race," 286.

64. Stuart Hall, "New Ethnicities," in *Stuart Hall: Critical Dialogues in Cultural Studies*, ed. David Morley and Kuan-Hsing Chen (London: Routledge, 1996), 446–447.

65. Victoria Pruin DeFrancisco and Catherine Helen Palczewski, *Communicating Gender Diversity: A Critical Approach* (Los Angeles: Sage, 2007), 21.

66. Sneja Gunew, "Feminism and the Politics of Irreducible Differences: Multiculturalism/ Ethnicity/Race," in *Feminism and the Politics of Difference*, ed. Sneja Gunew and Anna Yeatman (Halifax: Fernwood, 1993), 1.

67. Herman Gray, *Cultural Moves: African Americans and the Politics of Representation* (Berkeley, CA: University of California Press, 2005), 110.

68. Leo Braudy, *The World in a Frame: What We See in Films* (Garden City, NY: Anchor, 1976), 35; Kristin Thompson, *Breaking the Glass Armor:*

Neoformalist Film Analysis (Princeton: Princeton University Press, 1988), 8–11; David Bordwell, *Poetics of Cinema* (New York: Routledge, 2008), 63–65.

69. Todd McGowan, *The Real Gaze: Film Theory after Lacan* (Albany, NY: State University of New York Press, 2007), 2.

70. Laura Mulvey, "Visual Pleasure and Narrative Cinema," *Screen* 16, no. 3 (1975): 8–14.

71. Mulvey, "Visual Pleasure," 8–14.

72. McGowan, *Real Gaze*, 8–9.

73. McGowan, *Real Gaze*, 11.

74. McGowan, *Real Gaze*, 11.

75. McGowan, *Real Gaze*, 12.

76. McGowan, *Real Gaze*, 3.

77. McGowan, *Real Gaze*, 17.

78. McGowan, *Real Gaze*, 7–8.

79. McGowan, *Real Gaze*, 13.

80. Kevin Goddard, " 'Looks Maketh the Man': The Female Gaze and the Construction of Masculinity," *Journal of Men's Studies* 9, no. 1 (2000): 34.

81. Mulvey, "Visual Pleasure," 11.

82. Kaja Silverman, *Male Subjectivity at the Margins* (New York: Routledge, 1992), 130.

83. Silverman, *Male Subjectivity*, 144–145.

84. Elizabeth Davis, "Structures of Seeing: Blindness, Race, and Gender in Visual Culture," *The Senses and Society* 14, no. 1 (2019): 74.

85. Davis, "Structures of Seeing," 74.

86. Diane Ponterotto, "Resisting the Male Gaze: Feminist Responses to the 'Normalization' of the Female Body in Western Culture," *Journal of International Women's Studies* 17, no. 1 (2016): 135.

87. J. Jack Halberstam, "The Transgender Gaze in *Boys Don't Cry*," *Screen* 42, no. 3 (2001): 294.

88. J. Jack Halberstam, *In a Queer Time and Place: Transgender Bodies, Subcultural Lives* (New York: New York University Press, 2005), 78–79.

89. Serano, *Whipping Girl*, 14.

90. Serano, *Whipping Girl*, 12.

91. Dean Spade, *Normal Life: Administrative Violence, Critical Trans Politics, and the Limits of Law* (Brooklyn, NY: South End Press, 2011), 102–115.

Chapter 2

1. In addition to the transgender comedies covered in this chapter, other examples include *Sylvia Scarlett* (1935), *Charley's Aunt* (1941), *Victor/Victoria* (1982), *Just One of the Girls* (1993), *Ladybugs* (1993), *Big Momma's*

House (2000), *100 Girls* (2000), *All the Queen's Men* (2001), *Juwanna Man* (2002), *The Hot Chick* (2002), *White Chicks* (2004), *It's a Boy Girl Thing* (2006), and *She's the Man* (2006).

2. Phillips, *Transgender on Screen*, 51–52.

3. Phillips, *Transgender on Screen*, 58–59.

4. Sara Ahmed, "Happy Objects," in Gregg and Seigworth, *The Affect Theory Reader*, 29.

5. Ahmed, "Happy Objects," 32.

6. John C. Meyer, "Humor as a Double-Edged Sword: Four Functions of Humor in Communication," *Communication Theory* 10, no. 3 (2000): 317-318.

7. Meyer, "Humor," 327–328.

8. Susan J. Douglas, *The Rise of Enlightened Sexism: How Pop Culture Took Us from Girl Power to Girls Gone Wild* (New York: St. Martin's Griffin, 2010), 65. The humor in transgender comedies is, of course, not solely derived from the transgender identities of the characters. Audience members may laugh at Tony Curtis's impression of Cary Grant in *Some Like It Hot* or the bumbling private detective's hand being smashed by a door while he tries to spy on Victoria in *Victor/Victoria*. Even humor involving transgender characters is not always the result of their transgender identities; Robin Williams's fake breasts catching on fire in *Mrs. Doubtfire* comes from a slapstick tradition for which the actor is well known rather than functioning as a specific comment on transgender women's bodies. The goal of this chapter is not to argue that all the humor in transgender comedies comes from the transgender identities of the characters but that the use of specific narrative conventions and visual codes supports a representation of the transgender characters as objects of ridicule.

9. Victoria Flanagan, *Into the Closet: Cross-Dressing and the Gendered Body in Children's Literature and Film* (New York: Routledge, 2008), 174.

10. Butler, *Bodies that Matter*, 126.

11. Garber, *Vested Interests*, 8.

12. Garber, *Vested Interests*, 70.

13. Straayer, *Deviant Eyes*, 44.

14. Daniel Lieberfeld and Judith Sanders, "Keeping the Characters Straight: Comedy and Identity in Some Like It Hot," *Journal of Popular Film and Television* 26, no. 3 (1998): 130.

15. Victor Turner, *The Ritual Process: Structure and Anti-Structure* (Piscataway, NJ: Aldine Transaction, 1995), 95.

16. Bell-Metereau, *Hollywood Androgyny*, 64.

17. Lieberfeld and Sanders, "Keeping the Characters Straight," 131.

18. Garber, *Vested Interests*, 70.

19. Maria Jesús Martinez, "*Some Like It Hot*: The Blurring of Gender Limits in a Film of the Fifties," *BELLS: Barcelona English Language and Literature Studies* 9 (1998): 150–151.

20. Martinez, *"Some Like It Hot,"* 149–150.

21. Straayer, *Deviant Eyes*, 43.

22. Bell-Meterau, *Hollywoood Androdyny*, 58–59.

23. Bell-Meterau, *Hollywoood Androdyny*, 59.

24. Bell-Meterau, *Hollywoood Androdyny*, 64.

25. Meiri and Kohen-Raz, *Traversing the Fantasy*, 199.

26. Meiri and Kohen-Ratz, *Traversing the Fantasy*, 198.

27. Lieberfeld and Sanders, "Keeping the Characters Straight," 131.

28. The purpose of this scene, as with the scene that opens *Big Momma's House* in which Malcolm disguises himself as an older Korean man in order to bust a dog-fighting ring, is to establish Michael's skill with makeup as a way of explaining how he is able to complete his transformation into Dorothy on his own. Matt in *100 Girls* and Daniel in *Mrs. Doubtfire* are also seen receiving help from a female friend and a brother, respectively. These more contemporary references to the help the characters receive or the skill they are shown to have are attempts to anticipate skepticism that audience members might otherwise have about how purportedly cisnormative men would know how to dress as women. Despite these references to the help of others, the actual process of transformation is still generally not shown.

29. Even the cultural icon that Michael becomes as Dorothy in *Tootsie* is based more on what he says than how he looks. When Michael auditions for the soap opera role as Dorothy, the producer decides to do a screen test. She tells the cameraman "I'd like to make her look a little more attractive. How far can you pull back?" to which the cameraman replies, "How do you feel about Cleveland?" The message is clear that Dorothy is not a very attractive woman. What Michael says is something he can control while defining his popularity in terms of a femininely attractive appearance might undermine his cisgender identity.

30. Frank P. Tomasulo, "Masculine/Feminine: The 'New Masculinity' in *Tootsie* (1982)," *Velvet Light Trap* 38 (1996): 5.

31. Garber, *Vested Interests*, 70.

Chapter 3

1. Other examples of transgender horror films include *The Silence of the Lambs* (1991), *Bad Education* (2004), *Split* (2017), and the sequels to *Sleepaway Camp*: *Sleepaway Camp II: Unhappy Campers* (1988), *Sleepaway Camp III: Teenage Wasteland* (1989), *Return to Sleepaway Camp* (2008), and *Sleepaway Camp IV: The Survivor* (2012).

2. Ahmed, *The Cultural Politics*, 65.

3. Halberstam, *In a Queer Time*, 78–79.

4. Ahmed, *The Cultural Politics*, 65.

5. Brian Massumi, "The Future Birth of the Affective Fact: The Political Ontology of Threat," in Gregg and Seigworth, *The Affect Theory Reader*, 54.

6. Ahmed, *The Cultural Politics*, 70.

7. Bell-Metereau, *Transgender Cinema*, 22.

8. Garber, *Vested Interests*, 115.

9. Robert Genter, "'We All Go a Little Mad Sometimes': Alfred Hitchcock, American Psychoanalysis, and the Construction of the Cold War Psychopath," *Canadian Review of American Studies* 40, no. 2 (2010): 135.

10. Genter, "We All Go," 151–153.

11. Naomi Kondo argues that *Psycho* is part of a prominent trend of portraying people with mental illness as violent killers. Like transgender people, this type of representation distances those with mental illness from the rest of society who fear their potentially violent behavior. Also, like transgender representations, these filmic representations are one of the few ways many people encounter mental illness. Critics often neglect to consider the very real implications these representations may have on the lives of those living with mental illness. Kondo, "Mental Illness in Film," *Psychiatric Rehabilitation Journal* 31, no. 3 (2008): 250.

William Indick, *Psycho Thrillers: Cinematic Explorations of the Mysteries of the Mind* (Jefferson, NC: McFarland, 2006), 32.

12. Thomas M. Sipos, *Horror Film Aesthetics: Creating the Visual Language of Fear* (Jefferson, NC: McFarland, 2010), 5.

13. Kendall R. Phillips, *Projected Fears: Horror Films and American Culture* (Westport, CT: Praeger, 2005), 5; R. Barton Palmer, "The Metafictional Hitchcock: The Experience of Viewing and the Viewing of Experience in *Rear Window* and *Psycho*," *Cinema Journal* 25, no. 2 (1986): 16.

14. Altan Loker, *Film and Suspense*, 2nd ed. (Victoria, BC: Trafford, 2005), 24.

15. Halberstam, *In a Queer Time*, 78–79; Peter N. Chumo II, "*The Crying Game*, Hitchcockian Romance, and the Quest for Identity," *Literature/Film Quarterly* 23, no. 4 (1995): 249.

16. Robin Wood, *Hollywood from Vietnam to Reagan* (New York: Columbia University Press, 1986), 148.

17. Ronald Librach, "Sex, Lies, and Audiotape: Politics and Heuristics in *Dressed to Kill* and *Blow Out*," *Literature/Film Quarterly* 26, no. 3 (1998): 167.

18. Linda Williams, "When the Woman Looks," in *Re-Vision: Essays in Feminist Film Criticism*, ed. Mary Ann Doane, Patricia Mellencamp, and Linda Williams (Frederick, MD: University Publications of America, 1984), 96.

19. Williams, "When the Woman Looks," 94.

20. Linda Williams has harsh words for the transgender identity of the killer in *Dressed to Kill*. "While supposedly about Bobbie's desire to castrate her male half, what the film actually shows is not this mutilation but another: the slow motion slashing of Kate's body as substitute for the castration Bob-

bie cannot yet perform on Elliot. In this light, Bobbie's vengeance on Kate can be viewed not as the act of a jealous woman eliminating her rival, but as acting out the *male* fantasy that woman is castrated, mutilated . . . The problem, in other words, is that she is not castrated; the fantasy solution of the male psychopath and the film itself is symbolically to prove that she is." Her argument implies that Bobbie strikes out at Kate because of unsatisfied male desires, completely negating Bobbie's transgender identity while also positioning it as the source of her rage. Williams' complete dismissal of the reality of Bobbie's transgender identity demonstrates the potential for approaching the transgender identities of characters in these films as separate from a supposedly true cisgender/patriarchal identity to devolve into outright transphobia. Williams, "When the Woman Looks," 97.

21. Ahmed, *The Cultural Politics*, 62–63.

22. Ahmed, *The Cultural Politics*, 64.

23. Ahmed, *The Cultural Politics*, 65.

24. Halberstam, *In a Queer Time*, 78–79.

25. Ahmed, *The Cultural Politics*, 65.

26. Ahmed, *The Cultural Politics*, 67.

27. William Rothman, *Hitchcock: The Murderous Gaze* (Cambridge, MA: Harvard University Press, 1982), 329.

28. Ahmed, *The Cultural Politics*, 65.

29. Indick, *Psycho Thrillers*, 32; Wood, *Hollywood from Vietnam*, 146.

Chapter 4

1. Robert W. Welkos, "The Secret of 'The Crying Game': Don't Read Any Further if You Haven't Seen This Film," *The Los Angeles Times*, February 18, 1993, https://www.latimes.com/archives/la-xpm-1993-02-18-ca-292-story.html.

2. Other transgender thrillers include *M. Butterfly* (1993), *The Last Seduction* (1994), and *Bad Education* (2004). The inclusion of films like *Myra Breckenridge* and *Ace Ventura: Pet Detective* in this chapter may seem like an unusual choice, since these films are generally understood to be comedies, but my reasoning is that the affective and emotional responses generated by these films fit the norms of thrillers regardless of how they are classified in terms of genre. The films are also structured to prompt these responses using the same narrative conventions and visual codes as other thrillers, so I made the decision to include the films with others that are similar in terms of construction rather than being constrained by genre expectations.

3. Neill D. Hicks, *Writing the Thriller Film: The Terror Within* (Studio City, CA: Michael Wise Productions, 2002), 34.

4. Hicks, *Writing the Thriller Film*, 34.

5. Hicks, *Writing the Thriller Film*, 32.

6. Robert Madrigal, Colleen Bee, Johnny Chen and Monica Labarge, "The Effect of Suspense on Enjoyment Following a Desirable Outcome: The Mediating Role of Relief," *Media Psychology* 14, no. 3 (2011): 268.

7. Halberstam, *In a Queer Time*, 78–79.

8. John McCarty, *Thrillers: Seven Decades of Classic Film Suspense* (New York: Citadel Press, 1992), 13.

9. Hanich, *Cinematic Emotion*, 156.

10. Hanich, *Cinematic Emotion*, 158–159.

11. Hanich, *Cinematic Emotion*, 158–159.

12. Ahmed, *The Cultural Politics*, 85.

13. Julia Kristeva, *Powers of Horror: An Essay on Abjection* (New York: Columbia University Press, 1982), 2.

14. Susan Strkyer, "My Words to Victor Frankenstein above the Village of Chamonix: Performing Transgender Rage," in Stryker and Whittle, *The Transgender Studies Reader*, 247.

15. Paul Martin Lester, "From Abomination to Indifference: A Visual Analysis of Transgender Stereotypes in the Media," in Spencer and Capuzza, *Transgender Communication Studies*, 152.

16. E. Cram, " 'Angie was Our Sister': Witnessing the Trans-Formation of Disgust in the Citizenry of Photography," *Quarterly Journal of Speech* 98, no. 4 (2012): 420.

17. Serano, *Whipping Girl*, 36.

18. Serano, *Whipping Girl*, 36.

19. Emma is John's transgender alter ego, reinforcing a trope already seen in the previous chapter on transgender horror films.

20. Flanagan, *Into the Closet*, 203.

21. Madrigal et al., "The Effect of Suspense," 268.

22. The box office success of *The Crying Game*, earning over $62 million in its initial US release, suggests that transgender identity is (or was in 1992) still enough of a taboo to tantalize large numbers of people, but it is still a taboo that people are supposed to be disgusted by, which is often the thrill of these kinds of films.

23. The difficulties scholars encounter in their own conceptions of gender are evident in the ways they are often at pains to classify Dil as a character. Nicola Evans calls her a "man who cross-dresses as a woman," Jane Giles refers to her as a "gay male transvestite, at home in golden sequins," Peter Chumo simply calls her a "woman who is false," and Kristin Handler describers her as a "man who appears to be, and identifies as, a woman." John Phillips notes that Dil is "extremely feminine in both appearance and behavior" but that she "does not manifest any of the anatomical characteristics of a male-to-female transsexual." I simply refer to Dil as a transgender

woman based on the positional approach I use in this book and the umbrella definition of transgender discussed in the Introduction. Nicola Evans, "Games of Hide and Seek: Race, Gender and Drag in *The Crying Game* and *The Birdcage*," *Text and Performance Quarterly* 18, no. 3 (1998): 199; Jane Giles, *The Crying Game* (London: British Film Institute, 1997), 63; Peter N. Chumo II, "*The Crying Game*, Hitchcockian Romance, and the Quest for Identity," *Literature/Film Quarterly* 23, no. 4 (1995): 249; Kristin Handler, "Sexing *The Crying Game*: Difference, Identity, Ethics," *Film Quarterly* 47, no. 3 (1994): 31; Phillips, *Transgender on Screen*, 120.

24. Handler, "Sexing *The Crying Game*," 41; Leighton Grist, "'It's Only a Piece of Meat': Gender Ambiguity, Sexuality, and Politics in *The Crying Game* and *M. Butterfly*," *Cinema Journal* 42, no. 4 (2003): 20-21; Jack Boozer, Jr., "Bending Phallic Patriarchy in 'The Crying Game,'" *Journal of Popular Film and Television* 22, no. 4 (1995): 174–175.

25. Phillips, *Transgender on Screen*, 124; Christopher Lockett, "Terror and Rebirth: *Cathleen ni Houlihan*, from Yeats to *The Crying Game*," *Literature/Film Quarterly* 33, no. 4 (2005): 297; Evans, "Games of Hide and Seek," 207.

Chapter 5

1. Other examples of transgender dramas include *Glen or Glenda* (1953), *The World According to Garp* (1982), *Just Like a Woman* (1992), *Ed Wood* (1994), *The Adventures of Sebastian Cole* (1998), *Princesa* (2001), *Tokyo Godfathers* (2003), *Normal* (2003), *Beautiful Boxer* (2003), *Soldier's Girl* (2003), *Breakfast on Pluto* (2005), *Dallas Buyer's Club* (2013), and *The Danish Girl* (2015).

2. Suzanne Keen, *Empathy and the Novel* (Oxford: Oxford University Press, 2007), 4.

3. Tania Singer and Claus Lamm, "The Social Neuroscience of Empathy," *The Year in Cognitive Neuroscience 2009: Annals of the New York Academy of Sciences* 1156, no. 1 (2009): 84.

4. C. Daniel Batson, Marina P. Polycarpou, Eddie Harmon-Jones, Heidi J. Imhoff, Erin C. Mitchener, Lori L. Bednar, Tricia R. Klein, and Lori Highberger, "Empathy and Attitudes: Can Feelings for a Member of a Stigmatized Group Improve Feelings Toward the Group?," *Journal of Personality and Social Psychology* 72, no. 1 (1997): 116–117.

5. Mary Beth Oliver, "Tender Affective States as Predictors of Entertainment Preference," *Journal of Communication* 58, no. 1 (2008): 55–56.

6. By *independent*, I am not referring to the mode of the production of the films as outside of the dominant corporate studio system, with most of these films having been produced and/or distributed by companies well

within this system, but, instead, to a stylistic form that most audience members associate with the label *independent*. Yannis Tzioumakis defines the view of independent film held by the "majority of people with a basic knowledge of American cinema" as "low-budget projects made by (mostly) young filmmakers with a strong personal vision away from the influence and pressures of the few major conglomerates that control tightly the American film industry." Though, of course, there are a wide range of films that fall under the indie label, independent film in this sense is typified by a more personalized form of narrative construction and character development rather than the product of particular noncorporate business arrangements, with "away from" in Tzioumakis's definition encompassing both production by companies outside of the dominant Hollywood studios and also more freedom within those studios. Yannis Tzioumakis, *American Independent Cinema: An Introduction* (New Brunswick, NJ: Rutgers University Press, 2006), 1.

7. Michael Z. Newman, *Indie: An American Film Culture* (New York: Columbia University Press, 2011), 87.

8. Geoff King, *American Independent Cinema* (Bloomington, IN: Indiana University Press, 2005), 107.

9. King, *American Independent Cinema*, 119.

10. King, *American Independent Cinema*, 123.

11. *Being read* is common terminology in the transgender community and refers to moments when someone recognizes you as transgender. It is of particular concern to transgender people, like Bree in this example, who are trying to be stealth about their transgender identities, meaning that they do not publicly share their identities with others.

12. While two transgender women, Emma Grashun and Tipper Sommore, do die in the first half of *Ticked-Off Trannies with Knives*, their deaths are meant more as a setup to the violent revenge meted out by their friends in the second half of the film than the serious reflection on the violence directed toward transgender people that Brandon's death is intended to be. Also, the transgender characters in chapter three above obviously kill other people, but with this statement, I am focused more on the deaths of transgender characters than the deaths perpetrated by them.

13. Nick Rees-Roberts, "La Confusion des Genres: Transsexuality, Effeminacy and Gay Identity in France," *International Journal of Cultural Studies* 7, no. 3 (2004): 293.

14. Kate Ince, "Queering the Family? Fantasy and the Performance of Sexuality and Gay Relations in French Cinema 1995–2000," *Studies in French Cinema* 2, no. 2 (2002): 95.

15. Ince, "Queering the Family?," 95.

16. Serano, *Whipping Girl*, 37.

17. Serano, *Whipping Girl*, 41.
18. Halberstam, *In a Queer Time*, 86.
19. Halberstam, *In a Queer Time*, 86.
20. Annabelle Willox, "Branding Teena: (Mis)Representations in the Media," *Sexualities* 6, no. 3-4 (2003): 420–421.
21. J. Jack Halberstam, "The Transgender Gaze in *Boys Don't Cry*," *Screen* 42, no. 3 (2001): 294.
22. Phillips, *Transgender on Screen*, 146.
23. Halberstam, "The Transgender Gaze," 296.

Chapter 6

1. Herman Gray, *Cultural Moves: African Americans and the Politics of Representation* (Berkeley: University of California Press, 2005), 113.
2. Aniko Bodroghkozy, "Negotiating Civil Rights in Prime Time: A Production and Reception History of CBS's *East Side/West Side*," *Television & New Media* 4, no. 3 (2003): 270.
3. Gross, *Up from Invisibility*, 262.
4. "Media Diversity Programs," *NAACP*, n.d., https://www.naacp.org/campaigns/media-diversity-programs/; "Entertainment Media," *GLAAD*, n.d., https://www.glaad.org/entertainment.
5. Kathryn C. Montgomery, *Target: Prime Time: Advocacy Groups and the Struggle over Entertainment Television* (New York: Oxford University Press, 1989), 217.
6. Viviane Namaste, *Sex Change, Social Change: Reflections on Identity, Institutions, and Imperialism* (Toronto: Women's Press, 2005), 45.
7. Jack Tomas, "ABC Cancels 'Work It,' But This Kind of Thing will Happen Again," *Tú Vez*, n.d., http://www.tuvez.com/abc-cancels-work-it-but-this-kind-of-thing-will-happen-again/workit/.
8. Lynette Rice, "Work It is Cancelled by ABC,'" *Entertainment Weekly*, January 14, 2012, https://ew.com/article/2012/01/14/work-it-cancelled/.
9. Daniel Reynolds, "*Adam* Director Rhys Ernst Addresses Critics and the 'War on Nuance,'" *The Advocate*, July 22, 2019, https://www.advocate.com/film/2019/7/22/adam-director-rhys-ernst-addresses-critics-and-war-nuance.
10. Rhys Ernst, "On 'Adam,'" *Medium*, June 5, 2018, https://medium.com/@rhys.ernst/on-adam-129982a3119b.
11. Jenni Olson, "'Adam is 2019's Most Controversial Queer Film—And Its Most Important," *New Now Next*, August 5, 2019, http://www.newnownext.com/adam-is-the-most-controversial-queer-film-of-2019-and-its-most-important/08/2019/.

12. Solvej Schou, "Roland Emmerich's 'Stonewall' Finds Controversy," *The New York Times*, September 18, 2015, https://www.nytimes.com/2015/09/20/movies/roland-emmerichs-stonewall-finds-controversy.html.

13. Ernst, "On 'Adam.' "

14. Laverne Cox, "Acting While Trans: A Look Back at 2011 for Transgender Actors in the Media," *The Huffington Post*, December 23, 2011, https://www.huffpost.com/entry/transgender-actors-2011_b_1162279.

15. William Keck, "*Hung* Takes a Transgender Turn," *TV Guide*, July 11–17, 2011, 14; also at https://www.tvguide.com/news/kecks-exclusives-hung-1034931/.

16. Keck, "*Hung*," 14.

17. Ron Becker, *Gay TV and Straight America* (New Brunswick, NJ: Rutgers University Press, 2006), 224.

Bibliography

Ahmed, Sara. *The Cultural Politics of Emotion*. 2nd ed. New York: Routledge, 2015.

———. "Happy Objects." In Gregg and Seigworth, *The Affect Theory Reader*, 29–51.

Alcoff, Linda. "Cultural Feminism versus Post-Structuralism: The Identity Crisis in Feminist Theory." In *The Second Wave: A Reader in Feminist Theory*, edited by Linda Nicholson, 330–355. New York: Routledge, 1997.

Aristotle. *On Rhetoric: A Theory of Civic Discourse*. Translated by George A. Kennedy. Oxford: Oxford University Press, 1991.

Bargetz, Brigitte. "Mapping Affect: Challenges of (Un)timely Politics." In *Timing of Affect: Epistemologies, Aesthetics, Politics*, edited by Marie-Luise Angerer, Bernd Bösel, and Michaela Ott, 289–302. Zurich: Diaphanes, 2014.

Batson, C. Daniel, Marina P. Polycarpou, Eddie Harmon-Jones, Heidi J. Imhoff, Erin C. Mitchener, Lori L. Bednar, Tricia R. Klein, and Lori Highberger. "Empathy and Attitudes: Can Feelings for a Member of a Stigmatized Group Improve Feelings Toward the Group?" *Journal of Personality and Social Psychology* 72, no. 1 (1997): 105–118.

Becker, Ron. *Gay TV and Straight America*. New Brunswick, NJ: Rutgers University Press, 2006.

Bell-Metereau, Rebecca. *Hollywood Androgyny*. 2nd ed. New York: Columbia University Press, 1993.

———. *Transgender Cinema*. New Brunswick, NJ: Rutgers University Press, 2019.

Berliner, Alain, dir. *Ma Vie en Rose*. 1997, Canal+.

Black, Edwin. "The Second Persona." In *Readings in Rhetorical Criticism*, 2nd ed., edited by Carl R. Burgchardt, 190–200. State College, PA: Strata, 2000.

Bodroghkozy, Aniko. "Negotiating Civil Rights in Prime Time: A Production and Reception History of CBS's *East Side/West Side*." *Television & New Media* 4, no. 3 (2003): 257–282.

Bogle, Donald. *Toms, Coons, Mulattoes, Mammies, and Bucks: An Interpretive History of Blacks in American Films.* 4th ed. New York: Continuum, 2001.

Boozer Jr., Jack. "Bending Phallic Patriarchy in 'The Crying Game.'" *Journal of Popular Film and Television* 22, no. 4 (1995): 172–179.

Bordwell, David. *Making Meaning: Inference and Rhetoric in the Interpretation of Cinema.* Cambridge, MA: Harvard University Press, 1989.

Bordwell, David. *Poetics of Cinema.* New York: Routledge, 2008.

Bornstein, Kate. "Gender Terror, Gender Rage." In Stryker and Whittle, *The Transgender Studies Reader*, 236–243.

Braudy, Leo. *The World in a Frame: What We See in Films.* Garden City, NY: Anchor Press, 1976.

Burke, Kenneth. *A Rhetoric of Motives.* Berkeley, CA: University of California Press, 1969.

Butler, Judith. *Bodies that Matter: On the Discursive Limits of "Sex."* New York: Routledge, 1993.

Cavalcante, Andre. "Breaking into Transgender Life: Transgender Audiences' Experiences with 'First of Its Kind' Visibility in Popular Media." *Communication, Culture & Critique* 10, no. 3 (2017): 538–555.

Chumo II, Peter N. "*The Crying Game*, Hitchcockian Romance, and the Quest for Identity." *Literature/Film Quarterly* 23, no. 4 (1995): 247–253.

Cloud, Dana L., and Kathleen Eaton Feyh. "Reason in Revolt: Emotional Fidelity and Working Class Standpoint in the 'Internationale.'" *Rhetoric Society Quarterly* 45, no. 4 (2015): 300–323.

Columbus, Chris, dir. *Mrs. Doubtfire.* 1993, 20th Century Fox.

Cox, Laverne. "Acting While Trans: A Look Back at 2011 for Transgender Actors in the Media." *The Huffington Post*, December 23, 2011, https://www.huffpost.com/entry/transgender-actors-2011_b_1162279.

Cram, E. "'Angie was Our Sister': Witnessing the Trans-Formation of Disgust in the Citizenry of Photography." *Quarterly Journal of Speech* 98, no. 4 (2012): 411–438.

Davis, Elizabeth. "Structures of Seeing: Blindness, Race, and Gender in Visual Culture." *The Senses and Society* 14, no. 1 (2019): 63–80.

DeFrancisco, Victoria Pruin, and Catherine Helen Palczewski. *Communicating Gender Diversity: A Critical Approach.* Los Angeles: Sage, 2007.

De Palma, Brian, dir. *Dressed to Kill.* 1980, Cinema 77 Film Group.

Douglas, Susan J. *The Rise of Enlightened Sexism: How Pop Culture Took Us from Girl Power to Girls Gone Wild.* New York: St. Martin's Griffin, 2010.

Downing, John, and Charles Husband. *Representing "Race": Racisms, Ethnicities and Media.* Thousand Oaks, CA: Sage, 2005.

"Entertainment Media." *GLAAD*, n.d. https://www.glaad.org/entertainment.

Ernst, Rhys. "On 'Adam.'" *Medium*, June 5, 2018. https://medium.com/@rhys. ernst/on-adam-129982a3119b.

Evans, Nicola. "Games of Hide and Seek: Race, Gender and Drag in *The Crying Game* and *The Birdcage*." *Text and Performance Quarterly* 18, no. 3 (1998): 199–216.

Flanagan, Victoria. *Into the Closet: Cross-Dressing and the Gendered Body in Children's Literature and Film*. New York: Routledge, 2008.

Garber, Marjorie. *Vested Interests: Cross-Dressing & Cultural Anxiety*. New York: Routledge, 1992.

Genter, Robert. "'We All Go a Little Mad Sometimes': Alfred Hitchcock, American Psychoanalysis, and the Construction of the Cold War Psychopath." *Canadian Review of American Studies* 40, no. 2 (2010): 133–162.

Giles, Jane. *The Crying Game*. London: British Film Institute, 1997.

Goddard, Kevin. "'Looks Maketh the Man': The Female Gaze and the Construction of Masculinity." *Journal of Men's Studies* 9, no. 1 (2000): 23–39.

Gottlieb, Lisa, dir. *Just One of the Guys*. 1985, Columbia Pictures.

Gray, Herman, *Cultural Moves: African Americans and the Politics of Representation*. Berkeley: University of California Press, 2005.

———. "The Feel of Life: Resonance, Race, and Representation." *International Journal of Communication* 9 (2015): 1108–1119.

———. *Watching Race: Television and the Struggle for "Blackness."* Minneapolis: University of Minnesota Press, 1995.

Gregg, Melissa, and Gregory J. Seigworth, eds. *The Affect Theory Reader*. Durham, NC: Duke University Press, 2010.

Grist, Leighton. "'It's Only a Piece of Meat': Gender Ambiguity, Sexuality, and Politics in *The Crying Game* and *M. Butterfly*." *Cinema Journal* 42, no. 4 (2003): 3–28.

Gross, Larry. *Up from Invisibility: Lesbians, Gay Men, and the Media in America*. New York: Columbia University Press, 2001.

Gunew, Sneja. "Feminism and the Politics of Irreducible Differences: Multiculturalism/ Ethnicity/Race." In *Feminism and the Politics of Difference*, edited by Sneja Gunew and Anna Yeatman, 1–19. Halifax: Fernwood Publishing, 1993.

Halberstam, J. Jack. *In a Queer Time and Place: Transgender Bodies, Subcultural Lives*. New York: New York University Press, 2005.

———. "The Transgender Gaze in *Boys Don't Cry*." *Screen* 42, no. 3 (2001): 294–298.

Hall, Stuart. "Culture, the Media and the 'Ideological Effect.'" In *Mass Communication and Society*, edited by James Curran, Michael Gurevitch, and Janet Woollacott, 315–348. Beverly Hills, CA: Sage, 1979.

————. "Encoding/Decoding." In *Media and Cultural Studies: KeyWorks*, revised edition, edited by Meenakshi Gigi Durham and Douglas M. Kellner, 163–173. Malden, MA: Blackwell Publishing, 2006.

————. "New Ethnicities." In *Stuart Hall: Critical Dialogues in Cultural Studies*, edited by David Morley and Kuan-Hsing Chen, 441–449. London: Routledge, 1996.

————. "The Work of Representation." In *Representation: Cultural Representations and Signifying Practices*, edited by Stuart Hall, 13–64. London: Sage, 1997.

Handler, Kristin. "Sexing *The Crying Game*: Difference, Identity, Ethics." *Film Quarterly* 47, no. 3 (1994): 31–42.

Hanich, Julian. *Cinematic Emotion in Horror Films and Thrillers: The Aesthetic Paradox of Pleasurable Fear.* New York: Routledge, 2010.

Heath, Stephen. *Questions of Cinema.* Bloomington: Indiana University Press, 1981.

Hicks, Neill D. *Writing the Thriller Film: The Terror Within.* Studio City, CA: Michael Wise Productions, 2002.

Hiltzik, Robert, dir. *Sleepaway Camp.* 1983, American Eagle Films.

Hitchcock, Alfred, dir. *Psycho.* 1960, Shamley Productions.

Ince, Kate. "Queering the Family? Fantasy and the Performance of Sexuality and Gay Relations in French Cinema 1995-2000." *Studies in French Cinema* 2, no. 2 (2002): 90–97.

Indick, William. *Psycho Thrillers: Cinematic Explorations of the Mysteries of the Mind.* Jefferson, NC: McFarland, 2006.

Jordan, Neil, dir. *The Crying Game.* 1992, Palace Pictures.

Keck, William. "*Hung* Takes a Transgender Turn." *TV Guide*, July 11–17, 2011, 14.

Keen, Suzanne. *Empathy and the Novel.* Oxford: Oxford University Press, 2007.

King, Geoff. *American Independent Cinema.* Bloomington, IN: Indiana University Press, 2005.

Kondo, Naomi. "Mental Illness in Film." *Psychiatric Rehabilitation Journal* 31, no. 3 (2008): 250–252.

Kristeva, Julia. *Powers of Horror: An Essay on Abjection.* New York: Columbia University Press, 1982.

Kuhn, Annette. *The Power of the Image: Essays on Representation and Sexuality.* London: Routledge, 1985.

Lester, Paul Martin. "From Abomination to Indifference: A Visual Analysis of Transgender Stereotypes in the Media." In Spencer and Capuzza, *Transgender Communication Studies*, 143–154.

Librach, Ronald. "Sex, Lies, and Audiotape: Politics and Heuristics in *Dressed to Kill* and *Blow Out*." *Literature/Film Quarterly* 26, no. 3 (1998): 166–177.

Lieberfeld, Daniel, and Judith Sanders. "Keeping the Characters Straight: Comedy and Identity in Some Like It Hot." *Journal of Popular Film and Television* 26, no. 3 (1998): 128–135.

Lockett, Christopher. "Terror and Rebirth: *Cathleen ni Houlihan*, from Yeats to *The Crying Game*." *Literature/Film Quarterly* 33, no. 4 (2005): 290–305.

Loker, Altan. *Film and Suspense*. 2nd ed. Victoria, BC: Trafford, 2005.

Lorde, Audre. "Age, Race, Class, and Sex: Women Redefining Difference." In *Out There: Marginalization and Contemporary Cultures*, edited by Russell Ferguson, Martha Gever, Trinh T. Minh-ha, and Cornel West, 281–287. Cambridge, MA: The MIT Press, 1990.

Luna, Israel, dir. *Ticked-off Trannies with Knives*. 2010, La Luna Entertainment.

Madrigal, Robert, Colleen Bee, Johnny Chen, and Monica Labarge. "The Effect of Suspense on Enjoyment Following a Desirable Outcome: The Mediating Role of Relief." *Media Psychology* 14, no. 3 (2011): 259–288.

Martinez, Maria Jesús. "*Some Like It Hot*: The Blurring of Gender Limits in a Film of the Fifties." *BELLS: Barcelona English Language and Literature Studies* 9 (1998): 143–152.

Massumi, Brian. "The Future Birth of the Affective Fact: The Political Ontology of Threat." In Gregg and Seigworth, *The Affect Theory Reader*, 52–70.

McCarty, John, *Thrillers: Seven Decades of Classic Film Suspense* (New York: Citadel Press, 1992).

McGowan, Todd, *The Real Gaze: Film Theory after Lacan* (Albany, NY: State University of New York Press, 2007).

McKee, Alan, *Textual Analysis: A Beginner's Guide* (Thousand Oaks, CA: Sage, 2003).

"Media Diversity Programs," *NAACP*, n.d., https://www.naacp.org/campaigns/media-diversity-programs/.

Meiri, Sandra, and Odeya Kohen-Raz, *Traversing the Fantasy: The Dialectic of Desire/Fantasy and the Ethics of Narrative Cinema* (New York: Bloomsbury Academic, 2020).

Metz, Christian, "Identification, Mirror," in *Film Theory and Criticism: Introductory Readings*, 7th ed., ed. Leo Braudy and Marshall Cohen (Oxford: Oxford University Press, 2009), 723-735.

Meyer, John C., "Humor as a Double-Edged Sword: Four Functions of Humor in Communication," *Communication Theory* 10, no. 3 (2000): 310-331.

Miller, Lucy J. "Becoming One of the Girls/Guys: Distancing Transgender Representations in Popular Film Comedies." In Spencer and Capuzza, *Transgender Communication Studies*, 127–142.

Montgomery, Kathryn C. *Target: Prime Time: Advocacy Groups and the Struggle over Entertainment Television*. New York: Oxford University Press, 1989.

Moretti, Franco. *Graphs, Maps, Trees: Abstract Models for Literary History*. New York: Verso, 2007.

Mulvey, Laura. "Visual Pleasure and Narrative Cinema." *Screen* 16, no. 3 (1975): 6–18.

Namaste, Viviane. *Sex Change, Social Change: Reflections on Identity, Institutions, and Imperialism*. Toronto: Women's Press, 2005.

Newman, Michael Z. *Indie: An American Film Culture*. New York: Columbia University Press, 2011.

Oliver, Mary Beth. "Tender Affective States as Predictors of Entertainment Preference." *Journal of Communication* 58, no. 1 (2008): 40–61.

Olson, Jenni. " 'Adam is 2019's Most Controversial Queer Film—And Its Most Important." *New Now Next*, August 5, 2019. http://www.newnownext. com/adam-is-the-most-controversial-queer-film-of-2019-and-its-most-important/08/2019/.

Palmer, R. Barton. "The Metafictional Hitchcock: The Experience of Viewing and the Viewing of Experience in *Rear Window* and *Psycho*." *Cinema Journal* 25, no. 2 (1986): 4–19.

Peirce, Kimberly, dir. *Boys Don't Cry*. 1999, Fox Searchlight Pictures.

Phillips, John. *Transgender on Screen*. New York: Palgrave Macmillan, 2006.

Phillips, Kendall R. *Projected Fears: Horror Films and American Culture*. Westport, CT: Praeger, 2005.

Pollack, Sydney, dir. *Tootsie*. 1982, Columbia Pictures.

Ponterotto, Diane. "Resisting the Male Gaze: Feminist Responses to the 'Normalization' of the Female Body in Western Culture." *Journal of International Women's Studies* 17, no. 1 (2016): 133–151.

Probyn, Elspeth. "Writing Shame." In Gregg and Seigworth, *The Affect Theory Reader*, 71–99.

Rault, Jasmine. "White Noise, White Affects: Filtering the Sameness of Queer Suffering." *Feminist Media Studies* 17, no. 4 (2017): 585–599.

Rees-Roberts, Nick. "La Confusion des Genres: Transsexuality, Effeminacy and Gay Identity in France." *International Journal of Cultural Studies* 7, no. 3 (2004): 281–300.

Reynolds, Daniel. "*Adam* Director Rhys Ernst Addresses Critics and the 'War on Nuance.' " *The Advocate*, July 22, 2019. https://www.advocate. com/film/2019/7/22/adam-director-rhys-ernst-addresses-critics-and-war-nuance.

Rice, Lynette. "Work It Is Cancelled by ABC.' " *Entertainment Weekly*, January 14, 2012. https://ew.com/article/2012/01/14/work-it-cancelled/.

Rothman, William. *Hitchcock: The Murderous Gaze*. Cambridge, MA: Harvard University Press, 1982.

Ryan, Joelle Ruby. "Reel Gender: Examining the Politics of Trans Images in Film and Media." PhD diss., Bowling Green State University, 2009.

Said, Edward W. *Orientalism*. New York: Random House, 1979; New York: Vintage Books, 1994.

Sarne, Michael, dir. *Myra Breckinridge*. 1970, 20th Century Fox.

Schou, Solvej. "Roland Emmerich's 'Stonewall' Finds Controversy." *The New York Times*, September 18, 2015. https://www.nytimes.com/2015/09/20/movies/roland-emmerichs-stonewall-finds-controversy.html.

Serano, Julia. *Whipping Girl: A Transsexual Woman on Sexism and the Scapegoating of Femininity*. Emeryville, CA: Seal Press, 2007.

Shadyak, Tom, dir. *Ace Ventura: Pet Detective*. 1994, Morgan Creek Productions.

Siebler, Kay. "Transqueer Representations and How We Educate." *Journal of LGBT Youth* 7, no. 4 (2010): 320–345.

Silverman, Kaja. *Male Subjectivity at the Margins*. New York: Routledge, 1992.

Singer, Tania, and Claus Lamm. "The Social Neuroscience of Empathy." *The Year in Cognitive Neuroscience 2009: Annals of the New York Academy of Sciences* 1156, no. 1 (2009): 81–96.

Sipos, Thomas M. *Horror Film Aesthetics: Creating the Visual Language of Fear*. Jefferson, NC: McFarland, 2010.

Spade, Dean. *Normal Life: Administrative Violence, Critical Trans Politics, and the Limits of Law*. Brooklyn, NY: South End Press, 2011.

Spence, Richard, dir. *Different for Girls*. 1996, BBC Films.

Spencer, Leland G., and Jamie C. Capuzza, eds. *Transgender Communication Studies: Histories, Trends, and Trajectories*. Lanham, MD: Lexington Books, 2015.

Straayer, Chris. *Deviant Eyes, Deviant Bodies: Sexual Re-Orientations in Film and Video*. New York: Columbia University Press, 1996.

Strkyer, Susan. "My Words to Victor Frankenstein above the Village of Chamonix: Performing Transgender Rage." In Stryker and Whittle, *The Transgender Studies Reader*, 244–256.

———. *Transgender History*. Berkeley, CA: Seal Press, 2008.

Stryker, Susan, and Stephen Whittle, *The Transgender Studies Reader*. New York: Routledge, 2006.

Thompson, Kristin. *Breaking the Glass Armor: Neoformalist Film Analysis*. Princeton: Princeton University Press, 1988.

Tomas, Jack. "ABC Cancels 'Work It,' But This Kind of Thing will Happen Again." *Tú Vez*, n.d. http://www.tuvez.com/abc-cancels-work-it-but-this-kind-of-thing-will-happen-again/workit/.

Tomasulo, Frank P. "Masculine/Feminine: The 'New Masculinity' in *Tootsie* (1982)." *Velvet Light Trap* 38 (1996): 4–13.

Tomkins, Silvan S. *Affect, Imagery, Consciousness*. Vol. I: *The Positive Affects*. New York: Springer, 1962).

Tucker, Duncan, dir. *Transamerica*. 2005, Belladonna Productions.

Turner, Victor. *The Ritual Process: Structure and Anti-Structure*. Piscataway, NJ: Aldine Transaction, 1995.

Tzioumakis, Yannis. *American Independent Cinema: An Introduction*. New Brunswick, NJ: Rutgers University Press, 2006.

Warner, Michael. "Introduction: Fear of a Queer Planet." *Social Text* 29 (1991): 3–17.

Welkos, Robert W. "The Secret of 'The Crying Game': Don't Read Any Further if You Haven't Seen This Film." *The Los Angeles Times*, February 18, 1993. https://www.latimes.com/archives/la-xpm-1993-02-18-ca-292-story.html.

Wilder, Billy, dir. *Some Like It Hot*. 1959, Mirisch Company.

Williams, Linda. "When the Woman Looks." In *Re-Vision: Essays in Feminist Film Criticism*, edited by Mary Ann Doane, Patricia Mellencamp, and Linda Williams, 83–99. Frederick, MD: University Publications of America, 1984.

Willox, Annabelle. "Branding Teena: (Mis)Representations in the Media." *Sexualities* 6, no. 3-4 (2003): 407–425.

Wolodarski, Wallace, dir. *Sorority Boys*. 2002, Touchstone Pictures.

Wood, Robin. *Hollywood from Vietnam to Reagan*. New York: Columbia University Press, 1986.

Index